BIRMINGHAM CITY
50 GREATEST MATCHES

BIRMINGHAM CITY
50 GREATEST MATCHES

Keith Dixon

DB PUBLISHING

First published in Great Britain in 2009 by The Breedon Books Publishing
Company Limited, Breedon House, 3 The Parker Centre, Derby, DE21 4SZ.
ISBN 978-1-85983-732-0

This paperback edition published in Great Britain in 2013 by DB Publishing,
an imprint of JMD Media Ltd

ISBN 978-1-78091-107-6

Printed and bound by Copytech (UK) Ltd, Peterborough

Contents

Introduction

It is never an easy task, as a lifelong supporter of a football club, to select 50 of the greatest matches from its history. The task is made even more difficult when that club has only won one major trophy in over 120 years of competition. Such was my dilemma when asked to produce this book. In the end I have been entirely subjective in my selections; there is no rhyme or reason behind the final choice. A few selected themselves – Cup Final appearances, excursions into Europe, promotions – but the vast majority are there just because they will mean something to Blues' supporters. Many of them symbolise what it means to be a Birmingham City Football Club fan – a glorious record of the optimism, blind faith and unswerving loyalty required to be a True Blue.

How many clubs would have included in their 50 most memorable games:

- **The first Golden Goal at Wembley**
- **The first match played on a Sunday**
- **A World Cup-winner's individual demolition of Southampton**
- **Being champions but not being promoted!**
- **A 16-year-old scoring all four goals in a match**

Acknowledgements

Grateful thanks to the following people for their help with this book, whether directly or indirectly: Julie, Holly, Harry, Matt and Ben Dixon – my family. Also my friends and fellow fanatical Bluenoses: Leigh Bosworth, Mike O'Brien and Martin Smallwood, who were kind enough to loan their priceless programme and memorabilia collections for inclusion in this book.

Foreword
by Ian Clarkson

Having supported, played and coached for Birmingham City, it was a real honour when I was asked to pen a foreword for this fascinating book. We all know that supporting Blues is a labour of love, which makes it far sweeter when the good times finally arrive. As a boy I can recall memorable games such as a 5–1 win over Manchester United and an unforgettable 4–3 triumph over Nottingham Forest; but a Boxing Day victory over the champions of Europe by a 3–0 scoreline in 1982 was undoubtedly the match that lives longest in my memory.

Each and every supporter will have their own memories, however, and I could wax lyrical for hours over Blues games that have sent a shiver down my spine, such as the Carling Cup thrashing of Ipswich. But I have chosen three games that are close to my heart for different reasons, which will always be in my own list of 'Memorable Blues matches.'

The match on 27 September 1988 saw Blues – who were a struggling Division Two side – lose 2–0 at home against Aston Villa in a League Cup second round first-leg clash. The game is probably only remembered by me, because I made my debut against the Auld Enemy. As a 17-year-old Blues nut, who had left school just over a year earlier, I walked around in a daze when Gary Pendrey pinned the team on the wall an hour and a half before kick-off. Kevin Gage and Andy Gray scored for Villa, and while most Blues fans will not give this game a second thought, I am sure they will remember my second pick, which was the catalyst for the official rebirth of the Blues.

Crowds had reached rock bottom, and we had just finished in mid-table in Division Three, so we could not sink any lower. But, under the no-nonsense style management of Lou Macari, we had reached the Leyland DAF Cup Final, and all of a sudden our first Wembley appearance for 35 years saw hordes of Blues fans rekindle their love affair with the club. There were an estimated 45,000 Bluenoses at Wembley to see a pulsating game, which we won 3–2 courtesy of a John Gayle overhead kick five minutes from time. Having led 2–0 and then been pegged back to 2–2 by Tranmere, it was typical Blues, but on this occasion we did not disappoint.

That game is featured in this book, but it was fitting that Gayle was hero of the day, as the giant striker from Kings Heath deserved his 15 minutes of fame. 'Gayley' was a man-mountain and always gave his all for the club. He seemed to click with Lou Macari's style of management, and he was almost unplayable on the day. He had to work hard to win over supporters initially, but never shirked a challenge, and I have never met a harder man during my football career. Any Blues fan over the age of 35 will recall that day with fondness and will have a tale to tell about the journey there, the journey back and, of course, the game!

IAN STEWART CLARKSON
Defender
159 + 13 Appearances

Clarky was born on 4 December 1970 in Solihull and was therefore a Bluenose from birth. Having played for Chapel Fields Primary school and Tudor Grange Senior school, he was signed under the Blues Youth Training Scheme (YTS) as a 16-year-old in June 1987, signing professional terms on his 18th birthday. Ian was a good reader of the game and was a resolute and committed defender, making the right-back position his own after the transfer of Kevin Ashley to Wolverhampton Wanderers. He transferred to Stoke City for £50,000 in September 1993, and after three successful years switched to Northampton Town in the summer of 1996. Ian moved into non-League football with Kidderminster Harriers in November 2000, helping them become the Nationwide Conference champions in the same year.

My last choice is the promotion-clinching game against Shrewsbury the following year in April 1992. The rebirth continued with promotion back into Division One, and I was lucky enough to be captain from the second game of season at the age of just 20. Nigel Gleghorn scored the only goal of the game against Shrewsbury, and with around 20,000 fans at St Andrew's the feel-good factor had undoubtedly returned. When David Sullivan arrived next season we were back on track.

The fact that Gleghorn scored the goal from an Ian Rodgerson cross was fitting as our two wingers were largely responsible for our promotion. The duo bagged somewhere close to 30 goals between them from wide positions, and with Simon Sturridge next top scorer there is no doubt Rodgerson and Gleghorn were the reason we were promoted that year. They were vastly different characters: 'Dodge' was a laid-back lad from Hereford, while 'Gleggy' was a worrier but always very vocal and a leader.

Anyway, I have rambled on for long enough. I am sure you all have a 'favourite 50', so sit back, revel in the good times and keep right on!

Game One

The First Official League Game

SMALL HEATH 5 BURSLEM PORT VALE 1

Date: 3 September 1892   **Venue:** Muntz Street
Attendance: 2,500   **Referee:** E. Aitchinson (Long Eaton)

Small Heath: Charsley, Bayley, Speller, Ollis, Jenkyns, E. Devey, Hallam, Edwards, Short, Wheldon, Hands.

Burslem Port Vale: Frail, Clutton, Elson, Farrington, McCrindle, Delves, Walker, Scarratt, Bliss, Jones.

Blues' first official League game in many ways set the tone for the way that their history would unfold over the next 117 years – all things with a touch of farce! The 1892–93 season, with the 'Heathens' as a founder member of the newly formed Second Division, began with 2,500 fans being left in the wet and windy Muntz Street ground awaiting the arrival of the opposition. Burslem Port Vale eventually arrived at 4.00pm (the planned kick-off was 3.30pm) with 10 men, as their centre-forward Beats had missed the train!

Blues chose to play with the gale-force wind at their backs against their 10-man opposition, and it was no surprise that Burslem Port Vale were very soon under immense pressure with Freddie Wheldon and Tommy Hands testing their defence. George Short hit the woodwork before Blues opened the score on five minutes. A smart move involving Wheldon, Short and Harry Edwards gave Wheldon the chance to score Blues' first official goal.

Both goalkeepers were involved during an intense period when Chris Charsley protected his goal from Burslem Port Vale pressure, while Frail, the opposition 'keeper, made a crucial mistake which resulted in Short scoring the second goal on 37 minutes. Just before half-time Wheldon got his second to give the home side a 3–0 advantage at the interval.

Burlsem Port Vale began the second period looking to take the initiative from Blues but on 50 minutes, Jack Hallam made it 4–0 with a 20-yard strike.

Burslem Port Vale scored their only goal through Bliss, but it was not to change the manner of Blues' dominance, and after several near misses from Edwards, Hallam and Wheldon, and with literally seconds to go, Edwards scored to make the final outcome 5–1.

CAESAR AUGUSTUS LLEWELLYN JENKYNS
Centre-half
90 appearances, 13 goals
8 appearances for Wales
Joined Newton Heath in May 1896.

Born in Builth Wells, Wales, on 24 August 1866, 'The Mighty Caesar' became the backbone of the Small Heath defence for eight seasons. Having played for local sides Southfield and St Andrew's Sunday School, he had a brief stay at Blues beginning in August 1884 before going on to play for Gas Unity. He returned to Blues in July 1888. A big, burly player, he had a fierce shoulder charge and a mighty tackle. A born leader, he captained every team he played for, including Wales, and was inspirational to his teammates. He could head a ball half the length of the pitch and once won a competition by sending a dead-ball kick fully 100 yards first bounce. He was certainly a tough character and was sent off several times in his career. He left Blues after being sacked for brawling with a Derby player whom he alleged had spat at him. He spent just over a year with Newton Heath before returning to the Midlands with Walsall in November 1897. His next job was as coach to Coventry City in 1902. He was a guest player for Saltley Wednesday FC in 1904, but he only played one game as he had not been reinstated as an amateur. He retired from football in May 1905 and died in Birmingham on 23 July 1941.

Game Two

Champions of Division Two

BLUES 3 ARDWICK 2

Date: 1 April 1893   **Venue:** Muntz Street
Attendance: 1,000

Small Heath: Charsley, Bayley, Pumfrey, Ollis, Jenkyns, Short, Hallam, Walton, Mobley, Wheldon, Hands.

Ardwick: Unknown.

This was the final game of Blues' first season in the Football League, and although they finished first in the League they were not promoted to the top division. Even though they had scored 90 goals in only 22 matches they were unable to claim that First Division spot due to their failure in the Test Matches – forerunners of today's Play-offs. So while this match saw them win the first-ever Second Division Championship, they were not promoted.

The Test Match was played at Stoke's Victoria Ground against Newton Heath on 22 April 1893. In front of 4,000 people the game was drawn 1–1, with Wheldon scoring for

Team group with Second Division shield, as featured in the 1906 'Opening of St Andrew's Souvenir Programme' *Top row, left to right:* Mr Alf Jones (secretary), T. Bayley, C. Charsley, C. Simms (trainer), G. Hollies, B. Pumfrey, F. Short, Mr J. Weston (director). *Middle row:* J. Hallam, W. Walton, F. Mobley, C.A.L. Jenkyns, F. Wheldon, T. Hands. *Bottom row:* W. Ollis, E. Devey.

PLAYER FACTFILE

JOHN HALLAM
Outside-right
151 appearances, 62 goals
1 appearance for Wales
Left Blues for Oswestry Town in 1885.

Born in Oswestry, Shropshire, in February 1869, Hallam played for two Oswestry sides before moving to Blues in September 1890: Oswestry Town (1885), Oswestry Crescent (1887–88) and Oswestry Town for a second time in August 1888. While at Blues he won a Division Two Champions' medal in 1893, followed by a runners'-up medal a year later. 'Jack' was a pint-sized winger with an amazing burst of speed, becoming an integral part of the prolific goalscoring attack of the time. He joined Swindon Town in August 1896, staying until May 1901 when he began working for the Great Western Railway.

the Blues. The replay was held five days later at Bramall Lane, Sheffield, and Blues suffered a 5–2 reversal, with Walton and Mobley scoring for Blues. The replay attendance was 6,000. Ever-presents this season were Wheldon, who scored 26 goals in 26 games, and Ollis.

Game Three

Promotion

BLUES 12 DONCASTER ROVERS 0

Date: 11 April 1903   **Venue:** Muntz Street
Attendance: 8,000   **Referee:** D. Hammond (Heywood, Lancashire)

Blues: Dorrington, Goldie, Wassell, Beer, Dougherty, Howard, Athersmith, Leonard, McRoberts, Wilcox, Field.

Doncaster Rovers: Eggett, Simpson, Layton, Murphy, Aston, Wright, Langham, Richards, Price, Ratcliffe, Robinson.

The *Birmingham Daily Gazette* correspondent described this victory as 'emphatic, characterised by expressiveness, forceful finishing and unselfishness.' Rovers were completely 'overwhelmed, outplayed in every department and their defenders were powerless against Blues' attacking.'

The Blues scored three times in the first 45 minutes, through Arthur Leonard (18 minutes) and Freddie Wilcox (29 and 40 minutes). Wilcox's second followed a magnificent run by Charlie Field, who went past four defenders in a 40-yard dribble before setting up Wilcox 10 yards from goal. Eggett, in the visitors' goal, performed

Team group with the Staffordshire Cup, the Mayor of Birmingham's Cup and Birmingham Senior Cup, as featured in the 1906 'Opening of St Andrew's Souvenir Programme'
Top row, left to right: C. Simms (groundsman), W. Norman (trainer), J. Glover, A. Robinson, W. Adams (president), F. Stokes, H. Howard, J. Dougherty, Dr. Stanley (Hon. Surgeon), Alf Jones (secretary). *Bottom row:* W.J. Beer, B. Green, A. Mounteney, W. Wigmore, W.H. Jones, F. Wilcox, C. Field.

Sport & Play – an example of the all sports magazine of the time.

miracles during the first period. He saved twice from Wilcox, once each from Field, Leonard, Charlie Athersmith and Bob McRoberts, and then deflected a stunning 30-yard drive from Billy Beer onto the crossbar with his outstretched leg.

McRoberts, who insisted on playing despite suffering from a heavy cold, had a hand in eight of the nine goals the Blues ran in during a one-sided second half. He and Leonard were in brilliant form. Rovers were torn to shreds as the rampaging Small Heath pressed home their advantage. The Blues, in fact, seemed to have far too much time, and both McRoberts and Field fluffed easy chances, then the floodgates reopened and the hapless Eggett in the visitors' goal could do nothing as the goals rained in.

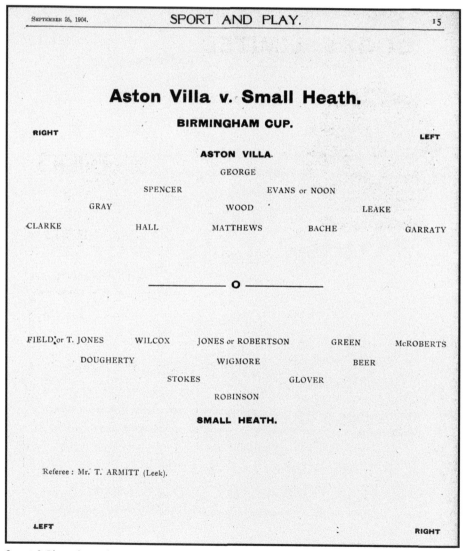

Sport & Play – how the teams lined up. This example is for a Birmingham Cup game on 26 September 1904.

PLAYER FACTFILE

ARTHUR RALPH LEONARD
Inside-right
75 appearances, 26 goals
Left Blues for Stoke in January 1904.

Leonard appeared under a pseudonym for the latter part of his career, as his real surname was Bamford. He joined Blues in strange circumstances; Blues saw him play with the Irish side, Glentoran, and were so impressed that they immediately signed him for £120. Leicester were also at the match and recognised him as their absentee player, Arthur Bamford. After being accused of this, he went missing for a few days, sending a telegram to his wife saying he had fled to America. He later re-emerged in Bristol and was persuaded to come back to Birmingham to face the accusations. He admitted he was Arthur Bamford, and the case was resolved when Blues paid Leicester an extra £20 for his signature. He was a big favourite with the fans, tricky with the ball and able to score goals and make them. His football career began in his birth town of Leicester, playing for 17th Leicestershire Regiment and Leicester Fosse in 1895 when he was 21. He continued to play for local sides like Rushden Town and Sheppey United before drifting over to Northern Ireland. He spent three years at Blues until joining Stoke in 1904. He then played for St Bernard, Clapton Orient, Plymouth Argyle and Reading.

Leonard and Wilcox each took their tallies to four goals apiece, Leonard's third coming from 40 yards after a brave run from full-back Archie Goldie. Wilcox's fourth was a superb right-foot volley after a devastating run and dribble by McRoberts. Athersmith, Field, McRoberts and Jack Dougherty rounded off the massacre, with Field's goal the 'pick of the bunch'.

Game Four

First Game at St Andrew's

BLUES 0 MIDDLESBROUGH 0

Date: 26 December 1906   **Venue:** St Andrew's
Attendance: 32,000

Blues: Robinson, Glover, Stokes, Wigmore, Beer, Dougherty, Anderson, Green, Jones, Mounteney, Southall.

Boro: Williamson, Hogg, Aitken, Barker, Jones, Davidson, Smith, Bloomer, Common, Cassidy, Cail.

For the first match at St Andrew's, Blues produced a special 'souvenir of the New Ground'. But there was a fear that few people would turn up, for snow turned the pitch into an expanse of white. The conditions were not conducive to good football, and Blues were worried their big day would be spoilt.

In the event, more than 32,000 attended the match, although the occasion was more memorable than the football. The goalless draw was inevitable – the brown ball would hardly move on what looked like a bed of cotton wool – and the majority of supporters went home frustrated. But Blues would have been happy with the event. Their average attendance that season was a mere 15,315 – less than half the official crowd for that first match at St Andrew's.

PLAYER FACTFILE

WILLIAM JOHN BEER
Wing-half
250 appearances, 35 goals
Retired while at Blues in May 1910.

Billy joined Blues for £700 in January 1902 from Sheffield United, where he had been a professional since 1898. While at Sheffield, Billy had won an FA Cup-winners' medal in the 1899 competition. He was best remembered for his subtle body swerve and cannonball shooting; indeed, he was a hugely successful penalty-taker for both Blues and the Blades, reputed never to have missed a kick. After retiring he spent some time in Australia, sheep farming, before returning to England, where he subsequently became manager of the Blues from May 1923 to March 1927.

An extract from the programme entitled:

The New Ground at St Andrew's

Mr Walter W. Hart, the Chairman of the club, should be a proud man to-day, for having steered the old club through the dark days recorded in the previous pages, he has realised an ambition upon which he set his heart some years ago — the club of which he was chairman to be known as the Birmingham Football Club, and in possession of an enclosure worthy of the city. It is now probably four years ago since the site was first mentioned by Mr Harry Morris, and an inspection by the chairman at once convinced him of the great possibilities of the position. Situated within a mile and a quarter of the centre of the city, and surrounded by an immense population, the site seemed in every way suitable for the realisation of the chairman's great ambition. After prolonged attempts to deal with the owner of the old ground for a renewal of the lease on favourable terms, or a sale of the freehold, a definite decision was arrived at early in the present year, and the removal to a new ground became inevitable. With commendable energy the chairman set to work to get promises of debentures sufficient to warrant the club going on with the scheme, and with Mr R.D. Todd setting a splendid example of courageous support, the money was at length forthcoming, so that last February it was decided to sign a lease for twenty-one years on advantageous terms. Then came the question of practically realising what had hitherto only appeared on paper. In Mr Harry Pumfrey, an old Small Heath school boy, the directors were fortunate to hit upon a diamond in the rough. His plans and drawings would have done credit to the most expensive professional architect, and there was every reason for the expressed astonishment of the directors who inspected them, when it is remembered that his position was little more than that of an ordinary working carpenter. But Mr Pumfrey's heart was in his work, and much of his spare time had been spent in the local School of Art, under whose auspices he executed work which was judged worthy of exhibition at South

The ground on which St Andrew's was built.

Kensington. Mr Pumfrey was therefore engaged at once as engineer and surveyor. A new ground committee was formed, consisting of Messrs T.W. Turley, W.W. Hart, R.D. Todd, H. Morris, and T. Whittell, Mr W.H. Bull being co-opted as soon as he joined the Board. Whilst everyone has borne his part in this big undertaking, it may fairly be stated that Messrs. Turley, Hart, and Whittell have been the hard-working men of that committee, the latter undertaking all the secretarial work involved. Mr Turley has displayed wonderful enthusiasm. Day after day he has been in the thick of the toil, and many a day he has put in fourteen solid hours' work in his anxiety to see things right, and the ground ready for opening at the earliest possible moment — and all this, mark you, without fee or reward, simply for sheer love of the old club. Probably Mr Pumfrey would be the first to admit that the job would have been too big for him without so able and energetic a clerk of the works. How many hundreds of pounds have been saved in fees by the work of these two men, only those who undertake heavy contracts can form an opinion. We have heard it put down to at least £2,000. A glance at the photograph of the state of the ground prior to work commencing [see page 21] will show that there was plenty to do when the work was taken in hand. The first consideration was, of course, the playing pitch, and to make this the two pools which were filled by artesian springs, and which form so prominent a feature of the picture had to be got rid of. The water was carried into a large drain placed diagonally across the field of play, with a manhole in the centre and another manhole at the opposite corner. Other drains were also trained into this main, and the whole covered with 2 feet of brick ends and ashes, on top of which was placed 18 inches of rubble, and some of the best turf it was possible to procure in the neighbourhood. All this was laid by the early weeks of June. The extent of the turf area is 123 yards by 83 yards, providing a four yards margin round a playing pitch which measures 115 yards by 75. This is surrounded by a six yards cinder running track, so that the spectators are a clear 10 yards from the touchline. The next item was to make up the embankment on the unreserved side. The site was offered as a tip and soon the loads of rubbish began to pour in. It is computed that no less than 100,000 loads, yielding an income of about £800, have been emptied to make up what has already been nicknamed 'Spion Kop'. At one

View of St Andrew's in 1906.

point there are 110 tiers of 13 inch tread rising to 5 inches to a height of 47 feet, and at the lowest point there are 82 terraces. It is computed that 60,000 people at 6d can see comfortably. At present, the ground will not permit a covering being erected, but so soon as the rubbish has settled sufficiently it is the intention of the directors to put up a covering behind the Tilton Road goal to protect at least 12,000 people from inclement weather. The grandstand, which runs for 123 yards on the Garrison Lane side of the ground, has twenty-nine rows of seats rising nine inches above one another. It will accommodate 6,000 people seated, another 5,000 being also able to stand on the 19 terraces in front. The roof, which measures 87 feet by 123 yards, is supported by steel stanchions, 41 feet high, let into from four to 10 feet of concrete. In its erection, 450,000 bricks have been used, together with 40 tons of corrugated iron, 100 tons of cement and a huge quantity of timber. There are five divisions for spectators, block A being priced at 1s., block B 1s 6d., block C 2s., block D 2s., Block E 1s 6d., block F 1s. The seats are approached by two flights of stairs, with a passage to each description of seat, all landings, passages, exits and entrances being lighted by electric light. Underneath, the space has been utilised for board room, offices, cycle store, four refreshment rooms, training room (containing a 9ft square plunge bath), dressing rooms and a spacious billiard room for the players, the whole heated by hot water apparatus. The latter room, by the way, has been generously furnished to the extent of 100 guineas, by Sir John C Holder, who has promised to perform the opening ceremony and thus once more identify himself in a special way with the public life of this big city. Thirty-six turnstiles will give admission to the ground, viz., sixteen for those paying 6d at Emmeline Street, where there are four exits of 10ft each; 10 at Garrison Lane, also for the unreserved, with three exits of a total width of 40 feet; and 10 at St Andrew's Street, for the stands and reserved portions of the ground, where four exits are also provided. Behind the railway goal terraced accommodation is provided for 4,000 people, at one shilling admission, so that in all 75,000 can be comfortably housed.

An extract from the souvenir programme for the opening of St Andrew's on 26 December 1906:

'HISTORY OF THE BIRMINGHAM FOOTBALL CLUB'

(Founded as 'SMALL HEATH ALLIANCE' in the year 1875)
Chronicled by Henry B. Lane

When compiling a brief history of Small Heath Football Club seven years ago, the writer stated that few famous clubs had survived a more chequered career. That remark is even more appreciated today, for whilst the Club at that day was making a gallant attempt to get out of the pecuniary difficulties incident to even a leading position in the Second League, at the present time it may be said to be securely placed in the First League, and hoping to enter on a wave of prosperity by taking possession of one of the finest football enclosures in the Kingdom. There will doubtless be some among the thousands expected to be present at the opening ceremony whose mind will go back to the days of 1875, when under the title of Small Heath Alliance, the club was first formed by Messrs. Edmunds, three brothers, Edden, and two brothers James. In those days a playing pitch for which rent was demanded was out of the question, and they were perforce content to play upon a piece of waste land somewhere near Arthur Street — strangely enough, within a stone's throw, as it were, of the present magnificent enclosure. It is recorded that the first game was played against the Holte Wanderers, as the name implies, an Aston team, the Small Heath eleven on that occasion being W. Edden, Arthur Wright, Fred James, Tom James, G.H. Edden, W.H. Edmunds,(capt.),T. Edden, David Keys, C. Barmore, C. Barr and J. Sparrow. After about two years of this 'free and open' kind of football, a move was made to an enclosed ground in Ladypool Lane, Sparkbrook, where a handful of spectators began to take an interest in the Club's doings. In 1877 the club moved to its late headquarters at Muntz Street, Small Heath, renting the ground for the sum of £5 from September to April, and with Arthur, Fred and Tom James, Sam Gessey and 'Billy' Edden amongst its most prominent players, progress in popularity and importance became rapid. A proper fixture card was drawn up for the first time, and the new ground evidently brought good luck, for of the twenty-two games played not one ended in defeat. Of the players mentioned, Arthur James was the most famous. From 1878 to 1885 he was 'the people's pet' and captain of the side. Many times he had the honour of representing the Birmingham Association in its matches against Sheffield, Glasgow, London and other Associations. W. Edden also represented the Birmingham Association as goalkeeper against London, Sheffield and Scotch Counties — matches which at that time were vested with unusual importance. The first time Small Heath Alliance and Aston Villa met was September 27th 1879, when the match, played at Muntz Street, ended in a victory for the Alliance by 1 goal and 1 disputed to 0. Mr. Edmunds was the first honorary secretary, and he was succeeded by Messrs. T.W. Hards, W. Edden, P.W. Harlow, S. Gessey, W.W. Hart, A. Jones and W. Starling, in the order named. A young fellow — quite a stripling then, but he had a big heart — turned out with the A team about this time. He is still actively at work on the club's behalf — as a Director nowadays. We refer to Harry Morris, who in all put in about eleven years' active service as a player for Small Heath. During his playing career his ability was recognised by the Birmingham Association, who selected him for one of their elevens in 1885. Harry Morris can fairly claim to be called one of the pillars of the Small Heath club. The 1882—83 season was a very successful one, for among other good performances the Walsall Cup was won, Wednesbury Old Athletic being beaten in the final tie at Walsall by 4 goals to one. With the present chairman (Mr W.W. Hart) as hon. Sec., and Messrs. Alfred Jones, W. Slater, W. Gent, A. Coles, E. Bailey, and the four of the James family as ardent workers, the club had a busy season during 1883—84, meeting among other clubs the Druids, Accrington, Great Marlow, Great Lever, Church, Dublin Association, Stoke, Aston Villa, and all the local teams. The next season when Alfred Jones had taken up the secretarial reins, was about the most successful of all the club's early years. The team ran into the semi-final of the English Cup, defeating Burton Wanderers (9—2), Darwen (3—1), Derby County (4—2), Davenham (2—1), Redcar (2—0), and at last succumbing to West Bromwich Albion in the semi-final at the Aston Lower grounds by four goals to none. The Small Heath team on that occasion was: — Hedges (goal), Hare and Evetts (backs), Fred James, Felton and Simms (half-backs), Davenport, Harry Morris, 'Eddy' Stanley, Figures and Hill (forwards). Only one of those players is to-day actively engaged with the club, viz., Charlie Simms, who now occupies the position of groundsman. About this time Chris. Charsley came from Stafford to Birmingham and threw in his lot with Small Heath, being elected a playing member in March 1886, and remaining a loyal amateur player for many seasons. He represented England against Ireland at Perry Barr in 1893, being the only player to gain English international honours whilst a member of Small Heath. On June 14th 1890, at a dinner given in his honour at the Albion Hotel, Livery Street, he was presented with a piano and purse of money as some recognition of his valuable services. Small Heath were among the first to adopt professionalism, which, about the years 1884 and 1885, caused such a flutter in football circles, their reason for so doing being that many of their players were working men who could not afford to lose the half-day which Saturday's football often involved, and the Association would not allow an amateur to be paid for lost time. It was in July 1885, that the club decided to adopt professionalism, and the present secretary could tell some interesting stories of how men who subsequently became famous in the football world came near throwing their lot with Small Heath, Dennis Hodgetts and Tom Green among the number. The first occasion on which Small Heath met Aston Villa in the English Cup occurred in the next season, when the teams were drawn together at Coventry Road in the second round, the game taking place on November 6th 1887, and ending in a victory for the Villa. There was no qualifying competition then. On July 24th 1888, Small Heath Alliance set the fashion to the world by adopting 'limited liability'. The word 'Alliance' was dropped and the club became known as the Small Heath Football Club Limited. This innovation surprised the football 'powers that be' years ago, but to-day we find the wisdom of its adoption confirmed by the football companies which abound on every hand. The first Directors of the company were Messrs. W.W. Hart (chairman), Starling and Greatorex (secretaries), W. Dormer, T. Denston, J.C. Orr, Alfred Jones, E. Badland, and J. Smith. Under the new order of things, the club had a successful season, paying a dividend of 5 per cent, out of profits. The team had an exceptional run of successes at the beginning of the season, but West Bromwich Albion beat them at Coventry Road, in the fifth round of the English Cup, by three goals to two, the home side leading till near the end by two goals. The team, with Harry Morris for captain, included, among other good players, Fred Speller and Caesar Jenkyns. Both these men subsequently helped the club to win many famous victories. In Speller's case regret was universal when his all-too-short career was terminated by a fractured leg against Darwen on October 29th, 1892. Of Jenkyns's valuable services, it is perhaps not too much to say that he was the mainstay of the side for close upon seven seasons. At the end of season 1888—89 the club was elected to a position in the Alliance, the organisation including such clubs as Sheffield Wednesday, Stoke, Notts Forest, Sunderland Albion, St George's & co., but during the three seasons they were members, Small Heath never achieved any remarkable success. In the first season they were bracketed with Notts Forest, with 17 points out of a possible 44. During this season Fred Wheldon joined the Heathens, and from March, 1890 until May 1896, when for the large fee of £100 and a match at Perry Barr guaranteed to produce another £250 he was transferred to Aston Villa, he performed brilliantly at inside left. Though opening the next season (1890—91) with a surprise victory of four goals to none over Aston Villa at Perry Barr, the club failed to achieve success in the Alliance, only scoring 16 points. This failure to win matches was no doubt due to the lack of interest in the club's doings, and, to stir up the enthusiasm, a public meeting was held in the Jenkins Street Board School, at which several of the local football magnates spoke and 207 more shares issued. The next year the club secured a higher position in the Alliance — many capital victories being recorded. After going through the Qualifying Competition of the English Cup, Woolwich Arsenal were met and discomfited by a heavy defeat of five goals to one at Small Heath, and the second round gave the Heathens Sheffield Wednesday as their opponents, when for a consideration of £200, the venue of the tie was changed to Sheffield, money then being very scarce with the Birmingham club. In July 1892, Mr T. Denston succeeded Mr W. Starling in the secretaryship and was the first paid secretary of the club, but he resigned office in the following October, and Mr Alfred Jones was elected, after an absence of several years from the secretariat, as his successor. He holds the office to-day, and is greatly

Page one of the Souvenir Programme which did not have team line ups within it.

esteemed by the Directors, who repose the utmost confidence in his judgement, while his straightforwardness has won him troops of friends among football officials throughout the country. It was in this season that the Alliance became amalgamated with the League, being called the Second Division, and not only was a Shield provided as the champion badge, but the three top clubs had an opportunity of promotion by meeting the three lowest clubs in Division I., the winners of the matches joining the first Division for the following season. Small Heath were the first to secure the shield, but in the test match against Newton Heath they were unsuccessful, the drawn game at Stoke being lost by five goals to two on the re-play at Sheffield. This was a most successful season, twenty-eight games being won out of forty-three played, and as the Directors were fortunate in keeping practically the same eleven together, it was not surprising that the success was repeated during the season of 1893—94. Though not champions this year, Liverpool heading them for that honour, the team placed the club among the first sixteen in the country by defeating Darwen, at Stoke, by three goals to one in the test match. April 28th 1894, was indeed a red letter day for the Heathens, and those who accompanied the team will probably never forget the excitement with which the victory was hailed by players and supporters. How the funnel of the engine was decorated with the club colours! — how the crowds thronged the platform at New Street on the return journey! — how everybody from Aston Villa downwards congratulated the plucky Heathens, not forgetting a most sportsmanlike letter from the defeated Darwen. As a record, it may be interesting to state that the following players constituted the eleven on that occasion: C. Charsley (goal); Fred Short and Purves (backs); Ollis, Jenkyns and E. Devey (half-backs), Hallam, Walton, Mobley, Wheldon and T. Hands (forwards). It was in this season that the reserve team were elected members of the Birmingham and District League, and mainly owing to the care of Mr Albert Coles, who at considerable sacrifice has devoted his whole attention to the eleven, they have always done well in the competition, the matches filling up the Saturday afternoons when the first team have been away in a manner that has met with hearty approval. The next season was not so successful as some of the club's ardent admirers could have wished, and though many capital performances were recorded, it was not until the last game was surprisingly won by two goals to none over Sheffield United, at Sheffield, that the ignominy of again appearing in the test matches was avoided. With 25 points to their credit, the club occupied the eleventh position — by no means a discreditable season's work, which opinion is strengthened by the remembrance that Derby County, Liverpool and Stoke had to play in the test games. The season which followed — 1895—96 — was a disastrous one. Nothing went right, and though strenuous efforts were made to pull the team together by engaging new players, the 'captures' mostly turned out to be failures. For the first time in the club's history Scotland supplied the eleven with recruits. For the following season, which perforce was spent in the Second Division of the League, a practically new team of players was engaged, wages and other expenses were curtailed, and a determined effort was made to regain the lost ground. Dennis Hodgetts was transferred by Aston Villa and captained the side for a few months, making his first appearance in Royal blue colours against Gainsboro' Trinity in October, 1896; but, in spite of a splendid run of victories towards the close of the season, the team could not reach a higher position than fourth. As a result of poor play during the season of 1897—98, the club fell two places lower in the Second League, and so inadequately were the efforts of the directors supported financially, that it was found necessary to organise a sports' meeting early in the summer, which assisted the funds to the extent of £211 16s 7d. During this summer, 'Bob' McRoberts was secured from Gainsborough. What a prize he turned out to be subsequent events proved beyond question, and it was with sincere appreciation of his worth that he was presented with an illuminated address on August 27, 1903, after five years' service. Two other notable additions were made to the club's strength about this time. Messrs. H. Morris and T.W. Turley being elected to the directorate, and right worthily they have justified the wisdom of the shareholders in inviting their co-operation. Under the captaincy of Alec Leake, a good-humoured and enthusiastic leader, the team won such increased support from the public that a profit of £755 18s 1d on the following year's working was recorded, but the First League was still a long way off, and with a view to procuring more money to enable the directors to secure stronger players, a bazaar was held at the Exchange Rooms, New Street, which brought in £312 9s 7d to the coffers of the club. Whilst playing at Stoke in an English Cup tie during March of this season, McRoberts was severely injured and the game drawn at Stoke was lost at Small Heath the following Wednesday. The loss of McRoberts's services at this juncture caused the directors to look around for a suitable successor, their choice falling upon the man who had succeeded him at Gainsborough, and here again it is surely unnecessary to point out how fortunate the directors were in persuading Walter Wigmore to come to Birmingham. From centre forward he has fallen back to centre half, to prove himself again and again the strong man of the side. The next season (1899–1900) was a continuation of the struggle for promotion, but with increased expenditure and decreased income, a heavy loss of over £800 on the season's working had to be faced, the only consoling feature being the high position of third in the Second Division. So keen were the directors in maintaining the foothold on the topmost rungs of the Second League ladder that they courageously faced the deficit, and firmly declined a tempting bait from Aston Villa to part with their clever and resolute centre forward — R. McRoberts. The best possible reward for their pluck came at the end of April 1901, when with 48 points to their credit, they proudly rejoined the select circle of the First Division after an absence of five years. During this season — on March 23 1901, to give the exact date — a memorable meeting took place with Aston Villa, in an English Cup tie, at Coventry Road. Most elaborate preparations were made, all prices were increased to 7s 6d., 4s., 3s., 2s.6d., 2s and 1s., but by stopping away the public showed their disapproval of what the directors considered proper precautions for keeping the crowd within manageable limits. For the comparatively small attendance, a 'gate' of £827 was considered most satisfactory. The result was a draw of no goals, Small Heath losing the replay at Villa Park by the only goal of the match, which was scored in the last minute of the extra time played. Profiting by this experience, ordinary prices were charged for the attractive League game with the Villa on October 12th 1901, and a record attendance of 29,000 spectators turned up to see the Villa win by 2 goals to 0. It was during this season, on January 28, 1902, that Mr William Adams, who had been elected to the presidency on July 22, 1901, first showed that interest and enterprise on the club's behalf which has made him so useful a member of the directorate by signing Beer and Field from Sheffield United, largely at his own financial risk. W.J. Beer has been a valuable addition, indeed, and many a time it must have surprised the Sheffield United directors to hear that he was the best half-back on the field after parting with him as a player 'with a past'. In spite, however, of the help of these splendid players, the last match found the Heathens with twenty-nine points and a victory necessary to escape relegation to the Second Division again. The unsportsmanlike tactics adopted by the Notts County players to keep their goal intact must still be fresh in the minds of everyone, and regret was universally expressed with the Heathens in their misfortune when the game ended in a draw of no goals and they dropped back again into the Second Division. Thanks to a magnificent response by McRoberts and his comrades, the necessary points for re-admission to the

First Division were secured the next season. In this connection an amusing incident may be cited. Anticipating victory at Barnsley on Easter Monday, a generous supporter of the club had secretly provided the trainer with a dozen bottles of champagne to enable the event to be properly celebrated at the conclusion of the match. The game was, however, lost by 3 goals to 1, so that, instead of jubilation, sorrow and seriousness was writ large on everybody's face, for another season in the Second League meant practically ruin to the club. No tidings had reached Barnsley of the other League games played that day, and it was only when New Street Station was reached shortly before midnight that a couple of enthusiasts met the party to inform them that Leicester Fosse had beaten Woolwich Arsenal at Woolwich and Small Heath were in the First Division again. Then the champagne was produced and everyone made merry, much to the astonishment of the few officials and passengers who were about the station at that late hour. The next season may be said to have witnessed the first real advance of the club towards the highest position of the League. Starting fairly well, more strength was added to the players by the engagement of Ben Green from Barnsley, Mr Adams astonishing the Yorkshiremen by agreeing to pay a transfer fee which they put on the player merely to 'choke him off', and again proving his splendid enterprise on the club's behalf. That the step was wise — bold as it may have been — the success of the side clearly proves. When Jack Glover, who offered his services in January 1904, was engaged to partner the classy Frank Stokes at back, another stalwart was added to the already strong team, and from that day to the present the club has held its own with the best in the football world. In chronicling this success two other players must be specially mentioned, Arthur Robinson (in goal) and W.H. Jones (as centre forward) have performed so ably that more than one victory may be ascribed to their efforts. Apart from a creditable position in the First League, the season of 1904—05 was notable for the fact that for the first time in the club's history, the Mayor of Birmingham's Charity Cup, the Birmingham Senior Cup and the Staffordshire Senior Cup were won, just in time, as it were, to get the old name of Small Heath inscribed thereon, for in March, 1905 at a special meeting of the shareholders, the name of Birmingham was unanimously adopted. The brilliant successes of last season are too recent to need mentioning, but as a record it may be written that for the first time in the club's history, Aston Villa were defeated in both League games, and were placed lower in the League table than Birmingham. Then the splendid show in English Cup ties will not readily be forgotten, when Preston, Stoke and Tottenham were defeated, and Newcastle United, after drawing luckily at Coventry Road, only won the replay after extra time, everyone agreeing that the latter game was about the finest ever seen on Tyneside. With the huge gates obtaining in these events, the necessity for a new and larger ground was brought home to the directors in no uncertain manner, around £2,000 being placed as a low estimate of what they missed by the old ground's inadequate accommodation. All the complaints should now be set at rest, for it is safe to assert that there are not half-a-dozen better enclosures in Britain.

Game Five

Arthur Reed?

BLUES 4 BURNLEY 0

Date: 6 April 1912   **Venue:** St Andrew's
Attendance: 35,000   **Referee:** T. Kirkham (Burslem)

Blues: Bailey, Ball, Womack, Gardner, Tinkler, Bumphrey, Gibson, Hall, Reed, Robertson, Hastings.

Burnley: Dawson, Reid, Taylor, McClaren, Boyle, Watson, Nesbitt, Hodgson, Freeman, Weightman, Harris.

When Burnley arrived at St Andrew's for this Second Division match, they were sitting proudly on top of the League table, their thoughts firmly set on winning promotion. The Blues were in the middle of the table and playing out the season, yet they dented Burnley's promotion hopes by outplaying them.

A crowd of 35,000 – the biggest of the season – saw a young amateur from Doncaster Rovers, Arthur Reed, make his debut for the Blues at centre-forward. He had a marvellous debut, scoring twice and giving the visitors' defence a 'right royal roasting'. The Blues had the advantage of a strong wind behind them in the first half, and Burnley had to face an intense sun. After Dawson, in the visitors' goal, had saved three good efforts from Jack Hall, George Robertson and Dickie Gibson, debutant Reed was denied a goal through offside.

The Blues went ahead after 20 minutes when some excellent work by Robertson and Albert Gardner set up Hall, whose powerful right-foot shot left the 'keeper stranded. Six minutes

PLAYER FACTFILE

RICHARD 'DICKIE' SAMUEL GIBSON
Outside-right
120 appearances, 19 goals
Joined Manchester United in June 1921.

Born in Holborn, London in February 1889, Dick began his football career with Sultan FC before joining Blues in September 1911. He was a flying winger with the tendency to overdo his dribbling skills. He began as an inside-forward, but when he switched to the wing his true ability became apparent. Dick had a quick temper and was often in trouble with officialdom. Before leaving Blues for Manchester United in June 1921, he recommended Percy Barton to St Andrew's. He stayed at Old Trafford until May 1922. During World War One he guested for Leicester Fosse.

later, Reed celebrated his first senior outing for the Blues, making it 2–0 with a sweetly struck shot from the edge of the area, after Hall and Walter Hastings had created the opening.

Dawson continued to perform heroics, stopping three efforts in four minutes as the Blues piled on the pressure. Blues were enjoying themselves and in the 61st minute, Gibson broke away down the right and, from his cross, Hastings cut in from the opposite flank and blasted in number three. With 15 minutes left Reed grabbed a fourth to give the Blues a notable victory.

Arthur Reed made 29 appearances and scored 13 goals. He was an unlikely looking footballer, being 5ft 5in tall with a 'roly-poly' physique. He only played one senior game for Doncaster Rovers, which was a Cup Final in which he scored the winning goal, only for the Rovers to be disqualified for playing an unregistered player.

Game Six

Hampton's Four-Goal Debut

BLUES 8 NOTTINGHAM FOREST 0

Date: 10 March 1920　　　　　　　　　　　　**Venue:** St Andrew's
Attendance: 15,000　　　　　　　　　　　　**Referee:** E.Pullan (Leeds)

Blues: Tremelling, White, Womack, Evans, Millard, Roulson, Burkinshaw, Hampton Lane, Whitehouse, Davies.

Nottingham Forest: Johnson, Barrett, Jones, Belton, Lowe, Armstrong, Davis, Spaven, Hart, Lithgoe, Shearman.

Blues introduced two new forwards to their line up: Harry Hampton (ex-Aston Villa and England) and Joe Lane (formerly of Blackpool, who cost a record £6,500). They got off to a great start as Blues registered their biggest win of the first post-war season.

The energy of Hampton was a revelation while Lane was all muscle and aggression in dealing with a combative defence. 'This new strike-force was unstoppable going down the centre of the pitch' reported the *Birmingham Gazette.* Blues were lying second in the table behind Tottenham Hotspur and were too good for their opponents even before they were reduced to 10 men when their centre-forward, Hart, was carried off with a fractured leg after 41 minutes.

Hampton opened the scoring in the 20th minute after George Davies's centre

PLAYER FACTFILE

JOSEPH HENRY 'HARRY' HAMPTON
Centre-forward
59 appearances, 31 goals
4 appearances for England
Joined Newport County in September 1922.

'Harry' was born in Wellington, Shropshire, on 21 April 1885. He began playing for Wellington Council School, Shifnal Juniors and Wellington Town in 1902 before signing for Aston Villa as a professional in April 1904. While at Villa Park he won the Division One Championship in 1910, a Division One runners'-up medal in 1913 and an FA Cup-winners' medal in 1905, 1913 and 1920. He joined Blues in February 1920 aged 34 and soon became a favourite of the fans with his all-action style. Known as 'The Wellington Whirlwind', he scored 242 goals in 376 games for the Villa, and he once charged over the 20st giant goalkeeper Willie Foulke in an attempt to score a goal. He prematurely retired while at Newport County in May 1923, only to rejoin Wellington Town in January 1924. He acted as coach at Preston North End from June to December 1925. He returned to St Andrew's as a youth coach from October 1934 to April 1936. 'Appy Arry' guested for Derby County and Nottingham Forest during World War One, and he played for the Football League XI on three occasions.

had beaten the Forest defence. The second came six minutes later when Hampton tapped in from six yards after Lane's shot had rebounded to him off Johnson's body and an upright.

In the second half Forest were completely outplayed.

48th: Lane hammered Davies's cross into the net, 3–0.

63rd: Hampton headed in a rebound of the crossbar from Lane's shot, 4–0.

68th: Lawrie Burkinshaw slammed in a 30-yarder, 5–0.

73rd: Burkinshaw turned in Davies's pinpoint centre, 6–0.

88th: Hampton turned in a rebound off Johnson from a Jack Whitehouse blockbuster, 7–0.

89th: Lane tucked away Davies's cross, 8–0.

Game Seven

Bill Harvey – Manager

BLUES 6 BOLTON WANDERERS 1

Date: 4 April 1927   **Venue:** St Andrew's
Attendance: 8,000

Blues: Tremelling, Womack, Barton, Liddell, Cringan, Dale, Bond, Crosbie, Bradford, Briggs, Scriven.

Bolton Wanderers: Gil, Greenhalgh, Finney, Cope, Round, Thornborough, Butler, Jack, Roberts, Gibson, Wright.

The two points secured ensured that Blues took a giant step towards Division One safety. The Board had removed Billy Beer as manager in March and appointed Bill Harvey as manager-secretary. He only had one full season in charge, being replaced for the 1928–29 season by Leslie Knighton. Harvey had an immediate impact with this scoreline, the highest of the season, beating the 4–0 drubbing of Manchester City in the previous home game. It was a weakened Wanderers that paraded in front of a meagre St

1926–27 team photograph. *Top row, left to right:* A.P. Brown, Brown, Bond, Bowden, Avon, Neale, Hibbs, Wood, Garratt, Viney, Moore. *Second row:* S. Scholey (trainer), Crosbie, Staley, Castle, Ashurst, Harvey, Tremelling, Barton, Cringan, Wharton, W. Kendrick (assistant trainer). *Third row:* Bradford, Bruce, Dale, Jones, Briggs, Womack, Harris, Hunter, Thirlaway, Liddell, Islip. *Bottom row:* Firth, Hamby, Leslie, Smith, Russell, Scriven.

PLAYER FACTFILE

WILLIAM HENRY TOMPKINS HARVEY
Outside-right
79 appearances, 2 goals
Joined Southend United in August 1925.
Blues assistant-manager-secretary in August 1926.
Team manager from March 1927 to May 1928.

Billy was born in Freemantle, Hampshire, on 12 April 1896. He played for Yorkshire Amateurs, 2nd Battalion West Riding Regiment and Sheffield Wednesday before joining Blues as an amateur in July 1921, signing a professional contract in the following November. He was a speed merchant on the wing, instantly recognisable by his heavy moustache. He joined the Shrimpers in 1925 before returning to Blues as assistant secretary in August 1926. He was promoted to team manager in March 1927, staying in post until May the following year. He then managed Chesterfield from June 1932 to June 1938 when he moved to Gillingham as manager until September 1939. While at Chesterfield they won the Division Three North Championship in 1936. Harvey gained a cap for the England Amateur team and also represented the FA on a tour of South Africa in 1920. He fell in love with South Africa and died there in July 1970. He was also a keen cricketer, playing for Warwickshire and Border province in South Africa.

Andrew's crowd, with four first-team regulars missing. Bradford and Briggs were exceptional upfront, exploiting great service from the midfield and wings. Scriven had his best game for the Blues, and Bond on the other wing created enough chances for Blues to have won by an even larger margin. Despite a strong cross wind, Blues' defence, marshalled by Liddell, never looked in danger, and it was no surprise when Blues took the lead after six minutes, Bradford converting easily after some great work on the right flank by Womack and Bond. A minute later Bolton exploited the wind, and although Tremelling caught the ball he was bundled over the line with it, and an equaliser was given, claimed by Gibson. Midway through the first half Blues regained the advantage, with Crosbie and Womack teeing up a heading opportunity for Briggs. Blues took total control in the second period, with goals from Cringan, Crosbie, Bradford and Crosbie again to make the final score 6–1.

Game Eight

FA Cup Third-Round Knockout?

BLUES 4 PETERBOROUGH & FLETTON UNITED 3

Date: 14 January 1928   **Venue:** St Andrew's
Attendance: 38,128   **Referee:** I. Stouther (Nottingham)

Blues: Tremelling, Womack, Randle, Morrall, Cringan, Leslie, Bond, Crosbie, Bradford, Davies, Ellis.

Peterborough & Fletton United: Whitehead, Hutchinson, Betteridge, Dickinson, Forrester, Irving, McGuigan, MacNaughton, Bruton, Lowson, Willis.

Blues were the bookmakers, favourites to humiliate non-League Peterborough & Fletton United easily in this third-round FA Cup-tie at St Andrew's. Peterborough & Fletton United were in new territory, having never got this far in the competiton previously, but they were well supported by over 4,000 travelling supporters.

The pre-game prediction seemed to be going to plan when Welsh cap Stan Davies scored on seven minutes, converting a cross from Benny Bond from 15 yards. This was the beginning of an onslaught, thought the St Andrew's faithful – and so it was for the first quarter of an hour which resulted in lots of Blues pressure but with no one capable of converting their numerous chances.

So it was no great surprise when Bruton equalised after 19 minutes, following up to turn in a rebound after Dan Tremelling had fumbled a Willis shot. Peterborough & Fletton United gained confidence and went into the lead after 24 minutes when a second fumble by the normally rock-solid Tremelling allowed Bruton to get his second.

After Davies had missed a sitter from close range, McGuigan gave the visitors a 3–1 advantage on 43 minutes. So at the interval it was a stunned St Andrew's contemplating an incredible Cup giant-killing feat.

After 60 minutes, Joe Bradford reduced the arrears and, as Peterborough & Fletton United began to tire, Bradford equalised with 15 minutes to go. With the visitors deserving a draw and a reply at home, a 30-yard defence-splitting pass from Johnny Crosbie enable Bradford to complete his hat-trick and send a lucky Blues side into the fourth round, where they beat Wrexham, only to lose to Manchester United in the sixth.

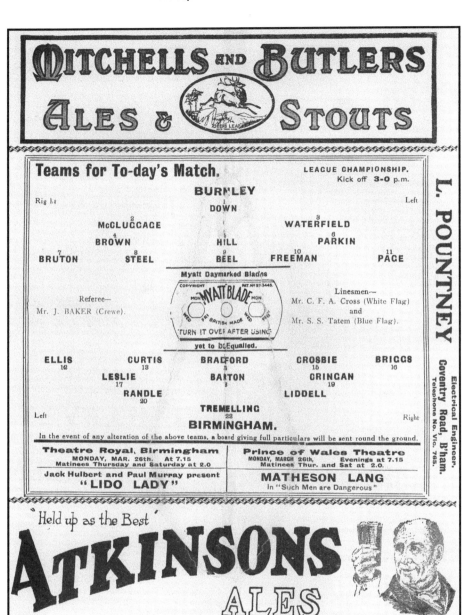

An example of how a programme looked in 1928.

RICHARD DANIEL TREMELLING
Goalkeeper
395 appearances, 0 goals
1 appearance for England
Joined Bury in May 1932.

Born in Mansfield Woodhouse, Nottinghamshire, on 12 November 1897, Tremelling played local football for Langwith Junction, Wagon Works FC and Shirebrook Juniors before joining Lincoln City as a professional in August 1918. Dan joined Blues on 13 May 1919, and he left on 13 May 1932, having spent exactly 13 years at the Blues and played in 13 FA Cup ties! He was totally reliable and a dependable goalkeeper, who when required could be brilliant. He became a 'keeper by accident when he was forced to go between the posts during an injury crisis at Langwith Junction, where he had played left-back until that fateful day. After his time at Gigg Lane he returned to Blues as an assistant trainer in June 1936, staying there until September 1941. He played for the Football League XI on three occasions. He died in Birmingham on 15 August 1978.

Game Nine

FA Cup Final

WEST BROMWICH ALBION 2 BLUES 1

Date: 25 April 1931   **Venue:** Wembley
Attendance: 90,368   **Referee:** Mr A. Kingscott (Derby)

West Bromwich Albion: Pearson, Shaw, Trentham, Magee, Bill Richardson, Edwards, Glidden, Carter, Billy Richardson, Sandford, Wood.

Blues: Hibbs, Liddell, Barkas, Cringan, Morrall, Leslie, Briggs, Crosbie, Bradford, Gregg, Curtis.

The road to Wembley
Round 3 Liverpool (a) 2–0 Curtis, Bradford
Round 4 Port Vale (h) 2–0 Bradford 2
Round 5 Watford (h) 3–0 Bradford, Curtis 2
Round 6 Chelsea (h) 2–2 Bradford, Curtis
Round 6 replay Chelsea (a) 3–0 Bradford 2, Firth
Semi-final Sunderland (Leeds) 2–0 Curtis 2

A wet but eager 90,368 crowd packed into Wembley to cheer the first all-Midlands Final for 36 years and Birmingham's first final in 50 years of trying. It was Blues from Division One against promotion-chasing Second Division West Bromwich Albion. The rain threatened to spoil the occasion, and it was the wettest Cup Final in years, ensuring both sides would be tested on the huge Wembley pitch in the mud. Blues settled to the conditions well and on their first real attack had the ball in the Albion net. A free-kick from Cringan was floated over towards the running Bob Gregg, who steered his header past a flat-footed Pearson for a perfect start; however, linesman Harold Mee of Nottingham surprised almost everyone in the stadium when he raised his flag to rule it out for offside. Blues, to their credit, put the disappointment to one side and were soon back attacking. Joe Bradford broke clear, but Pearson rushed out to smother the Blues forward, then Curtis sent in a dangerous-looking cross, which again was clipped away from Bradford, this time by centre-half Magee. Albion then countered, and Barkas just managed to catch and then clear from Glidden, who had raced free from a hopeful long-ball clearance. It was now a good end-to-end game, with both teams looking likely to score, and after 25 minutes Albion went in front. A fiercely hit Glidden cross struck Barkas on the hand, and before the Albion players made any appeal Richardson latched onto the loose ball. His first-time shot was blocked by Hibbs, but he followed up to smash in the rebound. Blues came close moments later with Bradford and Crosbie, who should have made more of their chances inside the Albion penalty area. Then, with half-time approaching, Bradford should surely have equalised when he stubbed his shot, and the ball bobbled past Pearson who scrambled across his line, grateful to see it roll wide of the post. Albion were better starters in the second half, and Hibbs pulled off a great save from Wood. On their next attack Wood hit the post with a belting shot from 20 yards as Blues held on and tried to settle the game down. As the Albion storm subsided, Blues counter-attacked. A long ball from Crosbie found Bradford, and as his fellow forwards looked to make space for a return pass he turned sharply and in the same movement shot past Pearson, and Blues were level on 56 minutes at 1–1. But with the Blues fans still celebrating the goal, Albion hit back with a sucker punch. After the ball was thumped forward Liddell failed to clear

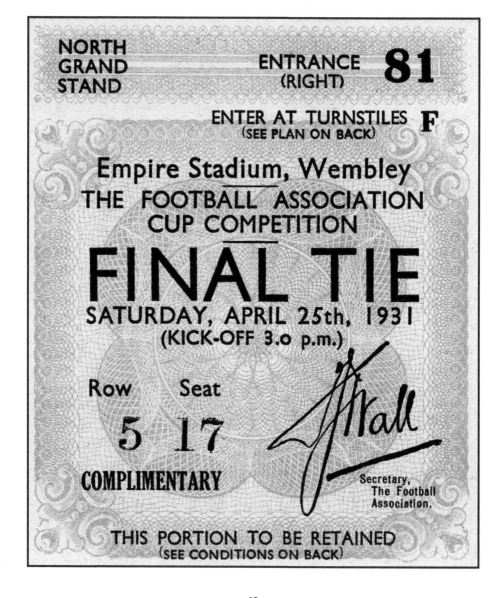

to any great distance and W.G. Richardson pounced to slip it past Hibbs from close range. Albion dominated the final moments of the game, and only the brilliant Hibbs kept Blues in with a slight chance with some brave diving saves, which kept the score down to 2–1. Blues will always rue the early disallowed goal, but Albion had earned their win and made it a Cup/promotion double when they won their last two League matches of the season.

THE 1931 FA CUP FINAL TEAM – WHERE DID THEY GO?

Name	All-time Apps	All-time Gls	Outcome
Hibbs, Harry	389	0	Retired, 1940
Liddell, George	345	6	Retired, 1932
Barkas, Ned	288	9	Chelsea, 1937
Cringan, Jimmy	285	12	Boston United, 1934
Morrall, George	266	7	Swindon Town, 1936
Leslie, Alec	143	0	Retired, 1932
Briggs, George	324	107	Plymouth Argyle, 1933
Crosbie, Johnny	431	72	Chesterfield, 1932
Bradford, Joe	445	267	Bristol City, 1935
Gregg, Bob	75	15	Chelsea, 1933
Curtis, Ernie	180	53	Cardiff City, 1933

A **1931 Birmingham team group.** *Top row, left to right:* Mr A. Leslie Knighton (manager), H. Hibbs, W.N. Blyth, K.C. Tewkesbury, G.R. Morrall, D.R. Tremelling, T. Fillingham, J. Bradford, A. Taylor (trainer). *Middle row:* J.A. Cringan, G. Haywood, G.R. Briggs, E. Barkas (Captain), G.W. Hicks, E. R. Curtis, A.J. Leslie. *Bottom row:* T.E. Robinson, W. Horsman, J. Randle, G. Liddell (inset), J. Crosbie, J. Firth, H. Booton.

PLAYER FACTFILE

EDWARD BARKAS
Full-back
288 appearances, 9 goals
Left Blues for Chelsea in 1937.

Ned Barkas was born in Wardley, Northumberland, on 21 November 1919. He played for St Hilda's Boys, East Bordern, Hebburn Colliery, Bedlington United, South Shields, Wardley Colliery, Norwich City and Bedlington United for a second spell before turning professional with Huddersfield Town in January 1921. While at Huddersfield he won the Division One Championship in 1924 and 1926 and won an FA Cup runners'-up medal in 1928 among 131 senior games. He joined Blues for a then club record transfer fee of £4,000 in December 1928. He was Leslie Knighton's first signing for Blues. He was a tough-tackling, hard-working full-back, which was exactly what you would expect from a player brought up in mining communities. Knighton signed him again, this time for Chelsea, in May 1937. After two years Ned returned to the Midlands to become player-manager of Solihull Town, and he then helped out Willmott Breedon FC in 1943–44 and Nuffield Mechanics in 1944–45, while working as a charge hand in a munitions factory. In the summer of 1926 he toured Canada with the Football Association.

The FA Cup Final Programme

Advertising

The programme for this match was the first ever to have product advertising on the front cover: 'DRINK BOVRIL – ONCE IT'S IN YOU IT'S SINEW' was the slogan – you obviously could not keep a good advertising man down, even in those days. The cost of the programme was sixpence or a tanner, and it consisted 36 pages, packed with information and advertisements, which are fascinating to read now:

OSRAM VALVES – The public's 'final' choice for radio – no transistors in those days.

MYATT DAYMARK BLADES – As supplied for the third time under Annual Contract to the whole British Army – product endorsement was around even then.

MADAME TUSSAUD'S announced: 'LOOK! THERE'S BARKAS and THAT'S GLIDDEN'. 'Here they are – at Madame Tussaud's – both rival captains!'

CLASSIC CURLY CUT TOBACCO – 10d per ounce – The 'extra-time' Tobacco.

LOCKWOOD & BRADLEY – Special Cup-Tie Tailoring Offer – All Wool Botany Serge Suits for 50 shillings.

The cover of the programme of the day, including advertising on the cover for the first time. An original would cost approximately £1,000.

RECKITTS BATH CUBES – FEET, FEET, FEET YOUR FEET NEVER GET A HOLIDAY.

BEMAX – Whatever your system needs – YOU'RE BOUND TO BENEFIT FROM BEMAX – The Natural Vitamin Tonic Food 2/6d.

TRUE STORY – 100 pages of thrilling real-life stories – fully illustrated 6d.

MACKINTOSH'S 'CHEWLETS' – The Great British Chewing Sweet – five for 1d.

ST. MARGARET – West Bromwich Albion are playing to-day in St. Margaret Jerseys.

The match-day programme was also used to promote other sporting events:

RUGBY LEAGUE FINAL – York v Halifax – best priced seats are 10/6d.

GREYHOUND RACING – Tonight at 8 – Public restaurant – Free Parking for Motor Coaches and Dancing Free.

ROYAL TOURNAMENT – Olympia – May 28 to June 13.

Just like in today's programmes, a section on 'HOW THEY REACHED THE FINAL' was included to appeal to the statisticians. This information is reproduced below.

BIRMINGHAM

		GOALS			
		F	A	Gate	Receipts
Third round.	v Liverpool (A)	2	0	40,500	£2,655
Fourth round.	v Port Vale (H)	2	0	44,119	£2,763
Fifth round.	v Watford (H)	3	0	49,757	£3,223
Sixth round.	v Chelsea (H)	2	2	55,298	£4,298
Replay	v Chelsea (A)	3	0	74,365	£5,147
Semi-final	v Sunderland	2	0	43,572	£3,939
(at Leeds)		14	2	307,611	£22,016

Goalscorers:
Bradford 7
Curtis 6
Firth 1
Total 14

WEST BROMWICH ALBION

		GOALS			
		F	A	Gate	Receipts
Third round.	v Charlton (H)	2	2	25,000	£1,574
First replay.	v Charlton (A)	1	1	18,700	£1,050
Second replay.	v Charlton (Villa Park)	3	1	27,700	£1,805
Fourth round.	v Tottenham H. (H)	1	0	40,850	£2,402
Fifth round.	v Portsmouth (A)	1	0	30,891	£2,410
Sixth round.	v Wolverhampton W (H)	1	1	52,300	£3,150
Replay	v Wolverhampton W (A)	2	1	46,860	£3,410
Semi-final	v Everton	1	0	69,421	£7,629
(at Old Trafford)		12	6	311,722	£23,430

Goalscorers:

W.G. Richardson	4
Wood	4
Carter	2
Glidden	1
Sandford	1
Total	12

So a total of 307,611 fans paid £22,016 to see Blues play in the FA Cup, excluding the Final. That equates to an approximate average admission charge per person of 1s 6d.

Entertainment

Throughout the afternoon there was a programme of musical entertainment laid on for the supporters.

PROGRAMME OF MUSIC
1.30 p.m. to 2.15 p.m. THE BAND OF HIS MAJESTY'S IRISH GUARDS
(By permission of Colonel H.V. Pollok, C.B.E., D.S.O.)
Director of Music — Lieut. J.L.T. Hurd L.R.A.M., P.S.M.

1. March	'The Mad Major'	Alford
2. Selection	'The Student Prince"	Romberg
3. Valse	'You Will Remember Vienna'	Young
4. Selection	'The Three Musketeers'	Friml
5. (a) Tango	'O Donna Clara'	Peterburski
(b) One Step	'There's a Good Time Coming'	Butler
6. Selection of Old English Airs arr. Myddleton		

Daily Express song sheet.

2.15 p.m. to 2.45 p.m. — COMMUNITY SINGING

Arranged by the 'Daily Express' National Community Singing Movement
Conductor — Mr T.P. Ratcliff
Accompanied by the Band of H.M. Welsh Guards (By permission of Colonel R.E.K.
Leatham D.S.O.)
Director of Music — Capt. Andrew Harris L.R.A.M.

2.50 p.m. to 2.55 p.m. — BANDS OF H.M. IRISH GUARDS
& H.M. WELSH GUARDS
GOD SAVE THE KING

3.45 p.m. — MARCHING BY THE COMBINED BANDS
After the Match — THE COMBINED BANDS WILL PLAY

Player Profiles
Pen pictures of the Birmingham stars appeared as is often still seen today.

PEN PICTURES OF PLAYERS

BIRMINGHAM

H. HIBBS (Goalkeeper) Born: Wilnecote. (Height 5ft 9 and half inches; Weight 12 st 2 lb.)

Without doubt the greatest goalkeeper in Great Britain and one of the finest who has ever played for England. There is no aspect of goal keeping at which Hibbs is not an expert. He has, of course, played many times for England and should continue to do so.

G. LIDDELL (Right Full-Back) Born: Durham. (Height 5ft 8 and three quarters of an inch; Weight 11 st 3 lb.)

Originally a half-back, Liddell has developed into a fearless and safe defender. Throughout the Cup competition Birmingham have been noted for stability and safety in defence, to which Liddell has contributed a fair share.

E. BARKAS (Left Full-Back) Born: Wardley Colliery. (Height 5ft 7 and three quarters of an inch; Weight 12 st 12 lb.)

Barkas has had experience of a Cup Final: he played with the Huddersfield team that lost to Blackburn Rovers in 1927–28. Captain of Birmingham, he inspires his men with his own deeds. He asks no quarter from any man, nor does he give quarter. Dogged and safe is Barkas, certain to fight to the last whether his side is leading or not.

J.A. CRINGAN (Right Half-Back) Born: Douglas Water, Scotland. (Height 5ft 9 inches; Weight 11 st 7 lb.)

Formerly a centre half-back, Cringan is now playing equally well on the wing. He is the type of player to succeed in any position, for he is untiring in action and most difficult to overcome; in fact, he is one of the most stubborn half backs in the First Division, for he never gives up.

G.T. MORRALL (Centre Half-Back) Born: Smethwick. (Height 5ft 11 inches; Weight 12 st.)

Before the England team to meet Scotland was chosen, Morrall was one of the newspaper favourites for the centre-half position. There are few better pivots in the game to-day. His height is of great advantage with the ball in the air, but wherever it is Morrall is reliable and sure. His tackling is keen and, if defensive play seems his stronger point, attack is not quite forgotten for his passes out to the wing are exceptionally accurate and worrying to the opposition.

A. LESLIE (Left Half-Back) Born: Greenock. (Height 5ft 8 inches; Weight 10 st.)

The lightest player on the field today; yet lack of ounces does not affect his play. With the possible exception of Magee, Leslie is probably the best attacking half-back in the match. His play is typically Scottish, his push passes through to the forwards being ideal for attack.

G.R. BRIGGS (Outside-right) Born: Wombwell, Yorkshire. (Height 5ft 8 inches; Weight 12 st.)

Another personality of the game. Briggs is a match winner; he may appear ordinary for some time, then he will pop up to score a great goal. In fact, there is no branch of forward play in which he does not excel and, as his weight might indicate, once he has the ball he takes some moving off it. It is said that he does not look the part of a footballer, but opposing defences know that appearances, when Briggs is concerned, are highly deceptive.

J. CROSBIE (Inside-right) Born: Glenbuck, Ayr. (Height 5ft 9 inches; Weight 10 st 5 lb.)

The master mind of the Birmingham attack. Cup Finals have been won by teams who had a star inside forward, and history may well be repeated to-day, for Crosbie is really a star. He rarely scores goals, he does not shoot very often; he really makes the openings for others. Without Crosbie the Birmingham team would be sadly handicapped — it is fortunate for this unlucky club that Crosbie has escaped serious injury.

J. BRADFORD (Centre-forward) Born: Pegg's Green. (Height 5ft 9 and three quarrtes of an inch; Weight 12 st 6 lb.)

A great all-round forward capable of scoring from any angle, Bradford has been for some seasons one of our finest footballers. Some weeks ago he was injured in a League game, and there were fears that he might have to miss to-day's game, it adequately sums up the value of Bradford to Birmingham to say that it would have been a tragedy had he not played.

J. FIRTH (Inside-left) Born: Doncaster. (Height 5ft 8 and half inches; Weight 12 st.)

Originally a right half-back, Firth came into the Birmingham team halfway through the Cup competition. He supplied the dash which had been missing. A most versatile and valuable man.

E. CURTIS (Outside-left) Born: Cardiff. (Height 5ft 7 and half inches; Weight 11 st 4 lb.)

Came from Cardiff City as an inside-left, in which position he has played for Wales. As a winger he has developed strength and his shooting power has become more marked. He scored both goals against Sunderland in the semi-final round. Curtis played for Cardiff City in the Final when the Cup was taken to Wales for the first time; he was then at outside-right.

The Match Preview

TODAY'S GAME
By
W.F. SANDERSON
Sports Editor, 'Sunday News'

This meeting to-day of two clubs who are neighbours — though it is not strictly correct to call it an all-Birmingham Final — once again brings into prominence the great attraction of the Football Association Cup Competition; anything can happen. Of the hundreds of clubs who have battled through the rounds, two are left whose grounds are but a few miles apart.

The captains shake hands.

There is more in the game, however, than this friendly, but keen rivalry. West Bromwich Albion a few seasons ago were slipping from the high place which has always been theirs in the game of football. The club saw the danger and acted. They decided upon a policy of rebuilding.

The team of to-day is the result. Youth was given its chance; young men were found and trained on in the tradition of West Bromwich Albion — to play good football. There was no haste or desire for quick results. Time was allowed to have its effect, and whatever happens this afternoon it is certain the Albion will play good football.

Turning to Birmingham, we see the result of amazing courage. There has been but one previous round when Birmingham were expected by the experts to win; always theirs was a frail chance. Yet they are here to-day and the others are gone. There is even more than that, I cannot recall a club who have been faced with such misfortune as have Birmingham.

Their number of seriously injured players in one season is a record. On the top of this they have had illnesses and set-backs. I think I am right in saying that not once in the Cup Competition this season have they been able to select their team until the morning of the game, and to-day there is a grave doubt about that great forward, Bradford. Theirs is a triumph over adversity.

Perhaps Birmingham do not play the same scientific game as West Bromwich Albion; it is impossible to do so with a much-changed team. Yet despite these things, Birmingham are effective, and that is what counts.

So the promise of to-day's game is good. There are no favourites, there can be no logical favourites in a Cup Final, and I am prepared to leave the game with the remark that whoever wins will well deserve the honour.

Game Ten

Bradford's Record

BLUES 4 PORTSMOUTH 0

Date: 24 December 1932 **Venue:** St Andrew's
Attendance: 10,000 **Referee:** W.J. Lewington (Croydon)

Blues: Hibbs, Booton, Barkas, Stoker, Morrall, Calladine, Briggs, Grosvenor, Bradford, Gregg, Curtis.

Portsmouth: Gilfillan, Mackie, Billy Smith, Nichol, Allen, Thackeray, Worrall, Jack Smith, Weddle, Easson, Rutherford.

Note: *Lewington missed the first five minutes of the match due to a train delay; his senior linesman Mr Bourne of Bristol replaced him for that period.*

Blues striker Joe Bradford became the most prolific goalscorer for one club in the Football League at this match. His fifth-minute goal, Blues' second, brought up a record-breaking 233, surpassing Bloomer's previous record of 232 for Derby County. Blues were at full strength apart from Calladine replacing Cringan who was injured.

Blues attacked the Railway End and after four minutes were awarded a direct free-kick following Billy Smith's handball. Stoker's kick was charged down, but a poor clearance from Nichol let Grosvenor fire the ball in from close range. Seconds later it was 2–0 when right-back Mackie made a mistake for the visitors, and Bradford got onto the loose ball to smash it past Gilfillan, who had advanced out of his goal to collect

A programme cover from the 1932–33 season.

JOSEPH BRADFORD
Centre-forward
445 appearances, 267 goals
12 appearances for England
Joined Bristol City in May 1935.

Still the greatest striker in the history of Birmingham City Football Club, Joseph Bradford could so easily have been an Aston Villa player. As a youth he was a goalscoring machine within Leicestershire, once scoring 13 goals in one game. He was invited for a trial at Villa Park, but they would not pay his travel expenses; Blues did, and he signed as a professional in February 1920. He made a few appearances in the 1920–21 Second Division title-winning side, but it was the following season that saw him secure a regular first-team place. He was at Blues for 14 seasons and proved to be Mr Consistency, scoring at least 10 goals in 12 of those seasons. He scored for Blues in the 1931 FA Cup Final to become the first player to score an equaliser at Wembley. As well as his England caps, he also represented the Football League side on five occasions.

Mackie's back pass. Bradford was mobbed by his teammates following his record-breaking goal. Midway through the half Gregg went off for treatment, but still Pompey could not make progress against 10 men. On his return four minutes later, Gregg struck the bar with his first touch. Blues next attack saw them increase their lead to 3–0 on 27 minutes, as Grosvenor scored with a 20-yard drive that flew into the top corner of the net. Blues dominated the second half, and if not for a tremendous goalkeeping performance from Gilfillan, then the score could have been double figures. Blues' final goal came in the 88th minute from Gregg, sending the crowd home happy after witnessing a record-breaking day.

Game Eleven

Relegation Was Avoided

LEICESTER 3 BLUES 7

Date: 28 April 1934   **Venue:** Filbert Street
Attendance: 18,000   **Referee:** J.S. Brown (Blackburn)

Blues: Hibbs, Booton, Barkas, Stoker, Morrall, Calladine, Moffatt, Roberts, Mangnall, Bradford, Guest.

Leicester: McLaren, Black, Jones, Smith, Heywood, Ritchie, Adcock, Maw, Chandler, Lochhead, Liddle.

There cannot have been many occasions in football history when a team avoids relegation by scoring seven goals away from home. While this was not the final game of the 1933–34 season, it was Blues' last away fixture. The teams facing relegation were: Chelsea, Middlesbrough, Newcastle United, Liverpool and Aston Villa. The table looked like this:

MIDDLESRBOUGH	37 points
ASTON VILLA	36 points
LIVERPOOL	36 points
CHELSEA	35 points
NEWCASTLE UNITED	34 points
BIRMINGHAM CITY	34 points
SHEFFIELD UNITED	RELEGATED

The message for the Blues' players was that a draw would not be enough and the two points for a win could prove crucial.

The Filbert Street pitch was a mud bath, which suited Blues' style of play, so much so that they went ahead after four minutes from Sid Moffatt. Harry Hibbs was in great form and protected Blues lead up to the 25th minute when Chandler equalised. With just over an hour gone, Blues regained the initiative through Billy Guest who went on to score a second 60 seconds later. It was 3–1 at half-time with McLaren in the Leicester City goal performing heroics to keep the score down. After the break on the hour, Chandler pulled another goal back for the home side before Maw equalised five minutes later. At 3–3 it seemed to the visiting fans that Blues had lost the chance of a win, and the best that could be achieved was to secure the draw and hope that other results went in our favour! While the crowd was pessimistic, the Blues players were undaunted and went back into the lead a minute later thanks to Dave Mangnall. A Leicester own-goal by Jones

DAVID MANGNALL
Centre-forward
39 appearances, 15 goals
Joined West Ham United in March 1935 for £2,500.

Born in Wigan on 21 September 1907, Mangnall played junior football for Maltby New Church FC and Maltby Colliery, which resulted in trials for Rotherham United and Huddersfield Town. He eventually signed as an amateur with Doncaster Rovers in August 1926 aged 19, but the opportunity to turn professional came in November 1927 with Leeds United. Two years later, in December 1929, he was transferred back to Huddersfield Town for a fee of £4,000, where in season 1931–32 he scored 42 goals. His final total for the Terriers was 61 goals in 79 games. He joined Blues in February 1934, but his time at St Andrew's was marred by injury problems. After just over a year he moved to West Ham United for £2,500 in March 1935, where he rediscovered his goal-scoring form. This resulted in a move to Millwall in May 1936, where he won a Division Three South Championship medal in 1937 and a Division Three South Cup-winners' medal in the same year. He moved to Queen's Park Rangers in May 1939, and he guested for Fulham, Millwall and Southend United during World War Two. In April 1944 he was appointed as manager at Loftus Road, where he stayed until he retired in May 1952.

with 20 minutes to go gave Blues a 5–3 advantage, which was increased to 6–3 at 72 minutes thanks to Roberts. The two points were finally secured when Guest completed his hat-trick with five minutes left. Blues lost their final home game to Huddersfield Town 3–1 on 5 May. But this precious victory kept them in Division One with Newcastle United going through the trapdoor of relegation

Game Twelve

Post-wartime Thriller

CHELSEA 2 BLUES 3

Date: 10 November 1945   **Venue:** Stamford Bridge
Attendance: 52,959   **Referee:** E. Flinstone (Newmarket)

Blues: Merrick, Duckhouse, Jennings, Harris, Turner, Mitchell, Mulraney, Dougall, Wilson Jones, Bodle, White.

Chelsea: Woodley, White, Tennant, Russell, Harris, Ross, Goudling, Williams, Lawton, Goulden, Bain.

Wearing red-and-white stripes, Blues appeared unrecognised by the season's largest crowd of 52,959. Regardless of their appearance, there was no mistaken identity as they continued their impressive run of form at the start to the season with an away win at Stamford Bridge.

CHELSEA FOOTBALL & ATHLETIC CO. LTD.

Official Programme

Directors :—Capt. J. H. MEARS, R.M. (Chairman), J. E. C. BUDD,
C. J. PRATT, H. J. M. BOYER, L. J. MEARS.

Manager-Secy. :—Wm. BIRRELL.

Ground :—STAMFORD BRIDGE, S.W.6. 'Phone :—FUL. 3321.

Saturday, November 10th, 1945.   Price Twopence

Table—Football League, South.

	P	W	D	L	For	Ag	Pts
Charlton A.	13	10	2	1	36	13	22
Birmingham	13	9	1	3	37	14	19
Aston Villa	14	8	3	3	42	21	19
Wolverhamp'n	13	7	3	3	22	15	17
Derby County	13	7	2	4	28	18	16
W. Bromwich	14	7	2	5	40	30	16
West Ham U.	13	6	4	3	21	18	16
Millwall	12	6	3	3	25	15	15
Brentford	13	6	3	4	19	11	15
Fulham	13	6	3	4	27	24	15
CHELSEA	13	7	1	5	26	28	15
Portsmouth	13	6	2	5	28	22	14
Coventry City	12	4	5	3	17	14	13
Notts Forest	13	3	6	4	20	16	12
Southampton	12	4	2	6	29	28	10
Leicester City	13	3	4	6	17	25	10
Tottenham H.	12	4	1	7	22	35	9
Arsenal	13	2	3	8	18	33	7
Newport C.	13	3	1	9	14	37	7
Luton Town	13	1	4	8	15	34	6
Swansea Town	13	3	0	10	23	53	6
Plymouth A.	13	0	5	8	14	36	5

GOALSCORERS.

Football League, South

Reg Williams	...	7
Len Goulden	...	5
Alex Machin	...	4
Jimmy Bain	...	3
Dai James	...	2
W. McCall	...	2
H. Brown	...	1
Opponents (own goal)	...	2

London Combination

Clements	...	7
Dolding	...	5
Bacon	...	3
James	...	3
Machin	...	2
Williams, T.	...	1
Friend	...	1
Dougall	...	1
Hallam	...	1
Donaldson	...	1
Scannen	...	1

Next Home Game

Tuesday, Nov. 13th

VERSUS

DYNAMO TEAM

of Soviet Russia

Kick off 2.30 p.m.

HALF-TIME SCORES.

A.	Brentford v. Spurs	....
B.	Swansea T. v. Charlton A.	....
C.	Arsenal v. Fulham ...	....
D.	Aston Villa v. Plymouth A.	....
E.	Southampton v. West Ham	....
F.	Millwall v. West Bromwich	....
G.	Coventry C. v. Notts Forest	....
H.	Derby County v. Wolves...	....
J.	Leicester C. v. Newport C.	....
K.	Luton Town v. Portsmouth	....
L.	Bolton Wand. v. Sunderland	....
M.	Everton v. Sheffield United	....
N.	Newcastle U. v. Liverpool	....
O.	Preston N.E.v. Manchester U.	....
P.	Sheffield Wed. v. Blackpool	....
R.	Manchester City v. Bury...	....

CHARLES WILSON JONES
Centre-forward
150 appearances, 69 goals
2 appearances for Wales
Joined Nottingham Forest in September 1947.

A red-haired, frail-looking player, who was always referred to as Wilson, he was born in Pentre, near Broughton, Wrexham, on 29 April 1914. He first played for Brymbo Green FC before going on trial at Blackburn Rovers. Wilson then went for a trial at Bolton Wanderers before signing professional terms with his local side Wrexham in August 1932. He joined Blues for £1,500 in September 1934 and within six months was leading the line for his country. He moved to Nottingham Forest three years later, and before retiring in June 1950 he also served Redditch United and Kidderminster Harriers. During World War Two he guested for Blackpool, Huddersfield Town, West Bromwich Albion and Wrexham. He died in Birmingham on 9 January 1986.

Blues had lost both George Edwards and Don Dearson, who were on duty with the Welsh International team, while Chelsea were strengthened by the arrival of their new £14,000 signing from Everton – Tommy Lawton.

After six minutes Blues scored their first when Wilson Jones converted Ambrose Mulraney's centre after a clever pass from Fred Harris. Although Blues were the stronger, Chelsea managed an equaliser on 15 minutes when Williams intercepted a Frank Mitchell pass, slipped the ball to Lawton who rounded Gil Merrick to score his first goal on his home debut for his new club. After 41 minutes, and with half-time approaching, Blues were awarded a penalty, and Arthur Turner made no mistake blasting the ball past Woodley in the Chelsea goal.

After 60 minutes Chelsea got their second equaliser, again through Lawton. Nineteen minutes later Blues scored the game's best goal to secure a well-earned victory; Turner, who was undoubtedly the Man of the Match, won the ball in his own half, sent a fine pass to Wilson Jones who, taking the ball on the run, 'nut-megged' the defender and delightfully clipped the ball over the advancing goalkeeper, Woodley.

Game Thirteen

Champions of Division Two

Blues 4 West Bromwich Albion 0

Date: 29 March 1948   **Venue:** St Andrew's
Attendance: 43,168   **Referee:** A. Baker (Crewe)

Blues: Merrick, Green, Jennings, Harris, Duckhouse, Mitchell, Stewart, Dorman, Trigg, Bodle, Edwards.

West Bromwich Albion: Heath, Pemberton, Kinsell, Millard, Vernon, A.J. Evans, Elliot, Drury, Walsh, Haines, Rowley.

T he 1947–48 season's Second Division Championship title fight had been at the mercy of these two West Midlands for most of the campaign. West Bromwich Albion had led the Division since September, only to be pushed out from first place by the Blues in December. Blues played with real class and quality to win this vital clash which was virtually worth double the points.

Blues were at full strength and unchanged, while the Baggies made one significant change: their kit wearing white shirts and blue shorts. The morning's deluge of rain had

The champions of Division Two with their trophy. Back row, left to right: Dave Fairhurst (trainer), Green, Duckhouse, Merrick, Mitchell, Jennings. Front row: Stewart, Dougall, Harris, Harry Storer (manager), Trigg, Bodle, Edwards.

MONDAY, MARCH 29th 1948 **PRICE TWOPENCE**

THE "BLUES" NEWS

OFFICIAL PROGRAMME OF THE
BIRMINGHAM CITY FOOTBALL CLUB

President—ARTHUR WARD, Esq., K.C.
Directors—H. MORRIS, (*Chairman*) D. F. WISEMAN (*Vice-Chairman*),
W. A. CAMKIN, H. DARE, W. H. DARE, L. J. MORRIS, J. WOOLMAN,
S. .F. L. RICHARDS.
Manager—H. STORER.   Hon. Medical Officer—Dr. E. GREGORY.   Secretary—W. H. GRADY.

Southampton proved themselves a good side at St. Andrews' last Saturday week. They were dour and well-disciplined in their play but admitted that they were a little fortunate to return home with a point.   Once again it must be recorded that missed scoring chances denied us a victory which our mid-field superiority warranted.   On three occasions though, when the ball hit the posts, only a couple of inches prevented us getting that vital goal.   We must pay tribute to a fine goalkeeping display by Black, who as a guest for the 'Saints' in our League South championship year, gave one of the most marvellous exhibitions possible in our match at The Dell.   Black, in our opinion, must be very close to securing Scottish International honours— our players certainly think it would be a deserved recognition.

o   o   o   o

Postal applications for the Sheffield Wednesday rail and match excursion tickets on 24th April are arriving in good number.   We repeat that these applications must be accompanied by a stamped addressed envelope and a remittance of £1.   Personal applications can be made at the Cattell-road offices of the club commencing Wednesday of this week, but only between the hours of two and four p.m.

o   o   o   o

Our reserves did well to bring two points back from Watford last Saturday week. As Leicester City lost, we regained our lead at the head of our section in the Football Combination Cup.   The team are as keen as mustard to enter the semi-final of this Cup and a win at Norwich to-day will set them well on the way to satisfying their desire.

o   o   o   o

The Railway Executive (Western Region) announced the new series of Excursion Trains for all our matches for the remainder of the Season which will be of especial interest to our Supporters on the South side of Birmingham.   Trains calling at all Stations between Leamington Spa and Bordesley will run each match day leaving Leamington at 11-47 a.m., 12-30 p.m. and 1-30 p.m.   The Excursion rate is the single fare for the return journey.   We are always pleased to announce any transport arrangements either by road or rail which are a convenience to our supporters.

made the pitch a virtual quagmire, making it difficult for all the players but especially the defenders. Blues took early advantage of the conditions when seven minutes into the game, following a George Edwards corner, two Albion players slipped in a goalmouth incident to allow Jackie Stewart to score from two yards. After 17 minutes the muddy ground was once again influential in Blues' second. Vernon, under no pressure, played a back pass to Heath, which skidded off the pitch, despite a despairing attempt by goalkeeper Heath, the ball went out for a corner. From Stewart's flag-kick Harold Bodle rose magnificently to head the ball home at the far post.

Blues remained in control throughout the 90 minutes, and second-half goals from Cyril Trigg and another from Stewart gave Blues an impressive 4–0 victory.

PLAYER FACTFILE

EDWARD DUCKHOUSE
Full-back/Centre-half
127 appearances, 4 goals
Left Blues for Northampton Town in 1950.

Born in the Shelfied district of Walsall in April 1918, Ted Duckhouse played in local football until he was signed by West Bromwich Albion as an amateur in August 1937, aged 19. Blues took over his amateur contract in July 1938, and he signed professional terms in August 1939. He was a solid, rock-hard defender who broke his leg in the 1946 FA Cup semi-final replay against Derby County when attempting to prevent the first goal – an incident which had a major effect on the outcome of the game, which Blues lost 4–0. He was transferred to Northampton Town on a free transfer in August 1950, ending his playing career at Rushden Town in 1955 after a three-year spell.

Game Fourteen

The First Post-war Derby

VILLA 0 BLUES 3

Date: 4 December 1948   **Venue:** Villa Park
Attendance: 61,632   **Referee:** Captain F.C. Green (Wolverhampton)

Blues: Merrick, Green, Jennings, Harris, Duckhouse, Mitchell, Berry, Stewart, Dougall, Bodle, Roberts.

Villa: Rutherford, Martin, Cummings, A. Moss, F. Moss, Lowe, Mulraney, Dorsett, Ford, Edwards, Smith.

Villa Park was packed with over 60,000 fans looking forward to the first 'Second City' derby since March 1939.

Nine years had been an eternity for the partisan fans of both sides to wait for the return of local football hostilities. Blues fielded two players who had played in the previous Derby game: Fred Harris and Dennis Jennings. Villa had a similar returning contingent in the form of Joe Rutherford and George Cummings. It was a reunion of a different kind for ex-Blues winger Jack Mulraney who had swapped 'Blue and White' for 'Claret and Blue.'

Jackie Stewart, who had been signed from Raith Rovers in the Scottish League was the star of the show, scoring two fine goals. His first was after 15 minutes, when Ted Duckhouse sent a long ball into Villa territory, and a neat

PLAYER FACTFILE

JOHN GEBBIE STEWART
Outside-right
218 appearances, 55 goals
Joined Raith Rovers in February 1955.

Born in Lochgelly, Fife, in Scotland on 4 September 1921, Jackie played for Lochgelly Welfare and Donibristle Youth Club before joining Raith Rovers in August 1939. Jackie was signed by Harry Storer in January 1948. Storer promised he was 'trying to sign a Scottish winger who would enable the team to gain promotion', and that is what happened. Jackie was fast, direct and all-action, qualities that soon endeared him to the St Andrew's faithful. He was only 5ft 5in, but he was tough and fearless. A former miner, he had a tremendous shot and once scored four goals in a match against Manchester City in September 1948. In February 1955 he rejoined Raith Rovers after suffering injury problems. Later he became trainer at Stark's Park, where he stayed until retiring in 1963. He died in 1990 in Cowdenbeath.

interchange with Neil Dougall resulted in the 24-year-old Scot rifling the ball past Rutherford into the right-hand corner of the net.

Stewart added a second goal with 24 minutes left on the clock after Harold Bodle had headed on Harris's free-kick. With Blues' long-ball approach dominating Villa's short passing game, Bodle completed the scoring on 71 minutes.

Ken Green and Jennings, the Blues' full-backs, negated the wing threats of Mulraney and Smith, which meant that the service to Trevor Ford was restricted, giving Duckhouse a relatively easy game against the physically intimidating Welshman.

Game Fifteen

Nine Goals

BLUES 9 LIVERPOOL 1

Date: 11 December 1954
Attendance: 17,514

Venue: St Andrew's
Referee: G. McCabe (Sheffield)

Blues: Merrick, Hall, Green, Boyd, Smith, Warhurst, Astall, Lane, Brown, Murphy, Govan.

Liverpool: Rudham, Lambert, Lock, Wilkinson, Hughes, Twentyman, Payne, Anderson, Liddell, Evans, A'Court.

Birmingham City were on the rise and heading for the Second Division title; Liverpool, pre-Bill Shankly, were in transition. There could be only one possible conclusion – a significant Birmingham victory. Blues went into the game missing the influential Welsh international Noel Kinsey, who was out injured, and his place went to Jackie Lane.

This was a day when it all went right for Blues and the only surprise was that they did not surpass double figures. It is hard to say whether Liverpool were dreadful because Blues were so good. It has often been claimed that this Liverpool team lacked good players, but this is not the case. They boasted Laurie Hughes, who had played in the 1950 World Cup as a defender for England, and Alan A'Court, who would play as a winger in the 1958 World Cup. And then there was Billy Liddell, one of the top 20 players in the club's history. On the day, however, it was Blues who fielded the class players.

EDWIN BROWN
Centre-forward
185 appearances, 90 goals
Joined Leyton Orient in January 1959.

Eddie was the original 'journeyman' footballer. Knowing he only had a few tricks in his repertoire, he knew he had to move from club to club before he was found out by the opposition defenders, hence the number of clubs he served: Preston North End, Southampton, Coventry City, Blues, Leyton Orient, Scarborough, Stourbridge, Bedworth Town and Wigan Athletic before retiring in December 1964. He was a showman and often entertained the St Andrew's crowd with his antics, such as shaking hands with the corner flag after scoring a goal. He very nearly became a priest before the lure of leather and grass took over. A lover of Shakespeare, he went on to become a games teacher in Preston, his home town.

Less than a minute had gone when Jackie Lane opened the scoring with a shot that took a wicked deflection off Lambert, which sent Liverpool's 'keeper Doug Rudham the wrong way. It was the perfect start on a difficult pitch that was just playable. The full-strength Liverpool side never recovered. Eddie Brown scored the second, latching onto Boyd's pass and firing an 18-yard shot in off the post. Blues' third was due to a goalkeeping error; a corner by Astall was dropped by the 'keeper right onto Brown's toe, and this chance was almost impossible to miss. Liddell reduced the arrears with a fine goal on 19 minutes, hitting a thunderbolt which left Merrick motionless as the ball whistled past him into goal. Any hope of a Liverpool recovery ended when Gordon Astall scored in the 27th minute with a pile-driver from the edge of the penalty area, and four minutes into the second half he scored Blues' fifth goal by putting the ball in the net with his chest from Lane's cross. The second half was surreal; probably the best that Blues have enjoyed in all their time at St Andrew's. They scored five goals and could have scored five more on top of that. It was that type of afternoon. Peter Murphy scored the sixth on 54 minutes, Alex Govan the seventh on 77, Murphy the eighth on 84, with Brown scoring the ninth before the celebrations for the eighth goal had ended. Brown's performance in scoring a hat-trick was as good an individual display as by any Blues player at St Andrew's.

Game Sixteen

Champions of Division Two

DONCASTER ROVERS 1 BLUES 5

Date: 4 May 1955   **Venue:** Belle Vue
Attendance: 21,303

Blues: Schofield, Hall, Badham, Boyd, Smith, Warhurst, Astall, Kinsey, Brown, Murphy, Govan.

Doncaster Rovers: Hardwick, Makepeace, Gavin, Hunt, Williams, Herbert, Mooney, Jeffrey, Jimmy Walker, McMorran, Geoff Walker.

Blues finally did it! Promotion at last to the First Division, where they had not been since they were relegated in 1950. In a double bonus they also secured the Second Division Championship, pipping Luton. A crowd of 21,305 watched the match, including many travelling Blues fans and also followers of Rotherham, who would have benefited from a slip-up by Blues. Blues had to win this game, and they did so with an emphatic four-goal burst in a one-sided second half, which eventually ended with a 5–1 scoreline.

The opening minutes were a typical tense clash of biting tackles and goalmouth excitement, Blues taking advantage of a strong wind by loading high crosses which Hardwick often had difficulty with; however, he kept them out with an array of improvised

65

"WE KNOW WHEN YOU'RE WITH US"

—says **GIL MERRICK**

I'M particularly happy to have this chance of adding a few lines to our booklet because it gives me the opportunity of paying a tribute to our supporters and explaining just what they mean to the team. And after such a successful season and at the beginning of a new one in the top division the club's followers are close to mind. I can assure you that one of the thoughts expressed at Doncaster after the win that made sure of promotion was that the return to the first division was going to be as much of a reward for the supporters as for the lads themselves.

There is no doubt that good genuine support can make a lot of difference to a team. In fact, there are times when it can mean points. A big crowd at St. Andrews always has a more inspiring effect on the players than a small one.

And the presence of supporters at away games is rarely missed by the players. I won't go as far as to say that it makes the difference between winning and losing — there are more factors to it than that — but the fact that our own people have travelled a long way to see us is not overlooked. I remember, for example, after the Ipswich Cup-tie one of the lads saying in the dressing room " what a disappointment it must have been for our supporters who have come so far." And there was sincere agreement from the team, who believe we at that early stage after the game were so down in the dumps they would have been forgiven for thinking only of their own misfortune.

But happily our thoughts about supporters on long away games are not always so regretful as at Ipswich.

Both at home and particularly away I think the presence of our supporters has a moral boosting effect in so much as it makes the lads, who, after all, are only human, feel that what they are doing must be worth while to attract people.

Birmingham have a great reputation up and down the country for being well supported. I remember a player at one away ground asking me " do you always get a following as keen as this away from home?" And when I told him we did I felt he was not only surprised but a little envious. I hope I shall always be able to say that — and knowing the strength of our followers and the enthusiasm of our Supporters Club, I'm sure I shall.

HOW WE CAME FROM NOWHERE TO WIN IT

Skipper LEN BOYD tells the story :—

SURELY the most remarkable thing about last season was that at one time we occupied the lowest position in the table since the war and yet we came out on the very top. And, indeed, on the day we topped the table for the first time in the season in the very last match that anyone played, we were champions !

And there were new experiences for everyone in those 9—1 and 7—1 defeats of Liverpool and Port Vale that helped us to become something of club history makers in that we scored more goals than any other Birmingham side in this century.

And yet at one stage of the season, after a third or so of the matches had been played, I honestly thought we might have to struggle to avoid relegation. Once a team gets on the slide it wants some stopping, and we were not doing very well with an away record that had brought us only one victory in our first ten journeys.

Why was it, then, that the team changed round so completely in form and the season ended in quite the opposite way to what had been threatened ?

I think I can summarise it under three headings.

(1) The arrival of Mr. Arthur Turner as manager, and the change he brought about with the same players in their attitude and approach to the game.

(2) The great fighting spirit and will to win in a new atmosphere of playing for the club and a place in every game.

(3) The final sustained effort of great determination and enthusiasm, in the face of the longest odds, that made home and away games one and the same thing.

I genuinely think that Manager Turner's first object was to get the side moving in the right direction again. More points and fewer losses and a respectable place in the table were, I am sure, his immediate aims.

He succeeded in that in some startling home form. Port Vale, Liverpool and Stoke City, the latter a strong promotion tip, were all beaten well. But away from home we still looked like another team.

Then gradually the influence began to tell. We won at Notts Forest on the Boxing Day to begin a run of away form that had not seemed possible a few weeks before. Soon afterwards we won a battle royal at Rotherham, where, for the first time away from home, we looked a really hard to beat proposition.

Of course we didn't realise it at the time, but if we had not squared up to the hard as nails Rotherham challenge when they threw it down— and believe me, it was hard ; Johnny Watts got knocked out so often he must have been listening for the count—our final effort would have been only a narrow disappointment.

It was good to see the difference in the side. Men were fighting for the ball harder and there was a better team spirit in so much as men were more ready to help each other. It all helped to make us look a better side because we were controlling more of the ball.

Then came the Cup that always brings the best out of us, and in the success in the competition our form both at home and away was consolidated.

But it was not until almost at the end of our Cup run that there was serious talk of promotion in the dressing room. And then it was no more than a possibility that opened up, simply because we had games in hand. We were, in fact, seventh in the table, but nine points behind, but if we could win the four games in hand we could catch up. But how often has that "bird in the hand" proverb been proved right. Setting a promotion target of 54 points, we wanted 22 points from 15 games to do it. They were indeed long odds.

Looking back now, I think the vital match that turned it for us was the mid-week game against Doncaster, after we had been knocked out of the Cup.

It is always a desperate moment to fail in the Cup when the competition is well on. You have been built up to win this and that and then comes sudden failure. You have a sort of guilty conscience and you are fighting against disappointment and depression. I don't think there is any doubt that it cost Notts County their promotion chance after being knocked out by York City. It wasn't quite so bad for us, going out to the favourites, Manchester City. But it was our ability to beat Doncaster in the League match, when our morale was at its lowest, that made me feel, " Well, if this is how the team are approaching the task then we must have a chance of promotion."

We did not talk about promotion anything like as much as you might imagine, but I knew the lads felt that on the strength of recent seasons and on their performance up to then, they were worthy of going up. We had beaten most of the teams above us and the whole approach to the task was right. But what a battle we had. It was the toughest spell I have ever had in football. In that last spell every team we met, even those who had no chance of winning anything, seemed out to prove they were as good as us.

Finally, we had to get five points out of six, and all away from home—and we did it with a wonderful, never-to-be-forgotten final at Doncaster.

---

goalkeeping manoeuvres. The importance of the first goal was such that Blues allowed gaps in defence to appear. Doncaster took advantage of these, and Schofield did well to keep out a Jimmy Walker attempt. Moments later the 'keeper again pulled out a spectacular save from a Geoff Walker shot that had been deflected on its way towards him. On 38 minutes, however, the pressure from Blues paid off when Astall scored. Latching onto a pass from Murphy, he outclassed the Rovers' defence and, although his shot was blocked by Hardwick, Astall followed up to hammer in the rebound. This brought about more pressure from Blues as they pushed for another to wrap up the game. Despite Birmingham forcing three quick corners, however, it was Doncaster on a breakaway who got the game's second goal just a minute before half-time. Jimmy Walker rose to plant his header past Schofield from only the second corner of the game. So

Programme cover signed by Eddie Brown and Jeff Hall.

PETER MURPHY
Inside-left
278 appearances, 127 goals
Left Blues for Rugby Town.

'Spud' was born in West Hartlepool on 7 March 1922. Having played for Dunlop FC, he had amateur spells with Coventry and guested for Millwall, before signing professional forms for Coventry in May 1946. Four years later, after scoring 37 goals in 119 appearances, he joined Arthur Rowe's famous 'push and run' Tottenham Hotspur team for £18,500 and was part of the set-up that won the Division Two Championship in season 1950–51, deputising for Les Bennett and netting nine times in 25 games. When Bennett returned from injury Murphy found himself playing out of position on the left wing and was therefore grateful for the chance to move on when Blues signed him in January 1952 for £20,000, with a Spurs tally of 21 goals in 49 matches. His Blues career took off when Tommy Briggs left to join Blackburn Rovers in December 1952, and he was soon terrorising goalkeepers with his shots from 30–40 yards out. He topped the Blues' scoring list on four separate occasions and was a key member of the forward line of Astall, Kinsey, Brown, Murphy and Govan, in which each member was capable of scoring spectacular goals; indeed, he scored a hat-trick on his debut in a 5–0 victory over Doncaster Rovers. In 1959 he was taken on as a coach for the youngsters, but was called back into the first team as they struggled against relegation, scoring four goals in seven games which resulted in the drop being avoided. He had a brief spell in non-League football with Rugby Town, as manager, guiding them to promotion to the Southern League Premier Division, and then looked after the Coventry City A team before retiring in May 1961. He died on 7 April 1975 aged 53.

typically Blues, after dominating and needing to win, were now level at the break and needing another goal. Again they would have to do it the difficult way.

The second half started much in the manner of the first, only this time Blues put their chances away. The first came after 55 minutes, Hardwick again only half-saving a shot by Murphy, who picked up the rebound to score via the inside of the post. Just 10 minutes later Brown controlled a cross from Hall skilfully enough to turn and fire past Hardwick. There was no restraining Blues now, and after 73 minutes Brown went through on a weaving run which opened up Rovers' defence again. He then waited at the edge of the area and lobbed a pass to Astall, who volleyed in Blues' fourth. A memorable night ended perfectly when, right on the final whistle, Govan scored a fifth goal, and the Championship celebrations started in earnest.

FA Cup Final

MANCHESTER CITY 3 BLUES 1

Date: 5 May 1956   **Venue:** Wembley
Attendance: 100,000   **Referee:** Mr A. Bond (Middlesex)

Manchester City: Trautmann, Leivers, Little, Barnes, Ewing, Paul, Johnstone, Hayes, Revie, Dyson, Clarke.

Blues: Merrick, Hall, Green, Newman, Smith, Boyd, Astall, Kinsey, Brown, Murphy, Govan.

The road to Wembley
Round 3 Torquay United (a) 7–1 Brown 3, Murphy 2, Astall, Kinsey
Round 4 Leyton Orient (a) 4–0 Brown 2, Murphy, Finney
Round 5 West Bromwich Albion (a) 1–0 Murphy
Round 6 Arsenal (a) 3–1 Astall, Murphy, Brown
Semi-final Sunderland (Sheffield) 3–0 Astall, Kinsey, Brown

On Saturday evening commemorative banquets were held for the players of FA Cup finalists Manchester City and Birmingham City in two London night spots no more than a stone's throw apart. Disappointingly, this was as near to the trophy

A team group. Back row, left to right: Lunnecor, Badham, Hall, Merrick, Smith, Lane, Warhurst, Green, Newham. Front row: Astall, Kinsey, Brown, Arther Turner (manager), Boyd, Murphy, Govan, Finney.

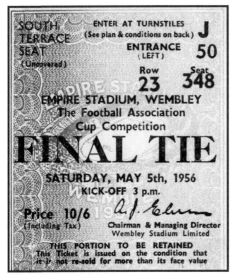 

A ticket for a South Terrace seat costing 10/6.   A ticket for the East Stand standing costing 3/6.

as Blues got all day. Blues lost their fighting spirit, an early goal, the battle in the Wembley cauldron, and most importantly, they lost their chance of a major trophy. The day seemed so promising, with the teams coming out to a huge roar from the 100,000 fans crammed into the home of English football, Wembley Stadium. On a lovely hot day, after the introduction to the Queen, the game kicked-off, and everything seemed perfect until the third minute, Revie starting the move 10 yards from his penalty area and swinging over a long pass, which cleared the head of Hall. Clarke raced in from behind to deliver a return ball to Revie who had made ground quickly. The ball was back-heeled square to Hayes inside the area, and he hit a crisp first-time shot past Merrick. Even then this was viewed as a stimulant – something to get Blues quickly into top gear. Unfortunately it simply did not, and this was the day's biggest disappointment. Although Blues hit back with a Kinsey shot which went in off the post to equalise 11 minutes later,

SUPPLEMENT TO 'BLUES NEWS', 24th MARCH, 1956

BIRMINGHAM CITY FOOTBALL CLUB

———

Good afternoon, Ladies and Gentlemen,

Before I commence writing this message to our supporters, I would like to say that our Chairman, Mr. Harry Morris, on behalf of his colleagues on the Board, wishes to be associated with all the sentiments I am about to express.

In the words from Sir Harry Lauder's famous song, "Keep Right on to the End of the Road," we are there at Wembley on May 5th, 1956, and if ever a team deserved to be there, we do.

Last week at Hillsborough, Sheffield, we earned the right to a Wembley Cup Final. My boys were grand, and played their hearts out against tough opposition, a display of fighting offensive and defensive football that was accorded by thousands of spectators as the best Semi-final seen for years.

How magnificent our defence stood up to the test when Sunderland turned on the heat ; how well our boys snapped up the chances by clear cut

70

The sheet music for *Keep Right On to the End of the Road*.

The cover of semi-final programme v Sunderland.

movements executed at a speed that bewildered our opponents ; how happy and confident we were that we could beat Sunderland.

I would not pick out individual players for mention from a game such as this, because this visit to Wembley has been earned by players who believe in the policy of the team and have the ability and courage to put it into operation.

I personally feel a very proud man, and I thank the players and staff for the co-operation, support and goodwill they have shown me since I became manager of this Club. We are a very happy club, and I can assure you all, that all efforts will be advanced to keep our Club in the top-flight of English football.

When the final whistle sounded at 4.40 p.m. last week I had tears of joy in my eyes, because of the success of our team, but also for the leading part that you, 'Our Supporters' have played in any success we have gained. It has been beyond our wildest hopes, we thank you very sincerely and we owe you a debt. To repay you all, we will pick up where we left off last week, to bring the Cup back for you. This has been your fight as well as ours, and how you have fought for us, words fail me.

Last week at Sheffield, in the words of Sir Winston Churchill, " this was your finest hour."

' Our Song ' born in the coach on the way to play Arsenal in the Sixth Round, and sung by you all on Saturday last, filled us all with emotion. We thank you all, it was like a charm, and how much the players responded to it.

Having played in the Semi-Final and lost, I would pay tribute to our opponents from Sunderland, for the sporting and clean manner in which they played; the blow is more heavy when you are so near to Wembley. They all wished us well in the Final, and I am certain I voice the wishes of all our supporters for their future progress.

For the huge number of letters and telegrams I have received and the good wishes of all, I thank you most sincerely. I could not attempt to answer them all so please accept this as my reply to you.

With team spirit and co-operation by all, I am confident we can win the Cup.

ARTHUR TURNER, Manager.

Blues autographs.

Daily Express Community Song Sheet.

there was still something lacking in their overall performance. Their spirit, prominent in other rounds, simply was not there when needed. When the Blues' famous battle cry 'Keep Right On' failed to raise the tempo after the goal, things began to look ominous. Blues held on until half-time with the scores remaining level, but they were clearly frustrated by the astute offside trap employed by Revie's men. Manchester City started off the better team in the second half, and were 2–1 up after 65 minutes. Johnstone, running at Green on the right, was presented with an opportunity to feed Dyson, who had run diagonally across the field to the edge of the area. A perfectly timed pass allowed Dyson to take the ball in his stride and fire past Merrick as he came out to narrow the angle. The winning team then put the game well beyond Blues' reach with a sucker-punch goal three minutes later. It came from a Blues attack: Trautmann dived bravely at the feet

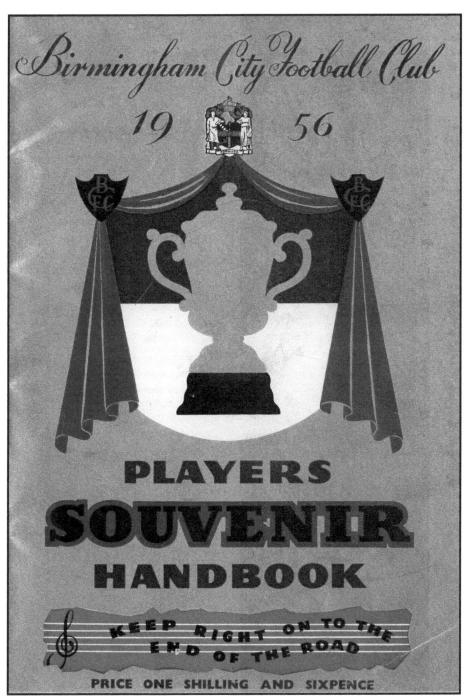

Cover of Players' Souvenir Handbook.

PLAYER FACTFILE

LEONARD ARTHUR MILLER BOYD
Wing-half
282 appearances, 14 goals
Retired from Blues in May 1956.

Len was a tall, elegant Cockney who joined Blues from Plymouth Argyle for £17,500 in January 1949, after playing a great game against the Blues at St Andrew's. At the time his transfer fee was a record for the Pilgrims. He was remembered for his long strides out of defence, while motivating his forwards into action with the nonchalant wave of his hand that became his trademark. He was a skilful player who worked hard and was therefore always respected by the Blues' fans. Unfortunately his career with Blues ended in difficult circumstances immediately after the FA Cup Final in 1956. There can be few players that can say that their last senior appearance for their club was a Wembley Final. The nature of his departure meant that Len fell out of love with the game, and he did not play again until he attempted a comeback with Hinckley Athletic in February 1959, which resulted him in finally finishing his football career at Redditch United, where he was coach and chief scout from 1960–65. As a captain of the club he led Blues to arguably their most successful season in 1955–56, when they were runners-up in the FA Cup Final and finished sixth in Division One.

of Brown, took the ball from him and kicked long upfield. It was flicked on by Hayes into the path of Johnstone, who had sprinted clear of the static defence. He finished with a lovely strike into the bottom corner. Moments later Trautmann received treatment after a collision with Murphy while saving Brown's header at goal. The goalkeeper played on despite holding his head in agony for 20 minutes. Any shot on target would have made a save impossible in his condition, but Blues failed to trouble him further. The game, and Blues' FA Cup dream, withered for another year.

THE 1956 FA CUP FINAL TEAM. WHERE DID THEY GO?

Name	All-time Apps	All-time Gls	Outcome
Merrick, Gil	551	0	Retired, 196
Hall, Jeff	264	1	Died, 1959
Green, Ken	443	2	Retired, 1959
Newman, John	65	0	Worcester City, 1957
Smith, Trevor	430	3	Walsall, 1964
Boyd, Len	282	14	Retired, 1956
Astall, Gordon	271	67	Torquay United, 1961
Kinsey, Noel	173	56	Port Vale, 1958
Brown, Eddie	185	90	Leyton Orient, 1959
Murphy, Peter	278	127	Retired, 1961
Govan, Alex	187	60	Portsmouth, 1958

Game Eighteen

First Kick in Europe

INTER MILAN 0 BLUES 0

Date: 15 May 1956   **Venue:** Milan
Attendance: 8,000

The Road to the Semi-final

Inter	Zagreb	Zagreb	Inter	Barcelona	Barcelona	Barcelona
(away)	(away)	(home)	(home)	(home)	(away)	(Basle)
Merrick	Merrick	Merrick	Merrick	Merrick	Merrick	Merrick
Badham	Badham	Farmer	Hall	Farmer	Hall	Hall
Green	Allen	Allen	Green	Allen	Allen	Farmer
Watts	Boyd	Watts	Watts	Larkin	Larkin	Watts
Newman	Newman	Green	Smith	Smith	Smith	Smith
Warmington	Warhurst	Warhurst	Warhurst	Watts	Neal	Neal
Cox	Lane	Cox	Astall	Astall	Astall	Astall
Kinsey	Finney	Orritt	Kinsey	Orritt	Kinsey	Orritt
Brown	Brown	Brown	Brown	Brown	Brown	Brown
Murphy	Kinsey	Murphy	Murphy	Neal	Murphy	Murphy
Govan	Murphy	Govan	Govan	Murphy	Govan	Govan

Inter-Cities Fairs Cup Qualifying Game

This was Blues' first game in this European competition. They finished top of their qualifying group with seven points from four games and moved on to meet Barcelona in the semi-finals.

The first Inter Cities Fairs Cup consisted of four groups of three teams, with the winners of each group progressing to the semi-final stage. The draw saw Blues in Group Three, pitted against Zagreb Select and Internazionale of Milan. London drew Frankfurt and Basle in Group One, Group Two consisted of Lausanne, Leipzig and Cologne, with Group 4 made up of Barcelona, Copenhagen and Vienna.

The first game played was London in Basle in June 1955, but Blues had to wait a further 11 months to make their European debut. In Zagreb an Eddie Brown goal after eight minutes gave Blues victory on foreign soil. It was not until 3 December 1956 that the return fixture took place in front of 40,144 fans. Blues ran out comfortable 3–0 winners with Orritt, Brown and Murphy the scorers on three, 60 and 67 minutes respectively.

The final group game was at home to Inter on 7 April 1957, and 34,461 gathered at St Andrew's to witness a titanic struggle. Blues won 2–1 with two Alex Govan goals either side

PLAYER FACTFILE

JAMES HARRIS
Forward
115 appearances, 53 goals
Left to join Oldham Athletic in July 1964.

Jimmy was born in Birkenhead on 18 August 1933. After impressing with Birkenhead Schools, he joined Everton Juniors in 1948, signing professional terms for the club in September 1951. A fast, two-footed, versatile striker, he spent nine years at Goodison Park before joining Blues for £20,000 in December 1960 with an Everton goal tally of 65 goals in 191 appearances. He kept up that extraordinary scoring rate while at Blues, leaving for Oldham in July 1964, where he made 29 appearances and scored nine. While at Blues he scored in the 2–1 victory over Inter Milan at the San Siro in the semi-final of the Inter-Cities Fairs Cup in 1962. This was the only time Inter Milan had lost at home to an English club until Arsenal repeated the feat 40 years later. After his time at Boundary Park, he moved to Tranmere Rovers in August 1966 and then Rhyl Athletic a month later. Eventually he retired in May 1967. His talent was recognised by an England Under-23 cap and an appearance for the Football League XI.

of half-time. Blues had to stave off tremendous pressure in the last two minutes after Lorenzi had scored in the 88th minute. Blues had topped the group and were now in the semi-final against Barcelona.

Barcelona arrived at Blues for the first leg on 23 October 1957 in front of 30,761 fans, who were lucky enough to witness a tremendous game, especially in the first 45 minutes. Blues took the lead through Brown in the second minute. The visitors replied in the 12th minute through Tejada, then went ahead through Evaristo on 27 minutes. Orritt brought Blues back on level terms after 35 minutes, only for Martinez to restore Barcelona's lead five minutes later. Murphy equalised to 3–3 in the 43rd minute, setting everything up for the final 45. It was Murphy that sealed a 4–3 victory with his second after 60 minutes. Blues had beaten the mighty Barcelona!

The second leg on 13 November drew a crowd of 60,000, and Blues' defence was magnificent until Kubala worked his magic in the 86th minute to draw the tie 4–4 on aggregate. The away goals rule did not apply then, so a replay was arranged in Basle on 26 November. A crowd of 20,000 saw Evaristo give Barcelona the lead after 33 minutes, only for Murphy to equalise on 48 minutes. Once again Kubala did the damage, scoring the winner on 83 minutes.

Just for the record Barcelona beat London 6–0 in the Final.

AN INTERVIEW WITH JIMMY WHICH APPEARED IN THE FEBRUARY 2007 EDITION OF THE BLUES MAGAZINE

I met goalscoring legend Jimmy Harris at his home, which is no more than 100 yards from Tranmere Rovers' ground, Prenton Park in Birkenhead. This is the house where he was born on 18 August 1933, which he inherited from his 'best friend', his mother. The modest terraced house holds an amazing collection of memorabilia from Jimmy's career, and during our conversation he dives into drawers and cupboards to produce fascinating items that support the stories he unfolds. 'I kept all this stuff to leave to my grandson, Robert, who is 14, lives in North Wales and supports Everton.'

Jimmy is a regular at Goodison Park and rates the signing of Lescott from Wolverhampton Wanderers as a better buy than that of Andy Johnson (ex-Blues). 'I worry about the lad when his pace goes because he has very little else!'

At 73 Jimmy goes to the gym three times a week 'to mess around', even though he has had five replacement hips and a new knee recently, courtesy of the Everton Ex-Players Foundation, which is run by a vicar based at the church within Goodison Park. Jimmy enjoys regular trips to his local, where he often drinks with Peter Johnson, who is a Tranmere Rovers Director and held a similar post at Everton. Jimmy recently made contact with an ex-girlfriend, Roberta, whom he now visits on his regular trips to Majorca.

As a schoolboy Jimmy was a left-half. 'I got a trial with Everton because my aunt was a grocer and she knew an Everton director who was a grocer wholesaler. She told him about me, and he invited her to send me along.'

'I signed professional forms when I was 18 and spent two years doing National Service in the Army. When I came out aged 20 they played me at centre-forward in an A-team game against Skelmersdale which we won 5–1, and I scored 4. I was a forward from that day on.'

Jimmy, who looks fit for his age, weighing 12st 10lbs, which is only a stone over his 'fighting weight', completed his apprenticeship as a printer before going full-time at the age of 21, scoring 72 goals in 207 appearances for the Toffees. He replaced Dave Hickson, who was a traditional bustling type of centre-forward, establishing himself as a quick, mobile striker with an eye for goal and the ability to operate down both flanks.

He knew his days at Everton were numbered when they signed Alex Young for £40,000. 'He had been bought as my successor, and the club needed to get some money back so it was obvious that I would be looking for a new club. Not long after Alex was signed I was travelling into training when I read in a newspaper that I would be signing for West Bromwich Albion, something I knew nothing about.'

'After training that day, which was a Thursday, John Carey, the manager, asked me to stay behind as he wanted to talk to me. He told me that West Bromwich Albion's people wanted to talk to me. I said I knew that, as I had read it in the paper.'

Jimmy did not sign for the Albion because he told Carey that he only wanted to play for big-city clubs. 'I felt justified in saying that, I was top scorer and had played for England Under-23s and the Football League. On the following Saturday Everton beat Sheffield Wednesday 4–2 and I scored two. Carey told me that 'a big-city club' wanted to meet me, so I met Gil Merrick at the Adelphi Hotel in Liverpool, and I agreed to join Blues for £20,000.'

'Gil told me to get to Birmingham on the following Monday, so I never had chance to say goodbye to the Everton lads, which was a shame. My signing-on fee was £1,750.'

'Everton were a big club — in 1948 Goodison was the only football ground to have stands on all four sides. Unfortunately they were a little mean with money as far as the players were concerned. After five years at the club I was entitled to a benefit of £750, a type of loyalty bonus. Everton decided to deduct £150 from my benefit because of the time I spent doing National Service, which grated a bit as they only paid me a retainer of £1 per week during those two years serving with the army in Germany!'

Aged 27, Jimmy signed in December 1960 and settled into digs in Moat Lane, Yardley. He made his first appearance against Boldklub Copenhagen at home, which Blues won 5—0 to get to the semi-final of the Inter-Cities Fairs Cup 9—4 on aggregate. Needless to say, Jimmy scored, which he did on a continuous basis for the Blues, averaging a goal in every other game. His first League goals came at home on 17 December 1960 against Bolton Wanderers in front of a crowd of 19,050, scoring both goals in the 2—2 draw.

Jimmy solved the number-nine shirt problem for Gil Merrick, as prior to his signing Blues had tried Don Weston, Robin Stubbs, Johnny Gordon and Bryan Orritt in an attempt to increase the goals tally.

In that first season he scored 13 goals in 24 League and Cup appearances.

'I had a great time at Blues with a great bunch of lads. The forwards were excellent, and we could always score goals, Mike [Hellawell], Jimmy [Bloomfield], Ken [Leek], Bertie [Auld] and myself were as good as anyone in the First Division. It was in the area of defence where we suffered. At full-back Stan [Lynn], George [Allen] and Brian [Farmer] were not the quickest, and while Terry [Hennessey] and Malcolm [Page] were good players they were inexperienced, so that put a lot of pressure on Trevor [Smith]. I remember the Spurs FA Cup tie which we drew 3—3 after going 0—3 down. That was typical, we were always coming from behind.'

Into a drawer and out comes Jimmy's runners'-up medal from the Inter-Cities Fairs Cup Final second-leg match versus AS Roma, which was lost 2—0 (4—2 on aggregate).

'We should never have played the first leg at St Andrew's as the pitch was frozen, but the return flight was booked for the Italians, and the game went ahead. Flights were not that regular in the early 1960s! Over in Italy the tunnel to the pitch was covered with a netting to protect the players from the crowd. What the fans did was fill plastic cups with sand, and then as we went out they threw them onto the netting, and the sand fell through on top of us, meaning we played the game with sand in our hair, ears, eyes and inside our shirts. There was one Italian player who throughout the game kept saying "English Ba****ds". It got on everyone's nerves, and at the end of the game Trevor [Smith] sorted him out.' Jimmy declined to give further details, but suffice it to say that the Italian stopped immediately.

After four seasons at the Blues, in which he gained a League Cup victory, Jimmy left in July 1964 after making 115 appearances and scoring 53 goals to join Oldham Athletic. He retired in May 1966 through injury, and after getting himself fit he played in Ireland for St Patrick's Athletic before joining Ellesmere Port as player-manager. During his time there he was approached by the Tranmere Rovers manager to see if he would join the coaching staff. Jimmy said he would think about it, and a day later he received a call from the manager saying not to bother thinking about it. He had mentioned it to a director who had said 'He didn't want to come to Tranmere as a kid so he can't come now!'

After that Jim spent 25 years at Vauxhall but was never a steward at Prenton Golf Club, although he admits 'it must have seemed like I was as I spent a lot of time there getting my handicap down to 2!' He remembers the occasion when Blues played Third Lanark at the Varsity Stadium in Toronto when both clubs were touring Canada in May 1961. Playing for them was a free-scoring centre-forward who caught Gil's eye and was eventually signed from Manchester City in the summer of 1963 to replace Jimmy. The striker's name was Alex Harley, and he lost the 'free-scoring' label on coming to St Andrew's.

During his time at Everton Jimmy never played in a Liverpool derby because 'Liverpool were never in the First Division in those days. I did play at Anfield, though, for the Football League against the Irish Football League in November 1950. I should have gained a full cap for England, but I didn't play well at Anfield and that was that! I did get an England Under-23 cap against the Scots. We won 3–1 and I scored. That was some team.'

Jimmy goes to another drawer and shows me a black-and-white team photograph. In the team are Don Howe, Duncan Edwards, Albert Quixhall, Johnny Haynes and Trevor Smith.

Why does Bertie Auld call you 'the Prince of Darkness?', I ask. Jimmy smiles a knowing smile and replies 'Oh that's just Bertie, he makes things up as he goes along.'

Changing the subject Jimmy pulls from a cupboard a white, Umbro, V-necked, short-sleeved football shirt. 'This is my England shirt. I was number eight.' On the front of the shirt are two sewn-on badges commemorating his two representative honours.

Jimmy recalls his days at Blues and the centre-halves of that time: 'I always did well against Billy Wright; he didn't enjoy my style of play, but my bogeyman was the Irish international Charlie Hurley of Sunderland — you knew it when he tackled you normally from behind. I think that is the biggest improvement in the modern game — the banning of the tackle from behind. People used to say that Stan Matthews never went for a 50/50 ball; well, why would he when defenders could injure him by tackling from behind? He'd get injured, which would affect his team and his ability to earn a living.'

All too quickly our time together is over, as Jimmy has to attend the funeral of the ex-Blackburn Rovers goalkeeper Harry Leyland, so we move into the back room, where the walls are full of photographic memories of his career, to take his photograph holding his League Cup Tankard and his Inter-Cities Fairs Cup Final Medal.

Game Nineteen

First Under Floodlights

BLUES 3 BORUSSIA DORTMUND 3

Date: 31 October 1956   **Venue:** St Andrew's
Attendance: 45,000

Blues: Merrick, Farmer, Green, Watts, Newman, Warhurst, Astall, Orritt, Brown, Larkin, Govan.

T
he match itself was irrelevant – although Blues did play well – but the occasion was significant. St Andrew's was able to boast floodlights for the first time. The stadium, which had opened on Boxing Day 1906, did without artificial light for half a century.

Birmingham were so pleased to be entering the world of floodlights that they produced a special programme for the occasion. Abandoning the usual blue-dominated colour, the club opted for gold. It remains one of the club's rarest post-war programmes.

It was Larkin who first threatened the Germans' goal, with full-back Wilhelm Burgsmuller having to clear one of his efforts off the line in the first few minutes. It came as a shock when the Germans took the lead after six minutes – even more of a shock to John Newman, as it was he who nodded the ball backwards into his own net after a teasing in-swinging cross from Wolfgang Press. As Newman was new to the team, it must have been fairly disheartening for him to make an error like that, especially as he really was under the spotlight! It took only five minutes for Blues to get back on level terms, with a typical goal from Alex Govan. Eddie Brown and he had developed a fine understanding over their years of playing together, and this was one of their typical moves. Brown hurtled down the right flank, completely outstripping the other full-back, Herbert Sandmann, and drawing the covering centre-half across to him. Govan, meanwhile, had spotted the gap and ghosted in from his left-wing position, into the blind spot in the goalmouth. When Brown's cross came over, he met the ball in his stride, administered a deft flick, and it flashed into the net for the equaliser. Blues powered forward, and Larkin missed a great chance,

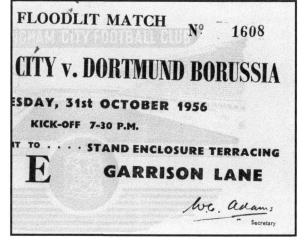

FLOODLIT MATCH   № 1608

CITY v. DORTMUND BORUSSIA

ESDAY, 31st OCTOBER 1956

KICK-OFF 7-30 P.M.

IT TO . . . . STAND ENCLOSURE TERRACING

E   GARRISON LANE

W.C. Adams
                                        Secretary

smashing the ball into the crowd, when the 'keeper was totally out of position and the goal was at his mercy. Brian 'Orrible' Orritt was giving a good account of himself and he got onto the scoresheet on 32 minutes. Astall had obviously taken a mental note of how easily Brown had outpaced Sandmann earlier and he decided it was his turn to exploit this perceived weakness. Sure enough, he left the full-back trailing in his wake, and he put over a fierce low cross, which Orritt met on the full and thumped home for a magnificent goal to give Blues a deserved lead. Two minutes into the second period Orritt scored his second. Brown was the provider after he had roamed along the left. His pinpoint cross left Orritt with only the 'keeper to beat, but he hurried his effort and hit the 'keeper's legs. Luckily for Orritt, the ball rebounded straight back to him, and his second attempt was put away with aplomb.

BLUES News

THE OFFICIAL PROGRAMME OF BIRMINGHAM CITY FOOTBALL CLUB

SEASON 1956-57   PRICE THREEPENCE

PLAYER FACTFILE

BRIAN ORRITT
Inside-forward
119 appearances, 27 goals
Appeared three times for Wales Under-23
Joined Middlesbrough in March 1962.

Born in Caernarfon, North Wales, on 22 February 1937, 'Orrible' played football and rugby at Caernarfon Grammar School, eventually opting for the round ball when joining Llanfair PG FC. He joined Bangor City in 1955, signing for the Blues in January 1956. He was nothing if not versatile, filling all 11 positions during his career, but at St Andrew's he was predominantly a winger or inside-forward. He represented Blues in the Inter-Cities Fairs Cup competition in both 1960 and 1961 to become one of the first Welsh-speaking footballers to take part in European competition. He was transferred to Middlesbrough in March 1962 and became their first-ever substitute, going on to make 118 appearances for the Ayresome Park outfit, scoring 22 goals in a four-year spell. In 1966 he emigrated to South Africa to play for Johannesburg Rangers and coached youngsters in Soweto. He gained three Welsh Under-23 caps.

The Germans' reputation as a come-back team was well known, and they certainly did not throw in the towel, despite this being only a friendly fixture. Just past the hour mark, Peters took a leaf out of Govan's book and, after a right-wing corner, netted a far-post goal. It looked as though Blues would run out winners, but in the very last minute Helmut Kapitulski won possession just inside the penalty area and hit the equaliser with great force.

Dortmund, who were one of the best teams in Europe at the time, played attractive football and belied the perception that Germans are all about ruthless efficiency. The two clubs forged a good relationship that lasted for a while. More than 45,000 people attended the match – an official attendance was not required and, therefore, not recorded – and St Andrew's had never looked better. The floodlights themselves were advanced for their time (four pylons, at each corner of the stadium, measuring 114ft high). There were 30 lamps on each pylon, each lamp being 1500 watts. MEB (Midlands Electricity Board) took a full-page advertisement in the programme to proudly put their name to 'The Big Switch On'.

The teams that lined up that night saw two of Germany's favourite internationals turning our for the opposition, goalkeeper Heinrich Kwiatkowski and captain Alfred Preissler.

Game Twenty

Fairs Cup Final First Leg

BLUES 0 BARCELONA 0

Date: 29 March 1960   **Venue:** St Andrew's
Attendance: 40,524

Blues: Schofield, Farmer, Allen, Watts, Smith, Neal, Astall, Gordon, Weston, Orritt, Hooper.

Barcelona: Ramallets, Olivella, Garcia, Segarra, Rodri, Gensona, Coll, Kocsis, Martinez, Ribelles, Villaverde.

The Road to the Final

Cologne (away)	Cologne (home)	Zagreb (home)	Zagreb (away)	St Gilloise (away)	St Gilloise (home)	Barcelona (home)	Barcelona (away)
Merrick	Merrick	Schofield	Schofield	Merrick	Schofield	Schofield	Schofield
Hall	Hall	Farmer	Farmer	Sissons	Farmer	Farmer	Farmer
Green	Allen	Allen	Allen	Farmer	Allen	Allen	Allen
Watts	Watts	Watts	Watts	Watts	Watts	Watts	Watts
Sissons	Smith	Sissons	Smith	Smith	Smith	Smith	Smith
Neal	Neal	Neal	Neal	Neal	Larkin	Neal	Neal
Hooper	Hooper	Hooper	Astall	Hooper	Hellawell	Astall	Astall
Gordon	Gordon	Gordon	Gordon	Gordon	Barrett	Gordon	Gordon
Brown	Brown	Stubbs	Stubbs	Orritt	Gordon	Weston	Weston
Orritt	Larkin	Larkin	Larkin	Barrett	Hooper	Orritt	Murphy
Murphy	Taylor	Taylor	Hooper	Taylor	Taylor	Hooper	Hooper

After beating Cologne, Zagreb and Union St Gilloise in rounds one, two and the semi-final respectively, Blues were in the Inter-Cities Fairs Cup Final – the first English club side to reach a European Final. It was not until 9 December that Blues knew who their opponents would be when Barcelona defeated Belgrade in the other semi-final 4–2 on aggregate. The tie at St Andrew's was described as a battle by the 40,524 crowd as the Spaniards came to defend and presented an 11-man wall for Blues to penetrate.

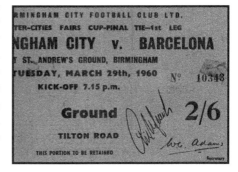

C.F. BARCELONA

THIS illustrious Club was formed in 1899 and we had the pleasure of playing them in Barcelona in 1925, when we were beaten 1-0 and 2-0. Joe Bradford, Dan Tremelling, Johnny Crosbie, etc., would remember these very pleasant outings. Since then they have made extraordinary progress, as the following achievements prove :—

Champions of Spain (The Generalisimo Cup) 13 times.
Winners of the League Championship, 6 times.
Winners of the Latin Cup, twice.
Winners of the Inter Cities Fairs Cup.

The fabulous Stadium which was opened in 1957 has to be seen to be appreciated fully. We thought the San Siro Stadium in Milan was terrific, and it certainly is, but this Barcelona Arena is out of this world. It will accommodate 150,000 spectators, 50,000 of whom can be seated. A further 30,000 are under cover. Incorporated in this spacious ground is a Chapel, a Hospital with Operating Theatre, and outside is a Car Park with room for 1,500 cars. Truly a colossal outfit.

It is interesting when you look back on the games between our two Clubs in 1957 :— At St. Andrew's we won 4-3, at Barcelona we lost 1-0, and the replay at Basle was lost 2-1 by a Kubala goal in the closing moments. In these games the following Barcelona players took part :—Ramallets, Estrens, Segarra, Gracia, Olivella, Flotats, Villaverde, Martinez, Evaristo, Tejada, Verges, Kubala, Brugue and Suarez. Ten of these players were in the Barcelona team in the two matches against the Wolves. One can judge the strength of this famous Club by the fact that seven players, viz. : Ramallets, Olivella, Gracia, Gensana, Segarra, Suarez and Martinez were selected for the Spanish international team which beat Italy 3-1 on March 13th.

FURTHER FACTS

Barcelona have 55,700 members, or Season Ticket Holders.

* * *

The Press Box in the Stadium has seating for 400.

* * *

The attendance last week in their game with Real Madrid was 120,000 with takings over £50,000.

4

The covers of two 'pirate' souvenir programmes.

It finished goalless, and Barcelona were happy to return to Spain without a deficit, confident that they would win the second leg on 4 May 1960.

Blues' task was made all the more difficult when they conceded a goal after just three minutes from Martinez and then three minutes later Czibor made it 2–0. Blues never recovered, and they went 3–0 down when Czibor scored his second three minutes into the second half. Coll added a fourth after 78 minutes before Hooper pulled a goal back four minutes later. It was no consolation to Blues, who were well beaten on the night, even if it was to one of the strongest European teams. The Camp Nou housed 75,000 fans that night.

The programme for the away leg.

PLAYER FACTFILE

TREVOR SMITH
Centre-half
430 appearances, 3 goals
Made two appearances for England.
Left Blues for Walsall in 1964

Born in Brierley Hill on 13 April 1936, Trevor captained the Brierley Hill & Sedgley Schools team to the first final of the English Schools FA Trophy, playing alongside Duncan Edwards, who later represented Manchester United before perishing in the Munich Air Disaster. He gained his selection due to his performances for the Quarry Bank Secondary Modern School, which also attracted the scouts from St Andrew's and other local professional clubs. He joined Blues as an amateur in July 1951 and signed as a professional in April 1953, helping Blues to win the European Youth Cup in 1954. After making his debut six months after signing professional terms, in a 4–2 victory at Derby County (and scoring an own-goal), he became a permanent member of the senior side, only missing out through injury or National Service commitments. At the age of 18 he was capped for England B against West Germany to add to his Schoolboy and Youth caps. Eventually he made two appearances for the B team, 15 appearances for the Under-23 side, before gaining two caps for the full England team against Wales and Sweden. Trevor also represented the Football League XI on two occasions, as well as playing for the Army Representative side for two matches. He became injury prone and was transferred to Walsall for £18,000 in October 1964, where he only made 12 appearances, forcing him to retire in February 1966. Later he was a permit player in the Lichfield Sunday League, and he was manager of Mile Oak Rovers in season 1970–71, while running a pub in the Tamworth area. He died in Essex on 9 August 2003.

Game Twenty-one

Fairs Cup Final First Leg

Blues 2 AS Roma 2

Date: 27 September 1961   **Venue:** St Andrew's
Attendance: 21,005

Blues: Schofield, Farmer, Sissons, Hennessey, Foster, Beard, Hellawell, Bloomfield, Harris, Orritt, Auld.

AS Roma: Cudicini, Fontana, Corsini, Giuliano, Losi, Carpanesi, Orlando, Da Costa, Manfredini, Angelillo, Menichelli.

A total of 21,005 fans filed into St Andrew's to see the first leg of the Inter-Cities Fairs Cup against Roma. Blues started on the attack early in the first half, with attempts from Bloomfield and Hennessey just a little off target. The Roma 'keeper, standing at over 6ft, was a great presence in the goalmouth and it was his skill and agility which kept Blues' scoring down to a bare minimum. Auld in the Blues attack was on particularly good form for this game. Hellawell put in a fine shot across the goal, but it posed no real threat and went to safety. The Italian side had a tough job on their hands and found it hard to break through Blues' midfield, consisting of Beard, Foster and Hennessey. Blues stood strong, but their efforts could not hold Roma forever. Orlando was fouled, but he evaded Sissons in defence to send the ball across goal to Manfredini, who put the ball into the back of the net in the 30th minute. The second half started with Blues attacking with the same enthusiasm with which they began the first period. Second attempts were sent across the goalmouth before being swept away out of danger. The Italians seemed to have slowed down in

ROBERT AULD
Outside-left
147 appearances, 31 goals
3 appearances for Scotland
Left for Glasgow Celtic for £12,000 in summer 1965.

'Bertie' was an energetic, skilful and often fiery player who was always a favourite with the Bluenoses. He joined Celtic as a professional in March 1955 as a 17-year-old, and after a season-long loan spell with Dumbarton in the 1956–57 season he established himself in the Hoops' first team, and Blues did well to gain his signature in April 1961, as there were a number of English and Scottish clubs keen to make him a member of their team. His stay at Blues was relatively short before he re-joined Celtic, which coincided with the most successful part of his career, culminating in him being a member of the first British team to win the European Cup in 1967. The honours simply poured in: Scottish League Champions in 1967, 1968 and 1970, Scottish Cup winners in 1965, 1967 and 1969, Scottish League Cup winners in 1967, 1968, 1969 and 1970. Celtic also won the World Club Championship in 1968. As well as his international caps he also played twice for the Scottish League XI. Upon his retirement as a player he managed a number of Scottish League sides, including: Hibernian, Partick Thistle, Hamilton Academicals and Dumbarton.

attack, so it was a wake-up call for Blues when they managed to slip through to score a second goal. Menichelli made an attempt at goal, but it was cleared by Beard, only to bounce to Manfredini who again sent the ball over the line with ease.

Blues were determined not to give in easily and put up a gallant fight, giving Cudicini in the Roma goal a heavy workout. Blues spent a good 15 minutes raining attempts on the 'keeper, and some of the saves he pulled off were outstanding. The scoreline showed Blues the cold hard fact that they were two goals down with just 10 more minutes of play remaining. Hellawell then had a go at goal himself, and this time Cudicini was well beaten by his shot. Blues took advantage and stepped up their attacks. Harris watched his shot bounce off the crossbar and rebound to Orritt, who won back possession. He sent the ball goalwards from close range, and it went over the line for the equaliser.

Game Twenty-two

Double Winners Humbled

BLUES 3 SPURS 3

Date: 6 January 1962   **Venue:** St Andrew's
Attendance: 46,096

Blues: Schofield, Lynn, Sissons, Hennessey, Smith, Beard, Hellawell, Orritt, Harris, Leek, Auld.

Spurs: Brown, Baker, Henry, Blanchflower, Norman, MacKay, Medwin, White, Allen, Greaves, Jones.

Tottenham Hotspur had done the League and FA Cup double in 1961 and were looking to return to Wembley the following year. St Andrew's was packed, eagerly looking forward to seeing the star names of the time.

At 3.32pm the visiting Spurs choir was in full voice with their famous hymn; *Glory, Glory Hallelujah*, as they had rocked Blues to the core by racing into a 3–0 lead. Spurs were described in that first half an hour as playing some glorious defence-splitting football on a swamp-like pitch, and Blues were reduced to chasing shadows in the gloom of a foggy day. After just seven minutes Greaves raced onto a through ball from Maurice Norman, and although Schofield dived at his feet, the ball squirted away and, quick as a flash, Greaves was back on his feet to slip the ball home. Schofield was

PLAYER FACTFILE

KENNETH LEEK
Centre/Inside-forward
120 appearances, 61 goals
13 appearances for Wales
Joined Northampton Town in December 1964 for £9,000.

Born in Ynysybwl, near Pontypridd in South Wales on 26 July 1935, Ken played for local sides Pontypridd Youth Club and Ynysybwl Boys FC before gaining a professional contract with Northampton Town in August 1952. In May 1958 he was transferred to Leicester City, which eventually saw him get into a dispute with the club that resulted in him being sensationally dropped on the morning of the 1961 FA Cup Final against Tottenham Hotspur, having scored in all the previous rounds. A month later he moved to Newcastle United for £25,000, but an unhappy few months in the North East was ended when he joined Blues. He signed in November 1961 for £23,000 and became a major force in a forward line which rivalled that of the mid-1950s in terms of its strike power: Hellawell, Harris, Leek, Bloomfield and Auld. He moved back to the Cobblers a year and a half after Blues' victory in the League Cup Final. The fee of £9,000 was virtually totally recouped when in November 1965 Bradford City paid for his services. From Bradford he returned to Wales to play for Rhyl Town in August 1968 and Ton Pentre in February 1970, before retiring four months later. Ken also made one appearance for the Welsh Under-23 side. He died in 2008.

then forced to pull off two tremendous saves from Cliff Jones and Greaves, but then after 29 minutes Jones, the Welsh international winger, made it 2–0 with a fantastic team move. The ball started its route to the back of the Blues net from the Spurs defence, Greaves eventually getting on the ball and firing a long pass out to Medwin, who was usually outside-right but had wandered over to the left wing. Medwin centred, and Jones crashed a tremendous cross shot past Schofield. Three minutes later Greaves was on the mark again when, following interplay between Dave MacKay and Les Allen, Allen's ball in was headed home by Greaves. The scoreline was 3–0, and the tie looked over.

Just a minute after the third Spurs goal, Jimmy Harris won possession after a Stan Lynn free-kick and slammed the ball past Bill Brown in Spurs' goal. This gave Blues some real hope, and both crowd and team upped their efforts for the final 12 minutes of the first half, although there was no further scoring before the break.

The second half got underway to an amazingly loud rendition of *Keep Right On To The End Of The Road*, and Malcolm Beard said later it was the best atmosphere he ever played in, which definitely seemed to unnerve the Spurs stars. Four minutes after the restart, Bertie Auld and Mike Hellawell had the Spurs defence in a tangle with long crosses from the wings, and an unmarked Harris headed home from close in. Fans invaded the pitch in their delight and were encouraged to return to their terrace positions by the players. Five minutes later those fans were back on the field of play once more, as Blues were back on level terms. Lynn got in one of his tremendous free-kicks on goal and although Brown dived to save it, he could not hold on. Ken Leek followed up and had the ball in the net in a flash. This was becoming a superb Cup tie and is still held as the best ever by many wise old blue heads.

Blues were on top now, and Terry Hennessey was running the show in the middle of the park, keeping Spurs penned back in their own half. Blues had many efforts and Leek went close on a number of occasions. Under great pressure as the game drew to a close, Spurs looked likely to crack, and then came the incident that has been often reported down the years and has never been forgiven by the Blues fans present that day.

Blues were throwing the proverbial kitchen sink at Spurs, and Ken Leek managed to get a shot in that beat the 'keeper. Norman was standing on his own goalline, and the ball evaded him and hit the back of the net. To the astonishment of everyone, the linesman's flag went up for offside. Malcolm Beard's opinion was that it was the best goal of the day – 'nothing wrong with it' – but Blues were denied.

The game went to a replay at White Hart Lane which Spurs won 4–2 and they went on to regain the trophy, beating Burnley 3–1 at Wembley in May.
Ken Leek recalls:
'Jimmy Greaves confirmed my feeling that the goal should have stood in his autobiography *Greavsie*. On page 182 he writes: "Two minutes from time with the score 3–3, the Birmingham centre-forward Ken Leek scored what looked to be the winner. Fortunately for us, the referee disallowed Ken's effort, though to this day I have no idea why. From where I was standing it looked like a perfectly legitimate goal".'

AN INTERVIEW WITH KEN WHICH WAS FEATURED IN THE DECEMBER 2006 EDITION OF THE BLUES MAGAZINE

In the pleasant suburb of Boughton near Northampton University is where you will find Birmingham City legend Ken Leek. At 71, 'Leeky' leads a contented retirement with his wife Janet, whom he has known since he was 17. He greets visitors with a warm smile and a Welsh accent that has not diminished since he moved to Northampton in 1952.

Born in Ynysybwl, near Pontypridd, Ken went to rugby-playing schools, but his father was soccer mad and introduced him to the game in a field behind their house, which was overshadowed by the Welsh mountains. He fondly recalls the days when the lads came home from the pit and impromptu 15-a-side matches were played.

Spotted playing in Welsh Boys' Club trials by Harry Hanford of Northampton, he moved into Mrs Matcham's digs and began a five-year apprenticeship with a local manufacturing firm. A year later the Cobblers asked Ken to give up his apprenticeship to concentrate on his football. Ken agreed and was immediately drafted into the National Service, spending the next two years in the RAF, 18 months of which involved a posting to Germany.

After signing full-time professional forms at the age of 20, it was not long before Ken gained his one and only Welsh Under-23 cap, replacing Roy Vernon in a game versus England at Wrexham. The Welsh won 2–1, with Brian Orritt scoring the winner after Trevor Smith had lost possession. The Blues connection was made.

Ken went on to win 13 Welsh caps and remembers his debut at Cardiff v Scotland, which Wales won 2—0. The goalkeeper that day, who was also Ken's roommate, was Gary Sprake.

Ken's international involvement continued after signing for Leicester in May 1958 when he was a member of the 1958 Welsh World Cup squad, and although he did not play in any of the games, at 22 it was a massively rewarding experience. He counts amongst his personal friends Ivor and Len Allchurch, Mel Hopkins, Mel Charles, John Charles, Cliff Jones and other Welsh greats, and he denies being born next door to ex-Blues favourite Don Dearson, although he acknowledges that Don came from the same village.

Following the disappointment of being dropped from the 1961 Leicester City FA Cup Final team on the morning of the Final, Ken was signed by Charlie Mitten, the Newcastle manager, on the recommendation of his Welsh international colleague, Ivor Allchurch.

Whilst Newcastle was a friendly club, it was too far away from his native Wales, and five months later Gil Merrick offered £23,000 to Newcastle (£2k less than they had paid Leicester), a £5-a-week rise to the Leek family to £35 and a club house in Sunnymead Road, Yardley, where Dennis Amiss, the Warwickshire cricketer, was a near neighbour.

Ken had played at St Andrew's for Leicester and loved the compactness of the stadium, which meant the crowd were close and loud. He also remembers that there was a great atmosphere in the Player's Lounge after the game, although in those days Ken's current favourite tipple, lager, was not available.

Ken spent four seasons at Blues, scoring 60 goals in 119 League and Cup appearances, and his most memorable goal was the one that was disallowed in the third-round FA Cup tie against Tottenham Hotspur in 1962 which, with two minutes to go and the score 3—3, would have resulted in the Blues knocking out Spurs, who ultimately went on to beat Burnley in the Final.

Jimmy Harris was Ken's best friend during his time at the Blues, and he recalls that Jimmy was alone in digs with one of the training staff, a Welshman, Dave Jones, so would very often come over to spend time with the Leek family. Indeed, when Jimmy's then girlfriend, Roberta from Liverpool, visited him, she would stay with Janet and Ken.

One of Ken's funniest moments, although it did not seem like it at the time, was when a number of his Welsh friends journeyed from home to Glasgow to see Ken play against Scotland. With five minutes to go Wales were losing 2—1 until Ken scored two to secure a dramatic victory. When Ken contacted his friends to ask them what they thought of his match-winning exploits they sheepishly replied that they had left the game 10 minutes before the final whistle to miss the crowds! Ken recalls that his home debut was against the team he supported as a child, Cardiff. The Blues won 3—1, with Ken scoring one, and from then on it was a goal every other game.

The prized possession in the Leek household is the tankard he received for winning the League Cup in 1963, after scoring two goals in the first leg 3—1 victory over Aston Villa. Although he delights in that victory, (his mate, Bobby Thomson, who played for the Villa that day, openly admits that Blues murdered the Villa in that game and should have scored six), he has a soft spot for the claret-and-blues, as his goalkeeper grandson Karl Darlow has been at their Academy for the past eight years.

The best players that Ken played with at the Blues, he considers to be: Terry Hennessey, Trevor Smith, Jimmy Harris and Bertie Auld in that order. One of the best things about his time at The Blues was the dressing-room atmosphere, as all the players got on with one another.

A typical day at the Elmdon Training Ground started at around 9.30, and as well as fitness and ball work there was always a six-a-side game and, for Ken — shooting practice! Every Wednesday

F.A. CHALLENGE CUP
3rd Round

BIRMINGHAM
V
TOTTENHAM

SOUVENIR

PROGRAMME

there was a 90-minute practice game: First Team against the Reserves. Players were asked to take it steady in the tackles, but that never really happened, recalls Ken. Gil Merrick conducted team talks every day at Elmdon, but on Fridays things got more focused, and that was when the team was announced.

On home matchdays players were expected to get to St Andrew's at least one hour before kick-off, and occasionally there was a lunch provided. Surprisingly a masseur was available to the players that required it, but more important to some of the players, particularly those of a nervous disposition, was that the trainer was able to dispense either whisky or sherry to calm their nerves.

Dave Bowen, who had managed the Welsh national side, was building a Northampton side that had already been promoted from the lower Leagues and was anxious to make it to Division One. So it was no surprise, in December 1964, when Ken moved to Northampton for £9,000 and promotion to the top division achieved.

Ken and Janet are always surprised about the way supporters of his clubs continue to make contact with him — he receives telephone calls, letters and knocks on the door from fans wanting autographs or simply to shake his hand.

Jimmy Harris and Ken have regular telephone contact, and during October Jimmy spent a few days with Ken after attending a reunion of the 1963 League Cup-winning squad in Birmingham.

At this event they met up once again with the magical Bertie Auld, and they kept each other amused throughout their stay with memories of their time at the Blues — very much the case of an Englishman, a Scotsman and a Welshman...

League Cup Final First Leg

Blues 3 Villa 1

Date: 23 May 1963   **Venue:** St Andrew's
Attendance: 31,580   **Referee:** Mr E. Crawford (Doncaster)

Villa: Sims, Fraser, Aitken, Crowe, Sleeuwenhoek, Lee, Baker, Graham, Thomson, Wylie, Burrows.

Blues: Schofield, Lynn, Green, Hennessey, Smith, Beard, Hellawell, Bloomfield, Harris, Leek, Auld.

Not since 1956 had Blues contested a domestic Final, and this was one they simply had to win, as the opposition were their neighbours and arch rivals, Aston Villa. Villa went into the match as the bookmaker's favourites, having been beaten Blues in a League match 4–0 two months earlier. Both sides were at full strength in front of a first-leg St Andrew's crowd of 31,580 who were licking their lips with relish in anticipation of this Birmingham derby, which to the winner was worth much more than just 'the bragging rights'.

Blues started well with near misses from Jimmy Harris and Ken Leek, both of which were well saved by the Villa goalkeeper Sims. Blues had their best chance to date soon after

---

PLAYER FACTFILE

STANLEY LYNN
Right-back
148 appearances, 30 goals
Left Blues for Stourbridge in 1966.

Stan 'the Wham' was one of the few players to cross over the City of Birmingham from Villa Park and become a true favourite of the fans. His terrific powerful shot, particularly when taking penalties, was the stuff of legend. Born in Bolton on 18 June 1928, his local football teams were Whitecroft Road School and Whitworth's FC. He joined Accrington Stanley as an amateur in August 1945 aged 17, before signing a professional contract in July 1947. He signed for Aston Villa for £10,000 in March 1950 and while there won the FA Cup in 1957, the Divison Two Championship in 1960 and the Football League Cup in 1961. He joined Blues in October 1961 for £2,000 when many people thought he was 'over the hill' at 33 years of age. This proved not to be the case; indeed, in 1964–65 he was the club's top goalscorer, and he won the League Cup for a second time in 1963. He went into non-League football with Stourbridge in August 1966 on a free transfer, eventually retiring in May 1968. He died on 28 April 2002.

when another shot from Harris was deflected onto the crossbar by Sims.

The competitiveness of both sides began to show when Bobby Thomson clattered Blues 'keeper Schofield with an unnecessary late challenge for the ball, and in another incident Leek sent Crowe flying with another late tackle, both fouls coming in the early stages, as the teams 'sorted each other out' in what was a typically eagerly fought out derby. There was a lot at stake! The first goal was scored by Leek after 14 minutes, much to the delight of the home fans. A ball from midfield by Harris released Bertie Auld down the left wing, and his cross was blasted home by Leek, this time giving Sims no chance of making a stop. Jimmy Bloomfield, with the tackles still flying in, became the first casualty, leaving to have a thigh injury dealt with, and he returned only to hobble on the wing so that he could run the

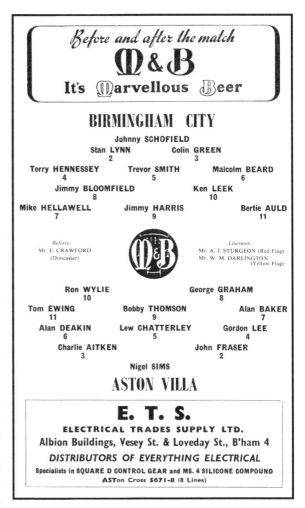

knock off. Villa were not beaten, however, and they got back into the game via an equaliser by Thomson. Gordon Lee started the move, and after driving into Blues' final third he sent in a hard, low cross which Thomson hit first time, which sped past Schofield as he was coming out to narrow the angle for the Villa man.

The second period began badly for Villa defender Sleeuwenhoek, who collided with his own goalkeeper which resulted in an injury that forced him to leave the field to receive treatment. Soon after that, Blues lost their centre-half as well when Trevor Smith was hurt in another rash tackle from Thomson. The first real chance to score was taken, and it restored the lead for Blues after 52 minutes. Again, Harris and Auld were the architects and Leek the goalscorer, with a low drive in the area from Auld's pinpoint pass. The match was still bad-tempered, and referee Crawford began to lose his patience with the persistent niggling fouling. Crowe became the next victim when he was elbowed in the face after a tussle with Auld. Charlie Aitken was then given a sharp tongue-lashing when he shoved Hellawell in the chest in yet another heated exchange. Fraser and Harris came close to blows as they squared up to one another and teammates had to drag them apart. Crawford also gave them a warning as they continued to infuriate the Doncaster official. Blues finally killed the game with their third goal after 66 minutes. From a Harris right-wing cross, Bloomfield dashed in unmarked (apart from the wound on his thigh) by Villa's sleeping defence to push the ball past Sims and in off the upright. Blues were leading 3–1, were in the ascendancy and strolled through the rest of the game, content to take their lead to Villa Park for the second leg. In the dying moments, Sims saved Villa once again, saving two excellent shots on goal from Leek then Auld. The final whistle came with Blues still holding a two-goal advantage and counting the bruises from this gruelling encounter.

THE 1963 LEAGUE CUP-WINNING TEAM. WHERE DID THEY GO?

Name	All-time Apps	All-time Gls	Outcome
Schofield, John	237	0	Wrexham, 1966
Lynn, Stan	148	30	Stourbridge, 1966
Green, Colin	217	1	Wrexham, 1971
Hennessey, Terry	203	3	Nottingham Forest, 1965
Smith, Trevor	430	3	Walsall, 1964
Beard, Malcolm	403+2	33	Aston Villa, 1971
Hellawell, Mike	213	33	Sunderland, 1965
Bloomfield, Jimmy	148	31	Brentford, 1964
Harris, Jimmy	115	53	Oldham, 1964
Leek, Ken	120	61	Northampton, 1964
Auld, Bertie	147	31	Glasgow Celtic, 1965

Ten-goal Thriller

BLUES 5 DERBY 5

Date: 9 April 1966   **Venue:** St Andrew's
Attendance: 13,083

Blues: Herriot, Fraser, Martin, Wylie, Foster, Beard, Jackson, Vincent, Fenton (Thomson), Vowden, Hockey.

Derby: Matthews, Richardson, Daniel, Webster, Saxton, Upton, Hughes, Buxton, Hodgson, Durban, Thomas.

Blues had established themselves in Division Two as a middle-of-the-table team with the eternal promise of more to come, but April 1966 saw Blues with no chance of promotion, nor of relegation, with Derby much the same, so understandably the crowd dropped to a little over 13,000.

The game began as most others, with little promise of the excitement to come. Blues took the lead on 15 minutes when Trevor Hockey, new to the ranks that season, smartly controlled a teasing right-wing cross from Jackson and fired a cross-shot past Matthews in the Derby goal. This stung Derby into action, and they pummelled Blues, taking only six minutes to equalise, Alan Durban tapping home after a corner was headed against Herriot by Derby's Thomas. Three minutes later, Derby were in front after

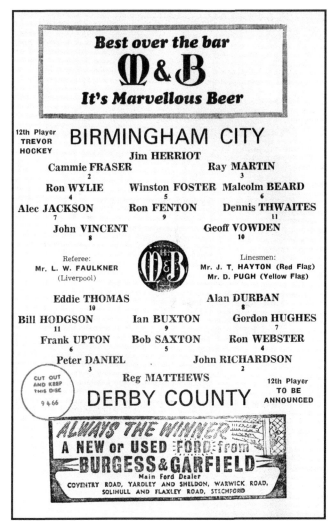

12th Player
TREVOR
HOCKEY

BIRMINGHAM CITY

Jim HERRIOT

Cammie FRASER   Ray MARTIN
2   3

Ron WYLIE   Winston FOSTER Malcolm BEARD
4   5   6

Alec JACKSON   Ron FENTON   Dennis THWAITES
7   9   11

John VINCENT   Geoff VOWDEN
8   10

Referee: Linesmen:
Mr. L. W. FAULKNER   Mr. J. T. HAYTON (Red Flag)
(Liverpool)   Mr. D. PUGH (Yellow Flag)

Eddie THOMAS   Alan DURBAN
10   8

Bill HODGSON   Ian BUXTON   Gordon HUGHES
11   9   7

Frank UPTON   Bob SAXTON   Ron WEBSTER
6   5   4

Peter DANIEL   John RICHARDSON
3   2

Reg MATTHEWS
12th Player
TO BE
ANNOUNCED

DERBY COUNTY

CUT OUT
AND KEEP
THIS DISC
9.4.66

Durban sprinted through Blues' defence to collect a long ball, drew Herriot out and fired a bullet shot across him into the net. Within a minute Blues had been awarded a penalty, which was converted by Beard, after Saxton brought down Jackson in the area. Blues redoubled their efforts, and Saxton's day got worse on 33 minutes when a Fraser cross from the right was instinctively turned into his own goal by the hapless defender. With no more scoring in the next 12 minutes, the score remained at 3–2 to Blues.

Derby took the field with renewed vigour for the second half, and they were back on level terms within two minutes of the restart, as Buxton chased a ball down the wing, caught up with it and cut into the area, where he fired low under Herriot's despairing dive. Just three minutes later, Blues were back in front, as a Hockey corner evaded Jackson's dive, but his movement transfixed the Derby defence and the ball ran through to Beard, who slammed it home off the underside of the crossbar. Derby countered again, and a wonderful save was needed from Herriot to deny Alan Durban his hat-trick, a save which took on more importance in the 67th minute, when Blues went 5–3 in front. A pinpoint cross from Hockey was powered home by Vowden's head, and Blues thought they had the points won.

Derby would have none of it, though, and they pressed at every opportunity. Finally, after 84 minutes, a high swirling ball deceived Blues substitute Thomson, who was all at sea and ended up deflecting the ball into his own net for the game's second own-goal. Derby took this good fortune as a sign and pressed forward in rejuvenated form, netting the equaliser just a minute later, with Durban finishing off good work from Buxton to claim his hat-trick and disappoint the Bluenoses.

TREVOR HOCKEY
Winger/Midfield
231+1 appearances, 13 goals
9 appearances for Wales
Joined Sheffield United in January 1971 for £35,000.

Born in Keighley on 1 March 1943, Hockey was another of football's journeymen, eventually playing on all 92 League Club grounds during his career. He was also another of those professional footballers that played rugby in their youth, and Trevor dabbled in both codes, playing union for Abertillery and league for Keighley. His early football included Eastwood School (Keighley), West Riding Under-19s and Keighley Youth Club, before joining Bradford City as an amateur in June 1958. His professional career began two years later when he signed professional forms for Bradford City in May 1960. Then his journey began: in November 1961 he joined Nottingham Forest for a fee of £15,000; a move to Newcastle (where he won a Division Two champions' medal in 1965) two years later for £25,000 preceded his arrival at St Andrew's in November 1965 for £22,500. He was a great favourite of the Bluenoses, with his energy-fuelled performances and his Beatles hair style. While he was not the most skilful of players, he was an aggressive midfielder who added bite whenever he played. In January 1971 he moved to Sheffield United for £35,000 and then to Norwich City in February 1973. At the age of 30 he went to Villa Park for a £38,000 transfer fee in June 1973. A stay of 12 months back in Birmingham ended with a move back to Bradford City in June 1974. In March 1976 he became player-manager to the Irish Club Athlone Town, before moving to start a career in the US, where soccer was being heavily promoted for the first time. He played for San Diego Jaws in the NASL in April 1976, then Las Vegas Quicksilver in March 1977 and San Jose Earthquakes in June 1977, before returning to the UK to become manager of Stalybridge Celtic in August 1977. He was one of the first players to appear in a Welsh shirt based on parental qualification. He died in Keighley on 2 April 1987.

Bobby Thomson recalls what might have been a contributory factor to his own-goal:
'I had had quite a late night and was relieved to be given the number-12 shirt. Sitting in the dugout, I had the sun in my bleary eyes throughout the game, and when I had to replace Ronnie Fenton I could barely see, due to the sun, I swear.'

Game Twenty-five

FA Cup Semi-final

WEST BROMWICH ALBION 2 BLUES 0

Date: 27 April 1968   **Venue:** Villa Park
Attendance: 60,831

Blues: Herriot, Murray, Martin, Wylie, Foster, Beard, Vowden, Green, Pickering, Page, Bridges.

West Brom: Osborne, Fraser, Williams, Brown, Talbot, Kaye, Stephens, Collard, Astle, Hope, Clark.

Fred Pickering remembers:
'My most memorable game was undoubtedly the 1968 FA Cup semi-final, and still to this day I do not know how we lost it. If I hit the post once it must have been umpteen times. I played really well that day, and my shots were bouncing off every part of John

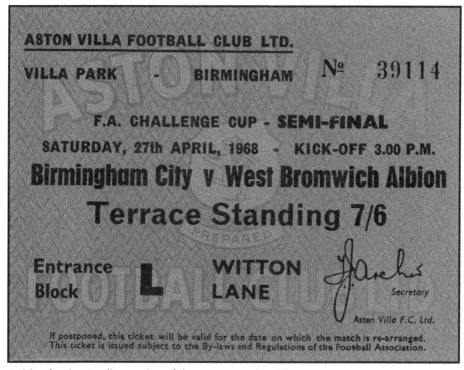

A ticket for the standing section of the terrace, costing 7/6.

FREDERICK PICKERING
Centre-forward
88 appearances, 32 goals
3 appearances for England
Left Blues for Blackpool in 1969.

Fred was born in Blackburn on 19 January 1941 and after playing in local football joined his home-town club as a junior in August 1956 before turning professional in January 1958. While there he was a member of their Youth Team which won the FA Youth Cup in 1959. He moved to Everton for £85,000 in March 1964 before signing for Blues for £50,000 in August 1967. He started out as a full-back but was converted into a hugely successful centre-forward, being fast, skilful and powerful and excellent in the air. He scored a hat-trick on his debut for England in the famous 10–0 demolition of the US. He left Blues for Blackpool in June 1969 before returning to Ewood Park in March 1971. After a trial at Brighton & Hove Albion in February 1972 he eventually quit first-class football in May 1973. As well as his full England caps he also played three times for the Under-23s and represented the Football League XI on one occasion.

Osborne's body, but they would not go in – I should have scored at least four! Our Cup run meant we did not get promotion as we only won four out of the nine games after we had beaten Chelsea in the sixth round. We finished fourth that season. After the game the team had a few drinks in the city centre before some of us decided to have a quiet drink at Moor Hall Hotel in Sutton Coldfield, which was where I and a few of the lads lived. Imagine how we felt when we walked in and found that Graham Williams, the Albion captain, had organised their celebration party to be held there. The first person I saw was John Talbot, their centre-half, who had spent the whole afternoon chasing after me! Needless to say, they bought the drinks all night.'

Barry Bridges recalls:
'I didn't play at all in that game. I don't know if I felt the pressure but I had played in three semi-finals before that, so perhaps it wasn't that. I make no excuses, I had a terrible game, but Freddy had a good game that day, but he just couldn't score. When I look back on it, the press were really building me up, and I don't now if I felt a bit more pressure than normal because people were relying so much on me. That sounds very conceited in saying that, but that was the feeling there was among Blues fans at the time because I was scoring goals for fun, as it were [Note: 27 goals in all games until that day]. Maybe that's what threw me because I didn't play at all. I had a terrible game, terrible. And that was my third semi-final defeat game in three years too – two with Chelsea and one with Blues, so the result didn't please me much either.'

AN INTERVIEW WITH FRED WHICH APPEARED IN NOVEMBER 2007 EDITION OF THE BLUES MAGAZINE

The goal machine, otherwise known as Fred Pickering (168 goals in 354 League appearances), lives quietly in a terraced house in Blackburn, the town where he was born within 300 yards of Ewood Park, the home of Blackburn Rovers, where his football story begins.

As a young boy he played as an inside-forward for Blackburn and Lancashire Schoolboys and at the age of 14 had scouts from the likes of Arsenal and Aston Villa knocking on his door, along with those from local teams like Preston and Burnley. He had decided that he would sign for either one of the 'big clubs' or Blackburn. As the only son (he has four sisters) his mother was reluctant for him to leave, so he signed apprentice forms for the Rovers while quitting his engineering apprenticeship with a local firm making looms for the textile industry.

He signed professional forms in January 1958 and received a signing-on fee of £10 that was exactly the same signing-on fee he got when he moved to Everton for £85,000.

As a full-back he captained the Blackburn youth team to win the Youth Cup in 1958—59 when they beat West Ham 1—0 at Ewood Park. The losers included Bobby Moore, Martin Peters and Geoff Hurst, who had a penalty saved! 'We were not a bad side in those days and as well as me we had two other players that went on to play international football, Keith Newton and Mike England.'

He converted to playing centre-forward after Derek Dougan had asked for a transfer on the eve of the 1960 FA Cup Final, 'once he had left they were short in the reserve side so I moved up front. Two weeks later I was in the first team scoring two goals in a 3—1 win over Manchester City, and the rest is history.'

'During my time at Rovers my maximum wage was about £20 per week less than some of the other first team, so I asked for an increase of £5 per week. Their response? Within two weeks I was transferred to Everton, even though I'd scored 72 goals in 146 appearances (and some of those were as a full-back) and been capped three times for the England Under-23 side.'

'Harry Catterick signed me for Everton, and I had three and a half years there, scoring 70 goals in 115 games, but I damaged my knee in a game against Liverpool and that was it with Everton. These days the top clubs spend time and money getting their top players fit after injury — look at Newcastle and Michael Owen, but in those days once you were badly injured you were moved on. The deal to join Blues was based on how many appearances I made.'

HOW DID YOUR MOVE TO BLUES COME ABOUT?

'I met Stan Cullis at a hotel in Knutsford, Cheshire, on the Thursday as the new season [1967—68] was due to start on the Saturday. Because of my injury I had had no pre-season, but a deal was agreed and, as I went home to get my gear, Stan formalised the details with Everton — in those days the players never got involved in the detail. I travelled down to Birmingham that night and went to St Andrew's on the following day. On Fridays, training was always held at the ground rather than Elmdon, and as I walked into the car park I bumped into Bert Murray and Barry Bridges who I knew from their Chelsea days. I told them I hadn't signed yet so they introduced me to the team. I could not believe the quality of the players and thought to myself with that team we've got a real chance of promotion to Division One. Remember, up until now I had only ever played in the top League. Anyway, I signed that afternoon and made my debut the following day.'

WHAT DO YOU REMEMBER OF YOUR DEBUT?

'We beat Bolton at home 4–0 ,and it was a delight to play alongside some great players: Ron Wylie, Johnny Vincent (who was just starting), Trevor Hockey, Geoff Vowden, Malcolm Beard and, of course, Bert and Barry. I was at least five games away from match fitness, and that's why it took me until 4 September to score my first goal. It was against Hull City in a game we won 6–2.'

WHERE DID YOU LIVE WHEN AT THE BLUES?

'I moved into the Sutton Coldfield area near Moor Hall Golf Club where a few of the team had houses. At the time I had a son aged five and daughter aged three, but my wife never settled and moved back north with the kids, leaving me alone in Birmingham for my two-year stay.'

The cover of a pirate programme.

WHAT WERE YOUR IMPRESSIONS OF THE BLUES?

'Everything was brilliant. I couldn't fault them from the players up to the boardroom. Clifford Coombs, the chairman, really cared about the football side of things and looked after the players' interests. It had a real family atmosphere, the best club I played for in that respect.'

WHO WERE THE CHARACTERS AT BLUES?

'Stan Cullis never really lived up to his reputation of being "the iron man". He was a lovely fellow; you couldn't wish to meet a nicer bloke. He never swore, always "flippin' this" and "floppin' that". Ron Wylie was a terrific man and a great captain. He was destined to go into management as he was always involved with the backroom boys, Joe Mallet and Bill Shorthouse. I remember Bobby Thomson turning up for training in a kilt one time!'

HOW DID YOUR CAREER END AT BLUES?

'I wanted to move back north to be with my family who were growing up fast. Originally I was destined to sign for Huddersfield, but I received a telegram from the Blues secretary, Alan Instone, asking me to call him. When I did I was told Blackpool wanted to sign me, so I had the chance to get back to Lancashire. That disappointed Ian Greaves, the Huddersfield manager. My final game was on 12 April 1969 when we lost 1—0 to Villa.'

TELL ME ABOUT YOUR ENGLAND APPEARANCES

'I played three times and scored five goals. My debut was in the 10—0 victory over the US. I played with a groin strain that I told no one about and scored a hat-trick — they were a load of donkeys! I was named in the initial squad of 40 for the 1966 World Cup, but my knee injury finished that for me.'

WHAT DID YOU DO AFTER YOU LEFT BLUES?

'At Blackpool we got promoted from Division Two as runners-up, but there was no medal — in fact I won nowt throughout my career! After a short return to Blackburn I went to Brighton for a trial at the request of their manager, Pat Saward. I only went because Barry and Bert were there, but it did not work out. Perhaps it would have had it been a more local team to my home, so I retired from the game in 1973. I then went to work in local factories as a fork-lift truck driver until I stopped full-time work when I was 58. I was diagnosed as being diabetic.'

Game Twenty-six

Greenhoff Scores Four but Misses a Penalty

BLUES 5 FULHAM 4

Date: 5 October 1968   **Venue:** St Andrew's
Attendance: 27,318   **Referee:** J. Finney (Hereford)

Blues: Herriot, Martin, Page, Wylie, Robinson, Beard, Hockey, Greenhoff, Vowden, Vincent, Summerill.

Fulham: McClelland, Pentecost, Dempsey, Matthewson, Ryan, Brown, Callaghan, Kerrigan, Large, Macdonald, Barrett.

What a game this was for the fans – nine goals, end-to-end action, a win for the Blues and a missed penalty!

It was a half-full St Andrew's crowd that got maximum value for their admission money! Blues had plenty of attacking options, with a midfield of Ron Wyliem, Malcolm Beard, Trevor Hockey and Johnny Vincent feeding Geoff Vowden, Phil Summerill and the relative newcomer, Jimmy Greenhoff. The counter to this was the Blues' defence frailties, which the Cottagers exploited to great effect to set up this memorable match.

Johnny Vincent began the goal avalanche after two minutes: it was 2–0 after 16

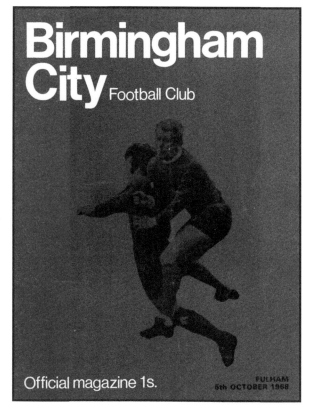

Birmingham City Football Club

Official magazine 1s.

FULHAM 5th OCTOBER 1968

JIMMY GREENHOFF . .
Another U-23 cap at St. Andrews ?

● It's taken **JIMMY GREENHOFF** no time at all to rival big Fred Pickering's popularity with the crowd at St. Andrew's and the former Leeds United utility man has made an auspicious start for us with five goals in six matches.

● This kind of scoring took Jimmy right into the reckoning for a place in the England Under 23 team before very long. His first Cap came against Wales on Wednesday night and . . .

● WHAT COULD BE BETTER THAN FOR HIM TO LINE UP AGAINST HOLLAND HERE AT ST. ANDREW'S ON NOVEMBER 13th?

● Youth International, Jimmy was an extremely versatile player for Leeds, playing at half-back or inside-forward. But his tremendous finishing power has made him one of the most effective strikers in the game.

● Already we think our £70,000 signing is looking a real bargain. His busy running off the ball makes yards of room for those around him and he always seems to have energy to burn.

● Jimmy's linking up well with another young man who has been tipped for Under 23 recognition before long — **JOHNNY VINCENT.** Last season Johnny started like a bomb with 13 goals by Christmas.

● He seemed to lose his spark on the heavier grounds in the New Year but he's back with his old sparkle and zip again this season. He has scored four goals already and that's not bad from a lad who does as much creative work as he does finishing.

● With Jim Herriot in the Scottish World Cup squad, Colin Green and Fred Pickering already full internationals, and Page, Greenhoff and Vincent all knocking on the door — it would appear the future's not so gloomy as it might seem after our disappointing start.

● **Keep it up chaps — you might get to Mexico in 1970 after all!**

A Jimmy Greenhoff article from the match-day programme.

minutes when Greenhoff netted his first. Before the first half-hour had ended Blues were three-up when a Vincent corner was converted by the ex-Leeds United striker.

In the second half the game was turned round in an incredible five-minute period in which Fulham got onto equal terms: on 48 minutes Large made it 3–1, a Dave 'Sugar' Robinson own-goal made it 3–2, before Large added his second to level the scores at 3–3.

After 64 minutes Greenhoff was fouled by Matthewson in the penalty area – Jimmy missed the resulting penalty-kick, but fortunately he rescued his reputation a minute later

JAMES GREENHOFF
Inside-forward
36 appearances, 15 goals
Played for England in five Under-23 games
Joined Stoke City in August 1969 for £100,000.

James 'Jimmy' Greenhoff was born on 19 June 1946 in Barnsley. He was a skilful forward and, although capped by England five times at Under-23 level, once as an over-age player, and playing for the Football League XI, he never played for the full side.Greenhoff started his career as an apprentice with Leeds United in June 1961, turning professional in August 1963. He moved to Blues for £70,000 in August 1968.He left Birmingham City in August 1969 for Stoke City in a deal worth £100,000. While at Stoke City he was a member of the 1972 League Cup-winning team and scored 76 goals, including a brilliant effort against Birmingham which won the acclaimed honour of 'Goal of the Season', in 274 League appearances before being sold to Manchester United in November 1976 for £120,000. While with Manchester United he helped the club win the 1977 FA Cup, scoring the winner in the Final, and played alongside his brother Brian, who also later played for Leeds United, signing in 1979. He won the Supporters' Player of the Year award in 1979. Greenhoff scored 36 goals in 123 appearances (including four substitute appearances) for Manchester United before leaving to join Crewe Alexandra in December 1980. He moved to NASL side Toronto Blizzard in March 1981, returning to the UK to play for Port Vale that August. He left Port Vale in March 1983 to join Rochdale, where he was player-manager up to March 1984, after which he returned to Port Vale as a coach. He retired in May 1985 to concentrate on coaching youngsters at holiday camps, which he combined with insurance work. He later developed his own insurance business, Greenhoff Peutz & Co., based in Audley, Staffs, and also worked for a paint company. At Leeds United he won a runners'-up medal in the Fairs Cup Final of 1967, upgrading to a winners' medal the following year.

with a shot from the edge of the box. It was 4–3, and Blues had regained the lead only to concede again three minutes later when Malcolm Macdonald put Fulham back on level terms.

An exciting tussle was eventually won following a goalkeeping error, when McLelland fumbled a Vincent effort, dropping the ball at the feet of Greenhoff with 19 minutes to go. Greenhoff made no mistake, and it was 5–4. The crowd left with a huge smile on their faces – this is what football is all about!

Game Twenty-seven

Four Goals at Sixteen

BLUES 4 BOLTON 0

Date: 20 February 1971   **Venue:** St Andrew's
Attendance: 25,600

Blues: D. Latchford, Martin, Pendrey, Page, Hynd, Robinson, Campbell, Francis (Bowker), R. Latchford, Summerill, Taylor.

Bolton: Boswell, Ritson, McCallister, Williams, Hurley, Rimmer, Waldron, Greaves, Fletcher, G. Jones, Phillips.

Bolton had chosen a defensive line up, and it was clear from the beginning that veteran defender Warwick Rimmer had been given the job of tracking Francis for the duration. From the off Rimmer was struggling to keep up with Francis, and it seemed only a matter of time before he would cause some real damage.

It took 16 minutes before Gordon Taylor headed down Ray Martin's free-kick for Trevor Francis to speed past his marker and lash in a fierce shot. Alan Boswell, the Bolton 'keeper, managed to parry the shot, but it looped up, and without hesitation Francis was on to it and Blues were 1–0 up. Four minutes later it was 2–0 when 'TF' latched onto a Phil Summerill effort and curled a shot past Boswell.

There was no further scoring until the 79th minute, although Dave Robinson had a goal disallowed and Taylor and Summerill had efforts against the woodwork. A Summerill shot was half-saved and, surprise, surprise, Francis was there to complete his hat-trick.

The game was won and Trevor Francis was in the history books, but it was not over yet. Four minutes later Robinson's left-wing cross was headed in for Francis's fourth.

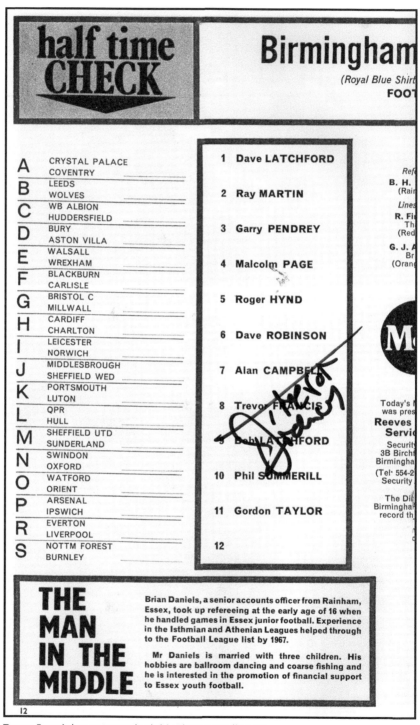

Trevor Francis has autographed this Blues team line up.

TREVOR JOHN FRANCIS
Inside-forward
327+2 appearances, 133 goals
52 appearances for England
Joined Nottingham Forest in February 1979 for £975,000 plus VAT and levy charges.

Born in Plymouth on 19 April 1954, 'TF' played for local sides in Devon before joining Blues as an apprentice in June 1969. After his two-year stint he joined the professional ranks in May 1971. He exploded onto the League scene with 15 goals in his first 21 games, demonstrating electrifying speed off the mark, fantastic dribbling skills, a powerful shot and a self-confidence which belied his youth. Throughout the 1970s, Francis's contribution undoubtedly kept Blues in the top flight, but it was inevitable that he would move onto bigger things. After eight years at St Andrew's he joined Nottingham Forest for £1 million to become the most expensive player in British football history. In his first season at the City Ground he won the European Cup, scoring the winning goal, and a year later he added a League Cup-winners' medal to his trophy cabinet. He was soon capped for England after five Under-23 appearances, going on to win 52 caps. In September 1981 he joined Manchester City for £1.2 million before moving to Italy when Sampdoria secured his services for £800,000 in July 1982. While there he gained an Italian Cup-winners medal in 1985. In July 1986 he moved within Italy to Atalanta for £900,000, but spent less than a year there before going to Scotland with Glasgow Rangers on a free transfer in September 1987. Once again honours came his way, this time with a Scottish League Cup success in 1988. He returned to England with Queen's Park Rangers in March 1988 and was appointed player-manager in the following December. In February 1990 he joined Sheffield Wednesday, serving them as manager from June 1991 to May 1995, securing the League Cup and Division Two promotion in his first season and FA Cup runners-up in 1995. After leaving Wednesday, Francis spent time working as a television pundit (something which he had done throughout his career) before going back to his spiritual home of Birmingham City as manager in 1996, aiming to regain their position as a top team. They reached the Play-offs three seasons running, in 1999, 2000 and 2001, but failed to be promoted. After losing the 2001 Football League Cup Final to Liverpool, Francis left later that year. He had a short spell in charge of Crystal Palace, who defeated Liverpool in an FA Cup fourth-round replay in February 2003.

Trevor had fallen awkwardly while scoring and was immediately substituted by Freddie Goodwin, which gave the St Andrew's crowd the chance to salute their young hero. 1970–71 was Trevor Francis's first season, and he recorded 21 League Appearances and one as a substitute, with a return of 16 goals. He also made two FA Cup Appearances and two in the League Cup.

Game Twenty-eight

Promotion

ORIENT 0 BLUES 1

Date: 2 May 1972   **Venue:** Brisbane Road
Attendance: 33,383   **Referee:** Mr M. Lowe (Sheffield)

Blues: Cooper, Carroll, Pendrey, Smith, Hynd, Whitehead, Campbell, Francis, Latchford, Hatton, Taylor.

Orient: Goddard, Arber, Rose, Hoadley, Harris, Allen, Lazarus, Brisley, Bullock, Walley, Bowyer.

This was the last game of the season, and one point was needed for Blues to be promoted to Division One after seven seasons in the Second Division. The Blues, whose travelling army of fans amounted to 18,000, were up for this match and confidence was high. The Brisbane Road crowd rose to 33,383 for the evening kick-off. Many were locals, but there was a contingent of supporters of the club who could benefit from a Blues slip up – Millwall, and they were clearly intent on causing problems should things begin not suit their expectations. Orient, the opposition in extremely important game, had nothing to play for other than their professional pride, and whatever the result it would not affect their position in the final Division Two table.

Blues started the match and right from the start it was clear that the pressure was telling in their performance; their game negatively impacted by the fear of making a single error. It was no surprise, therefore, that the opening exchanges were almost entirely held in midfield arena, Blues were happy to soak up any pressure and earn their point through a stern defence, which was often placed deep in the Orient half. A rare scoring chance came Blues' way, but Bob Latchford snatched at it and the ball ballooned over the bar. At the other end Garry Pendrey bravely threw himself forward to block a goal-bound shot from Lazarus, and striker Mickey Bullock (who played for Blues from 1962–67) almost broke Blues' hearts, but his shot brought out a great diving save from Paul Cooper. Blues' best chance came just before the first 45 minutes and elapsed when Goddard acrobatically tipped over a shot from Bob Hatton.

Blues began the second half with a lot more confidence, and obviously Freddie Goodwin's half-time team talk had worked. They were no longer showing signs of fear, and they began to chase the game to secure the result that every Blues fan desperately wanted – it was as if they had been told only a win, not a draw, was needed. Immediately you could see that Trevor Francis, who had been conspicuous by his absence in the first half, was now looking for the ball, and when he received the ball for the first time after the restart he struck a beauty from outside the area which Goddard saved brilliantly. Then minutes later he sent a spectacular volley from Gordon Taylor's cross just inches wide. Blues looked increasingly the more likely to score, and on 58 minutes they took a huge step onto the Division One ladder's bottom rung with a goal from Bob Latchford. A corner from Taylor was headed in by the Blues centre-forward whose progress was being badly hampered by being pulled back by the 'keeper. The goal sparked chaos all around – Orient's players surrounded the referee, complaining that Latchford had in fact fouled Goddard, and while this was going on the Blues fans invaded the pitch for a goal celebration, followed shortly after by the Millwall fans. Chaos reigned for quite some time as the police tried to get the fans back to their places on the terraces. Once play eventually restarted with just

the players and officials on the pitch it was Blues who dominated. Taylor broke through and almost made the game safe, but he was denied again by a great instinctive save from Goddard. This started what had been pending for some time – another pitch invasion, only this time it was the Millwall fans. Play was halted again, and after the second restart Blues carried on where they had left off – attacking the Orient goal. A lob by Hatton just cleared the bar in the closing minutes, which brought from the Blues element in the crowd a resounding version of their battle hymn *Keep right on to the end of the road* which was the loudest ever. The referee finally signalled the end of the game after almost 100 minutes of activity, including stoppage time, and the players raced off fearing for their safety.

Blues fans stormed the pitch, and a promotion party started. Even the announcement of a bomb in the ground did not stop the celebrations, but after being ignored the police took over and everyone was evacuated. Everyone, it seems, apart from the Blues team and chairman Keith Coombes who were still in the dressing room, choosing not to leave. Coombes summed up the mood of the club by saying after the game, 'I didn't care even if it was a real bomb, I can go happy now I know we are back in Division One'.

ROBERT DENNIS LATCHFORD
Striker
190+4 appearances, 84 goals

Born in King's Heath, Birmingham, on 18 January 1951, Bob signed as an apprentice for the Blues in May 1967, signing professional terms in August 1968. Latchford was the complete centre-forward: good in the air and on the ground. Despite his size, he was very fast over short distances, making him a great 'poacher' of goals, and he also scored with some great diving headers. He was a member of the 1967 Blues youth team that were runners-up in the FA Youth Cup. He was transferred from Birmingham City to Everton for £350,000, a British transfer record fee at the time. Howard Kendall and Archie Styles were transferred to Birmingham City as part of the same deal, with Birmingham being paid just £80,000. At Everton, Latchford was the top scorer for six successive seasons, scoring 30 goals in the 1977–78 season, a feat he had completed at Blues in 1971–72. During the mid-1970s Latchford was widely considered as one of the top English forwards of his generation. He earned his first full cap for England in a World Cup qualifier against Italy in 1977. He won a runners'-up medal at Everton in the League Cup of 1977. Latchford made 288 appearances for Everton, scoring 138 goals. He left Everton for top flight Swansea in July 1981 for £125,000, scoring a hat-trick on his debut for the Swans. He won the Welsh Cup twice in 1982 and 1983. He moved to Holland to join NAC Breda (15 appearances, 13 goals) in February 1985. He moved back to Wales for a loan spell with Newport County during January to May 1986. In August 1986 he joined Merthyr Tydfil, winning the Welsh Cup in 1987. He was a Director of Alvechurch FC and later returned to Blues to work in both the commercial and the youth development departments.He played 12 times for England, scoring five goals, to build upon the fact that he had six Under-23 and four Youth caps, as well as an appearance for the Football League XI.

Game Twenty-nine

We Was Robbed

LIVERPOOL 4 BLUES 3

Date: 2 December 1972   **Venue:** Anfield
Attendance: 45,407

Blues: Kelly, Martin, Want, Pendrey, Hynd, Harland, Hope, Calderwood, Latchford, Hatton, Taylor.

Liverpool: Clemence, Lawler, Lindsay, Storton, Lloyd, Hughes, Keegan, Cormack, Heighway, Toshack, Callaghan.

Blues had just been promoted to what was then the First Division in the days before Premierships and Championships. Liverpool were in their halcyon days and England and Europe seemed to be gripped by red hands. They were again leading the First Division, and the arrival of Blues at Anfield looked like a banker home win for the non-committed. But to this day Blues will always believe they were robbed of a famous victory by a referee's decision that beggars belief!

A crowd of 45,407 were packed into Anfield – this was the Liverpool managed by Bill Shankly and including Keegan, Toshack, Hughes and Thompson. In goal for Blues was Mike Kelly, who at the time was the reserve-team coach and had been pressed into service because of a goalkeeping crisis, with Paul Cooper and Dave Latchford being injured. Liverpool had not dropped a point at home, and Blues had only scored six goals in their previous 11 away fixtures.

The Kop was stunned when Gordon Taylor fired Blues into the lead, and after Alex Lindsay had levelled the scores Bobby Hope scored his first goal for the Blues after his summer signing from West Bromwich Albion. Bob Latchford then scored to make it 1–3. Just before half-time Peter Cormack pulled a goal back for Liverpool, and by the 56th minute Lindsay had scored again to make it 3–3.

In what was easily Blues' best away performance for years, the 73rd minute brought the moment that angered Goodwin and every member of his team. Blues were on the offensive, and Garry Pendrey's centre ended with Trevor Storton heading into his own net. At 3–4 Blues could well have gone on to win the match. But that is when the referee, Mr A. Hart of Kent, took a hand. He disallowed the goal. Yes, that's right, he disallowed an own-goal!

In the opinion of the referee Bob Hatton had pushed Storton. The Blues players and fans were stunned, and to make matters worse Liverpool went down the other end and John Toshack put them ahead for the first time.

Bobby Hope recalls:

'To this day, people still talk about it – there was no way that Bob pushed him. There might have been a small amount of contact, but it was more to the point that the two Liverpool players collided. I believe, as we all did at the time, that had that goal stood, then it would have sealed the points for us. There is no secret, that even today, if you go to Anfield, you rarely get anything. It was an intimidating place to go to try to get anything and more so then than now. These were the days when it was standing only at the Kop, and they could make some noise. If that goal had been disallowed these days, then the TV cameras would have every angle covered, and I am sure it would have shown we were right to complain, but it would not have changed a thing.'

Tony Want recalls:

'This was my most memorable game for the Blues. After the setback of having Bob Hatton's goal disallowed Liverpool scored the winner, but we were robbed and the Liverpool players knew it as they clapped us off the pitch!'

PLAYER FACTFILE

ROBERT JOHN HATTON
212+6 appearances, 73 goals
Joined Blackpool in July 1976.

Bob was born in Hull on 10 April 1947. He played in more than 600 matches for a variety of clubs and scored at a rate better than one goal in every three matches. Wolverhampton Wanderers signed him from Wath Wanderers as an apprentice in June 1963. He turned professional in November 1964. He joined Bolton Wanderers in March 1967 before moving to Northampton Town in October 1968. When the Cobblers were relegated to Division Four his services were secured by Carlisle United at the start of the 1969–70 season for £8,000. Bob was well known even then for his hard work and finishing prowess in front of goal and could easily have commanded a higher fee. Bob Stokoe, the Carlisle United manager, was not about to argue, though, and signed Hatton on a two-year deal. He scored 14 goals in 50 appearances in his first season to finish as the club's top scorer. In 1970–71 he scored 24 goals in 46 appearances and signed a new contract in the summer of 1971, much to the delight of everyone concerned with the club. What no one had realised, though, was that it had a release clause. After just 15 games of the 1971–72 season the shock news filtered out that Bob Hatton was moving to Blues for a club record fee of £80,000. His ability to score with both feet and his head, together with his tireless energy, endeared him to the Bluenoses, and his role in the striking trio of Latchford, Francis and Hatton should never be underestimaated. After five years at the Blues he moved to Blackpool in July 1976. This was followed by moves to Luton Town in July 1978, Sheffield United in July 1980 and Cardiff City in December 1982. He retired from playing in May 1983.

Game Thirty

Kenny to the Rescue

BLUES 2 NORWICH 1

Date: 27 April 1974   **Venue:** St Andrew's
Attendance: 44,182

Blues: Latchford, Martin, Pendrey, Kendall, Hynd, Roberts, Campbell, Francis, Burns, Hatton, Taylor.

Norwich: Keelan, Butler, Benson, Stringer, Forbes, Grapes (Davies 45), Steele, MacDougall, Suggett, Boyer, Sissons.

Nothing changes! The final game of the 1973–74 season threw up that regular event – Blues had to win to stay in the First Division, and a tense and dramatic game was once more eagerly awaited and anticipated by near-capacity crowd. Both teams stepped on to the pitch knowing a victory would leave them safe, with the loser hoping that Manchester United would fail to get a point from their game in hand against Southampton, who were bottom and already relegated.

It was an in-form Blues hoping that they could add another game to their four-game unbeaten run; in fact, they had taken 16 points from the last possible 26, losing just three times, one of which was to Norwich 2–1 at Carrow Road. It had not escaped the fans' notice that their improved performances had coincided with the arrival of Howard Kendall. Both sides were unchanged for the game and were at full strength. The atmosphere inside the ground was intense, and Bluenoses were right behind their team, so for the visitors it must have felt like playing against an extra man as they kicked-off the match.

The crowd were tense, which seemed to be having an affect on the home side, as it was a nervous Blues who went a goal down after just four minutes. Garry Pendrey brought a Steve Grapes run to an illegal conclusion, and from Suggetts' free-kick Dave Stringer rose unmarked to head the ball past a flat-footed Dave Latchford. The game restarted with the St Andrew's faithful stunned into silence, but the team were determined to get back into the game as soon as possible, and it was not long before they managed to create a goalscoring opportunity. A good move between Gordon Taylor and Trevor Francis allowed Alan Campbell to shoot, and his effort hit Steele on the arm, but there was no intention to handle the ball even though the Bluenoses pleaded for a spot-kick. On 20 minutes Blues had a real clear-cut chance when Taylor cut inside his full-back, and once within range his fierce cross-shot was well saved by Keelan the Norwich goalkeeper. Moments later, Francis tried a long-range shot, which again Keelan saved, although this time the save was less spectacular.

The wrong date was printed on this match-day programme cover.

Blues were in the ascendance and in their eagerness to get forward were leaving gaps at the back, giving Norwich the chance of a breakaway. Pendrey, who had got forward, tried a shot from distance, but it was blocked by Boyer who collected the rebound and easily outpaced the Blues full-back as he broke away. Luckily Roger Hynd was covering well and came across to steal the ball away from the speedy Norwich forward. With the break approaching, Blues finally got back on level terms on 41 minutes when Kendall, who had been involved in all of Blues' quality play, once more collected a loose ball and threaded a lovely weighted through pass to Hatton who beat the advancing Keelan with a simple tap-in. Blues fans were still in seventh heaven when just two minutes later another great cross from Taylor was met by a bullet-like dive from Kenny Burns, who at full stretch placed his header across Keelan and into to the top corner. Blues could not have timed their two-goal strike better as moments later the whistle for half-time was blown, giving them the chance to regroup and give everyone in the crowd a chance to settle down. The job was only half done. The second half was less frantic, and Blues started to pass intelligently rather than trying to find their forwards with a succession of long balls. The first

PLAYER FACTFILE

KENNETH BURNS
Defender/centre-forward
195+9 appearances, 53 goals
20 appearances for Scotland
Joined Nottingham Forest in July 1977 for £150,000.

Glaswegian Kenny joined Blues from Glasgow Rangers as an apprentice in June 1970 as a 17-year-old. Turning professional a year later, he enjoyed six years at St Andrew's before joining Nottingham Forest for £150,000. He was a versatile player equally at home in either an attacking or a defensive role; indeed, he became a successful replacement for Bob Latchford when he joined Everton. Burns was a great hero to the fans with his aggressive, never-say-die attitude – with Kenny in the team you knew he and all his teammates would give 100 per cent. He joined Nottingham Forest during the Brian Clough era and won the European Cup twice in 1979 and 1980, the Division One title in 1978, the Football League Cup in 1978 – the same year in which he won the coveted title of Footballer of the Year. After four years at the City Ground he was signed by Leeds United for £400,000 in October 1981.

opportunity to score came through a free-kick awarded to Bob Hatton after he was fouled by Forbes. Kendall hit the free kick beautifully only for the ball to narrowly miss the target as it clipped the crossbar. With the match now virtually over and victory and survival in sight for the home side, the Canaries produced their best chance of scoring since the fourth minute. Blues failed to clear a right-wing cross, and Latchford was called to pull off an incredible double save from Sissons and then MacDougall. Blues played out the final minutes of the game without further trouble, and when the final whistle blew there was mass hysteria and a pitch invasion from the joyous Blues fans.

Howard Kendall remembers:
    'My proudest moment during my time at Blues was the avoidance of relegation at the end of my first season. We finished 19th. After the game I was in the bath [individual ones in those days] along with the rest of the team, when Freddie [Goodwin] came in and said "They're still out there, they won't go until you go out and do a lap of honour". So as captain I had to organise the lads to get dry, get back into their kit and do a lap of honour for the fans. I could not believe it – a lap of honour for avoiding relegation. I had done the job Freddie had bought me for!'

FA Cup Semi-final Replay

FULHAM 1 BLUES 0

Date: 9 April 1975   **Venue:** Maine Road, Manchester
Attendance: 35,205

Blues: Latchford, Page, Bryant, Kendall, Gallagher, Pendrey, Hendrie, Francis, Burns, Hatton, Taylor.

Fulham: Mellor, Fraser, Strong, Mullery, Lacy, Moore, Mitchell, Conway, Busby, Slough, Barrett.

Blues took 25,000 fans to Manchester and were relieved to see the in-form Bryant restored to the opening line up. Pendrey was moved forward to partner Gallagher, replacing John Roberts, who had been given a torrid time by Mitchell at Hillsborough. The only other change was the injured Campbell being replaced by Hendrie.

Blues battered the Fulham goal from the off but yet again they were thwarted by the composure of the ageless Bobby Moore, who played as brilliantly in this game as he did at any time in his career! Alongside him, his protégé John Lacey turned in a performance of such maturity which belied his youth, while 'keeper Peter Mellor was akin to the 'India Rubber' man in goal, wrecking his reputation of being inconsistent and weak on crosses. He won simply everything that the tireless Hatton, Burns and Francis threw at him that night, blocking shot after shot from every conceivable angle, including one awesome tip onto the post from a Burns pile-driver. He would be the first to admit he had the game of his career; Dave Latchford, by comparison, was a mere spectator.

Despite all the goalmouth action, amazingly it was stalemate at full-time, but Blues went into the extra 30 minutes looking the fitter, stronger and more determined side. Surely it was just a matter of time before Blues broke the deadlock, such had been their dominance. However, they could not find a way through, and then the unthinkable happened. With just a minute to go, a last-ditch Blues attack broke down. Fulham's Alan Slough belted a 50-yard hit-and-hope wide down the right wing to John Dowie, who instinctively nodded into the path of Mitchell. He dummied Gallagher and, with just big Dave Latchford to beat, the Blues' 'keeper raced out and blocked the Fulham striker's shot. The ball hung in the air, Latchford was spreadeagled on the deck and Gallagher tried in vain to scramble back, but collided with Latchford.

A ticket for the semi-final replay against Fulham.

HOWARD KENDALL
Midfield
134 appearances, 18 goals
Played six times for England Under-23
Joined Stoke City in August 1977 for £40,000.

Kendall was born on 22 May 1946 in Ryton-on-Tyne. While playing for Ryton & District Schools, he signed as an apprentice with Preston North End in 1961, turning professional in May 1963. He played in the 1964 FA Cup Final against West Ham United, becoming the youngest player to appear in a Wembley Final, aged 17 years and 345 days, a record he held until 1980. He joined Everton for £80,000 in March 1967, completing 'The Holy Trinity' with Alan Ball and Colin Harvey. Everton won the First Division title in 1969–70 and he was appointed captain of the Toffees. In February 1974 he was transferred to Blues in a deal valued at £350,000, involving Bob Latchford and Archie Styles. He left Blues for Stoke City for £40,000 in August 1977, where he became player-coach, helping them to promotion to the First Division in the 1978–79 season. Although a gifted player, Howard never pulled on a shirt for the full England side, although he played for England's Under-23 side, Youth and Schoolboys. He also played once for the Football League XI. In June 1979 he was appointed player-manager of Blackburn Rovers, gaining promotion to Division Two in the 1979–80 season. In May 1981 he returned to Everton as player-manager, becoming the youngest man to achieve this position at the age of 34 years and 351 days. He only played four games before retiring as a player. While manager of Everton he won the Division One title in 1985 and 1987, the FA Cup in 1984, the European Cup-winners Cup in 1985 and the Charity Shield in 1984, 1985 and 1986. He left Goodison Park in June 1987, frustrated by the ban from Europe of English teams, to manage Athletic Bilbao in Spain. His unsuccessful spell ended with the sack in November 1989. He returned to England to manage Manchester City from December 1989 to November 1990 before returning to Everton. He failed to repeat the successes of the 1980s and resigned in December 1993. He had six months in Greece with Xanthi from May to November 1994, before joining Notts County in January 1995. After a turbulent 11 months he moved to Sheffield United in December 1995, where his success was measured by the fact that he saved the club from relegation and then took them to the Play-off Final in 1997. He returned to Everton for a third time in August 1997, but resigned at the end of the season, having avoided relegation on the last day. Another spell in Greece, this time with Ethnikos Piraeus, ended in the sack in March 1999 after only four months in post. He remains the last English manager to win a European competition with an English club.

Meanwhile, the ball fell kindly to Mitchell, who many maintained controlled the ball with his arm, and it bobbled agonisingly over the line just inside the post. It seemed to take forever. When the final whistle went seconds later, Blues fans were silent, totally silent – you could have heard a pin drop but for the celebrating 3,000 Fulham fans. The Wembley dream was over.

NB: the first game was played at Hillsborough, Sheffield, on 5 April 1975 and was a 1–1 draw, Gallagher scoring in front of 54,166. The team was: D. Latchford; Page, Pendrey; Kendall, Gallagher, J. Roberts; Campbell, Francis, Burns, Hatton, Taylor.

Howard Kendall recalls:
'It was my unhappiest experience at Blues losing that game after we had played them off the park. Their 'keeper, Peter Mellor, was unbelievable. That was without doubt the hardest night in my football career. The players were just stunned, and we went off to our hotel in Buxton where we had planned to celebrate going to Wembley. As skipper I had missed the chance to lead out a team in an FA Cup Final. The lads had a few beers and went to bed; the atmosphere was very sombre. At five o'clock in the morning, Freddie [Goodwin] said to me "Get the lads up, we're going home". We were devastated.'

Joe Gallagher recalls:
'For a footballer to lose a semi-final is bad enough, to lose in a replay is a double whammy, but to lose in extra-time of a replay was a triple whammy! The whole team was down; there is no word to describe the feeling of utter devastation, disbelief and emptiness we all felt.'

AN INTERVIEW WITH HOWARD WHICH APPEARED IN THE OCTOBER 2007 EDITION OF THE BLUES MAGAZINE

I met 61-year-old Howard in Alan Stubbs's wine bar, Woodwards, in Formby Village, near Liverpool, a place where Howard has returned to live whenever his career has allowed him. Our time together is punctuated by him being greeted by other customers, a measure of the popularity of the man in this area of the United Kingdom, where he has a regular column in the Liverpool Echo and a full diary of after-dinner speaking engagements.

Howard grew up in the North East, where his father was a miner, moving to Washington when his father gave up the pit due to ill health. After playing for local sides he was selected for England Schoolboys, and the scouts from local clubs, Newcastle and Sunderland among them, began to show an interest in signing the young Kendall. As an only child his family took a great interest in where his football career should start, and it was a case of whether he left school and signed as an apprentice, or stayed in full-time education and played for a club at the same time.

'My cousin was on Newcastle's books, and he said that there were lots of lads signed to the club who weren't getting regular games, so his advice was to become an apprentice as it virtually guaranteed regular football.'

'Reg Keating, the chief scout at Preston North End, had become a family friend so he invited me, my mum and dad to visit Deepdale and look at the facilities and also to see where my digs would be. I think mum and dad went along hoping to pick holes in the set up as they wanted me to stay at home, but Preston had a really friendly and family atmosphere, so I signed in June 1961 on apprentice forms. I was just 15. My dad said "It's better to get with a smaller club, do the business and then the bigger clubs will be in for you." He was absolutely right. I signed pro in May 1963, played in an FA Cup Final and was then signed by Everton for £80,000 when I was 21.'

FULHAM

versus

BIRMINGHAM

CITY

1-0   John Mitchell celebrates Fulham's goal

F.A. Cup
Semi-Final
Replay

at Maine Road,
Manchester
Wednesday,
April 9, 1975
kick-off 7.30pm

1-1   Joe Gallagher celebrates the equaliser

Official Programme 15p

HOW DID YOUR MOVE TO BLUES COME ABOUT?

'I had been at Everton seven years, and Billy Bingham was the manager. He decided that the club needed a centre-forward and that he could progress the club without me. He had targeted Bob Latchford and Denis Tueart of Sunderland. In fact I was expecting to move to Sunderland before I met Freddie Goodwin at Knutsford Services on the M6.

It was a really complicated deal: in exchange for Bob, Everton gave Blues £350,000, me and Archie Styles. The deal nearly stalled over a loyalty bonus I felt I was due. It was only £5,000, but that was a lot of money in 1974. Freddie was very helpful and supported me, saying that I should hold out for the payment as they had already introduced Bob at Goodison Park, therefore the deal was done.'

WHAT WERE YOUR INITIAL THOUGHTS OF THE BLUES?

'When I turned up at the Elmdon training ground it was like an air-raid shelter compared to what I had been used to at Everton. My value in the transfer deal was estimated at £180,000. That was the biggest transfer fee Blues had paid, a fact that John Roberts used against me on my first day. At Elmdon there was no washing facility, so training tops that were dirty were simply dried and then worn the next day. The lads' tops were covered in mud, and John said to me "Come on, you're the most expensive player ever, go and complain about the condition of our tops!" I looked at Archie, who like me had been issued with a brand new top, and said "Nothing wrong with mine", and I walked out leaving John open-mouthed and the rest of the lads in stitches. Freddie had bought me to ensure that we stayed in Division One and immediately made me captain, a job I had performed at Everton.'

WHAT DO YOU REMEMBER OF YOUR DEBUT?

'I always got nervous on debuts. I had a real nightmare on my Everton debut, and my performance against the Wolves for Blues was only average. It was a really heavy pitch, and we lost 1—0 on 10 February in front of a crowd of 33,821. We had some real personalities in my debut team: Gary Sprake (what a character!), Ray Martin, Joe Gallagher, Roger Hynd, Garry Pendrey, Trevor Francis, Kenny Burns, Bobby Hope and Gordon Taylor. We were very close to being a really good side.

I felt sorry for Gary because he had the reputation for making mistakes, and when he was at Leeds he had a team in front of him that could make up for his errors. At Blues he never had that luxury, so his mistakes on occasions cost us dear. He was replaced by Dave Latchford after my debut game and only played a further two games for the Blues first team. There was real competition between the sticks as Paul Cooper was third choice!'

WHAT WAS YOUR OPINION OF FREDDIE GOODWIN?

'Although Willie Bell was his assistant, they weren't very close, so Freddie used to talk to me in my capacity as captain to gain my thoughts on a number of topics. He was always the boss and made the final decision on his own, but he valued my opinion. The way he was with me had a positive influence on my decision to stay in the game as a manager, in fact I started to gain my coaching qualifications at Lilleshall while at Blues. Thank you Freddie.'

HOW DID YOUR CAREER END AT BLUES?

'Freddie had left, and in September 1975 Willie Bell was appointed as caretaker manager. On 11 October we were due to play away at Liverpool, and he dropped me. It was only the second time in my career, and I was not best pleased. It was as if he wanted to assert himself as being his own man and dropping me was a way of showing this to the Board. We lost 3—1, and I was reinstated for the following match. While I didn't leave until the end of the 1976—77 season, things were never the same after that, and he left the month after my move to Stoke City for £40,000. George Eastham was the Stoke manager then, and he had been my boyhood hero. Not long after my signing he was replaced by Alan Durban, who offered me the player-coach role, and I was on the managerial ladder.'

HOW DO YOU RATE THE BLUES V VILLA DERBIES AGAINST THE LIVERPOOL V EVERTON GAMES?

'I've played in both, and believe me the Blues v Villa games are unbelievable in terms of passion and equal to that of the Merseyside derbies. I played in four games against the Villa and won three of them!'

WHAT ELSE DO YOU REMEMBER ABOUT YOUR TIME AT BLUES?

'I got on really well with Jimmy Calderwood, now manager at Aberdeen. When he was at Dunfermline I met him on a beach in Majorca walking with his chairman. He was on the phone to Aberdeen about a possible move, while obviously not wishing to alert the chairman to his intentions. I shouted out that if Jimmy ever left I could be his replacement. I thought it was really funny, but Jimmy was not best pleased. Thankfully it didn't affect our friendship long term, and when he was playing in Holland he would feed me information about the game over there.'

WHAT WAS YOUR OPINION OF TREVOR FRANCIS?

'I rate TF as one of the two best players I have seen in the English League — he had everything! The fact that the other player was Alan Ball is testament to how highly I rated Trevor.'

YOU HAD A DECENT RATIO OF GOALS AT BLUES. CAN YOU REMEMBER ANY?

'I can remember my first goal for Blues in a 4—0 win over Queen's Park Rangers on 23 April 1974. Phil Parkes was the 'keeper, and he paid me the compliment of acknowledging that it was one of the best goals he ever conceded. It was a strike from outside the box with my left peg!'

5–1 Victory

BLUES 5 MANCHESTER UNITED 1

Date: 11 November 1978
Attendance: 23,550

Venue: St Andrew's

Blues: Freeman, Tarantini, Dennis, Towers, Gallagher, Page, Dillon, Buckley, Givens, Calderwood, Fox.

United: Roche, Nicholl, Houston, McCreery, B. Greenhoff, Buchan, Coppell, J. Greenhoff, Jordan, Macari, McIlroy.

Rooted at the bottom of the First Division table, and with no win on the record books, to all the neutrals it was a forgone conclusion that Blues would lose heavily when Manchester United arrived at St Andrew's. Relegation was already on the cards!

The statistics did not make good reading: 13 games played, 10 defeats, only seven goals scored. Jim Smith, the Blues manager, had used over 20 players in the games, and the defensive line up had changed with every game. It was a period of instability, and confidence was low, but unlike Blues money was being spent both home and abroad: Alberto Tarantini, a World Cup winner with Argentina four months before, had been signed for a fee of £295,000, suggesting that Blues were thinking like a big club if not necessarily playing like one. On the other end of the scale Alan Buckley, a striker from Walsall, had also joined the club on a free transfer.

The script was being played out perfectly when United opened the scoring in the 13th minute through Joe Jordan after Malcolm Page was dispossessed by Lou Macari. It seemed nothing was going to change for the St Andrew's crowd, so the prospect of a heavy defeat was threatening the atmosphere around Small Heath. But within 10 minutes the home side were back in it. Kevin Dillon scored with a fierce strike that avoided the vain attempts of Paddy Roche in the United goal. Buckley then scored, in the 32nd minute, heading home at the far post after an

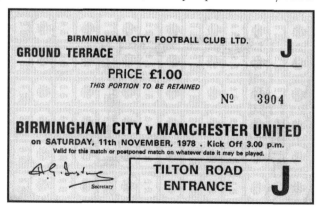

ALAN PAUL BUCKLEY
Inside/Centre-forward
25 +4 appearances, 8 goals.

St Andrew's was a one-season stop off from Walsall. He joined Blues in October 1978, having spent over five years at Fellows Park, only to return there in July 1979 as manager. In 500 games for the Saddlers he scored over 200 goals, representing a return of a goal in every 2.5 games, which he virtually emulated at Blues. As manager of Grimsby Town he achieved a Wembley double in 1998 when the Mariners won the Auto Windscreens Shield and gained promotion by winning the Second Division Play-off Final. His time at Blundell Park also saw him achieve promotion from Division Four and Division Three in two successive seasons, 1989–90 and 1990–91. The Buckleys are a footballing family, with Alan's brother, Steve, and his two sons, Adam and Simon, all playing at professional level.

interchange between Don Givens and Tarantini, and that man Buckley scored again just before the break. United were attacking Blues without any real thought about the defensive frailties they were creating that could be exploited by the opposition. Blues were thankful, and they exploited the situation to the full with further goals by Givens and Jimmy Calderwood.

Unfortunately this result did not spark a change in Blues' fortunes, and their record in the First Division made bleak reading. By 13 February, when they lost 1–0 away to Liverpool, Blues' record in the First Division was played 25, won 2, drawn 4, lost 19. There was a slight improvement after that but not significant enough for Blues to avoid relegation. They finished in 21st position, despite winning their final match of the season, 3–1 away to Queen's Park Rangers.

BIRMINGHAM CITY NEWS

THE OFFICIAL MATCHDAY MAGAZINE OF BIRMINGHAM CITY F.C. 20p

Football League – Division One
Saturday 11th November 1978 – Kick-off: 3-00pm
BIRMINGHAM CITY v MANCHESTER UNITED
Season 1978-79 (Issue Number 8)

INSIDE ★ NEW buy Alan Buckley in action
★ NEW pin-up team group

Game Thirty-three

Promotion

BLUES 3   NOTTS COUNTY 3

Date: 3 May 1980   **Venue:** St Andrew's
Attendance: 33,863   **Referee:** Mr K.G. Salmon (Barnet)

Blues: Wealands, Broadhurst, Lees, Curbishley, Gallagher, Todd, Ainscow, Givens, Bertschin, Gemmill, Dillon.

Notts County: Avramovic, Richards, O'Brien, Benjamin, Stubbs, Kilcline, McCulloch, Masson, Christie, Hunt, Mair.

B irmingham City were boasting one of the best home records in the Division as they went into this decisive match against mid-table opposition needing just a draw to ensure promotion. Bearing in mind that Blues' record in achieving success in this type of game was 'mixed' to say the least, nothing was being taken for granted. The crowd, which grew to 33, 863, arrived at St Andrews hopeful that the Blues would beat the Magpies and make sure of a promotion spot with a victory.

Blues soon dominated a County side playing for nothing other than their professional pride. A goal for City was always on the cards, and it came early enough to hopefully steady the nerves within the crowd, scored by Keith Bertschin after 18 minutes. A neat move saw Kevin Dillon beat his full-back on the right, put in a clipped cross to Don Givens who, rather than shoot from an acute angle, screwed the ball across the face of the goal for Bertschin to nod in at the far post. It was all going far too well, and this was reinforced when Blues added a second, four minutes later, leaving even the pessimists expecting a successful and positive outcome. The goal came straight from an Alan Curbishley free-kick from 25 yards, after Givens had been fouled by Kilcline. Minutes

LLEWELLYN CHARLES CURBISHLEY
Midfielder
153+2 appearances, 15 goals

Alan was born in London on 8 November 1957 and joined West Ham United as an apprentice when he was 16, signing professional forms in July 1975. Blues acquired his signature for £225,000 in July 1979. Having played for England at Schoolboy, Youth and Under-21 level, he brought skill and class to the Blues' midfield, plus a sweet right foot. Another favourite of the fans with his competitiveness and all-action approach, he left Blues for Aston Villa in March 1983 for £100,000 and that tremendous Bluenose, Robert Hopkins. Charlton Athletic and Brighton & Hove Albion followed, before he returned to the Valley to take up the managerial reins, where he won promotion to the Premiership in 1998 and 2000.

later, the crowd were on their toes when Avramovic brilliantly saved an Archie Gemmill free-kick from almost the same spot as Curbishley's previous strike. But as all Blues supporters know, we never do things easily, and a lapse in the Blues defence allowed County back in the game at 2–1. A great cross from Hunt on the right was met by Mair, who nipped in to poke the ball past Jeff Wealands at the near post. Just four minutes later, Mair was again involved, this time as a goal provider when he put Christie through after Kevan Broadhurst had slipped. Taking the ball on, the County striker made the one-on-one with the 'keeper look easy, with a low shot past the oncoming Wealands.

It was now all-square, and reality had arrived – there was every chance that Blues could lose this game as County began to take the initiative. But within minutes Blues were back in the lead through Dillon. Bertschin's cross from the right was too long for Dillon and Givens in the centre; however, Givens chased the loose ball and centred from the left, the ball fell to Bertschin who laid the ball off to Dillon who swept in a low left-foot drive into the corner of the net. It was half-time and Blues were winning 3–2 – happy days? The nerves were back immediately after the restart when Mason's fierce shot was brilliantly saved by Wealands, an early sign that the County players were not going to let Blues have the points without a fight. With just 27 minutes of the game remaining, Brian Kilcline got forward for a set piece and scored an equaliser to ensure a heart-stopping finale to a game that had already left most people drained of all feeling. It seemed like an eternity waiting for the final whistle as every forward pass by County had the crowd expecting it to ruin the dream; however the Blues defence of Broadhurst, Terry Lees, Joe Gallagher and Colin Todd remained strong until the long-awaited final whistle. A mass, but good humoured, pitch invasion followed, and the promotion party got into full swing when the players arrived in the main stand directors area to thank the crowd, who in turn thanked them for the season's achievements and for that unforgettable 90 minutes of football.

Game Thirty-four

The First Sunday Game

COVENTRY CITY 4 BLUES 4

Date: 16 February 1986   **Venue:** Highfield Road
Attendance: 14,271   **Referee:** Mr K. Lupton (Stockton-on-Tees)

Blues: Seaman, Ranson, Roberts, Hagan, Whitton, Kuhl, Bremner, Clarke, Kennedy, Geddis, Hopkins.

Coventry: Ogrizovic, Borrows, Downs, Bowman, Kilcline, Peake, Bennett, Turner, Regis, Brazil, Pickering.

This was Blues' first ever League game to take place on a Sunday, and the new arrangement seemed to find favour with the fans as over 14,000 turned up at Highfield Road for this Midlands derby. It was thrilling game, with eight goals and three points shared – a result, which will have frustrated both Blues fans and players alike as they deserved the win.

Andy Kennedy put the Blues ahead after two minutes, and 16 minutes later the visitors were leading by two goals when Steve Whitton scored after Kennedy's second attempt had been blocked by Ogrizovic. The feeling was for an away win, but misses by David Geddis, who hit the post, and Wayne Clarke's header which also bounced off the woodwork meant that the home side were still in the game at half-time. After the break Coventry looked the

stronger and more determined team. Their efforts paid off quickly, with Dave Bennett opening the scoring for the home side on 51 minutes, slotting in a headed cross from Brazil. Just seven minutes later Coventry were awarded a penalty after Brian 'Harry' Roberts had fouled Bennett in the area. Kilcline took the kick and put it away with ease.

Blues got back into the lead on 60 minutes with a shot from Martin Kuhl, which forced its way into the roof of the net, but shortly afterwards

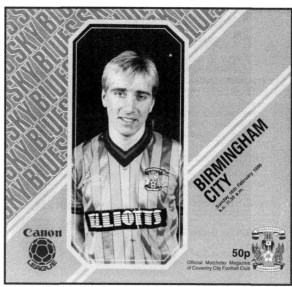

ANDREW JOHN KENNEDY
Centre-forward
62+25 appearances, 21 goals
Joined Blackburn Rovers in June 1988 for £50,000.

Andy was born in Stirling, Scotland, on 8 October 1964. He played in Scotland for Sauchie Athletic and Glasgow Rangers before going on loan to Seiko FC in Hong Kong. He joined Blues in March 1985 for £50,000. A hard-working player, always willing to take on defenders, he was a great favourite with the Bluenoses. In his first season he was the club's leading scorer with nine goals, which said it all about the team at that time. After a loan spell with Sheffield United in March 1987, he joined Blackburn Rovers for £50,000. In August 1990 he signed for Watford for £60,000. After another loan period, this time with Bolton Wanderers in October 1991, and a two-year stint he signed for Brighton & Hove Albion in September 1992. Another two years saw him joining Gillingham as a non-contract player in September 1994. In March 1995 he tried his luck in Ireland with Portadown and Shelbourne before returning to Hong Kong with Happy Valley.

Coventry drew level again. Brazil managed to get Jim Hagan out of position and passed to Bennett, who shot in a superb 20-yard drive. The visitors again took the lead seven minutes from the end when Kennedy grabbed his second goal of the game, but the lead did not last long. Kilcline's first penalty awarded to the home side was entirely questionable, but it was nothing compared to their 88th-minute gift. The referee ruled that Ray Ranson had fouled Nick Pickering in the box, although it seemed to all the Blues' fans in the crowd that Pickering had in fact tripped over the Blues defender's leg after he nudged the ball away. Wayne Clarke was booked for dissent after expressing his view of the matter to the referee, and Kilcline stepped up, totally unaffected by the situation to slot the ball home with ease from the penalty spot.

The Leyland DAF Cup Final

BLUES 3 TRANMERE ROVERS 2

Date: 26 May 1991   **Venue:** Wembley
Attendance: 58,576   **Referee:** Mr J.E. Martin (Alton, Hants.)

Blues: Thomas, Clarkson, Overson, Matthewson, Frain, Yates, Peer, Robinson, Gleghorn, Gayle, Sturridge (Bailey 62).
Substitutes, unused: Hopkins.

Tranmere Rovers: Nixon, Higgins, Bronman, McNab (Martindale), Hughes, Vickers (Malkin), Morrissey, Irons, Steel, Cooper, Thomas.

Road to Wembley
Walsall (a) 1–0
Lincoln (h) 2–0
Swansea (h) 0–0 won on penalties 4–2
Mansfield (h) 2–0
Cambridge (h) 3–1 area semi-final
Brentford (h) 2–1 (a) 1–0 area Final won 3–1 on aggregate

The introduction of these 'modest' competitions for the lower League clubs seemed to be more for the benefit of the sponsors rather than the clubs taking part, but Wembley was not complaining on this occasion as it would benefit from a much increased turnover following this invasion of the Blues' fans.

There were 48,000 Blues fans in a crowd of 58,576, and the twin towers vibrated with the expectation of seeing the Blues lift their first Cup at the home of English football. On this occasion the Bluenoses were not to be disappointed. Led by Manager Lou Macari and Brummie John Gayle providing the inspiration Blues dominated as much on the field as the Bluenoses did in the stands. After an energetic start Blues went into the lead on 21 minutes when a long

LEYLAND DAF
CUP FINAL
Sunday 26th May 1991
Turnstiles Open at 1.00 pm
Please take your position by 2.15 pm
Kick Off at 3.00 pm

WEMBLEY STADIUM
LEYLAND DAF
Cup
TO BE RETAINED

TURNSTILE J

BLOCK   ROW   SEAT
146   13   91
£14.00
32100   209 130491 141704A

clearance was headed on by Gayle to the nippy Simon Sturridge who raced on to beat Nixon with a neatly placed shot just inside the penalty area.

Blues settled on the lead and were happy to control the game, keeping Tranmere under their influence. The tactic worked well, and Tranmere rarely troubled Martin Thomas in the Blues goal. As half-time approached a pass out of defence came to Gayle, who allowed the ball to go under his foot, enabling him to gain a few yards on his marker. He pulverised a rising shot which easily beat Nixon from just inside the 18-yard box to give Blues a 2–0 advantage on 41 minutes. Blues could have had a third goal when Dean Peer's volley was brilliantly saved by Nixon.

While the half-time break was always welcome, Blues did not

want it on this occasion as it often meant that teams lost their momentum. Blues, as it is often the case, are a team who never do anything the easy way, and sure enough when the second half started Blues were not the same team that left the pitch on 45 minutes. Tranmere rallied after the break and gave themselves a real chance on 61 minutes when Cooper pulled a goal back. Blues got nervous, and five minutes later Tranmere were level through Jim Steel. The game then ebbed and flowed, and everyone felt that he next goal would be the winner. With the game entering its final few minutes it seemed that extra-time would be inevitable; however one moment of magic remained, and up stepped 'Gayley'. A free-kick was awarded to Blues near the halfway line, and Ian Clarkson floated the ball into the Tranmere area. Vince Overson beat Higgins in the air, glancing his header to Gayle, who was not in the best position to deal with Overson's knock-down. With his back to goal, however, he performed an incredible scissor-kick, and the ball smashed into the corner of a bemused Nixon's net in the 86th minute. The goal was indeed the winner. What a goal, and Blues were Wembley winners at long last!

Robert Hopkins recalls:
'In preparation for the Final we went to Reading University, where there were no luxuries and no TV as we slept in the Halls of Residence. On the day before the game, Peer, Sturridge, Robinson and myself were spoken to by Lou Macari, the manager. He told us

that there were three places up for grabs in the starting line up for the Final and who got them would be decided on the outcome of a race. The first three to complete four laps of the athletic track would get a place. I told him what I thought of the idea and came last.'

Ian Clarkson remembers:
'The Final was played some three weeks after the season had finished. Two weeks before we had a full-scale friendly against the Albion that we won 5–3. It was Bobby Gould's punishment for the Albion players for getting relegated! We were stationed at Reading University in the lead up to the Final, in the Halls of Residence. It was a bit primitive but it served its purpose, as we had a lot of young Brummie lads in the team and the pressure for tickets etc was high, so it was good to get away from it all. Lou Macari had been appointed in February 1991, and it was a good appointment for me. He was all about hard work and running. Reading University was obviously not chosen for its facilities, as we had to drive around the middle of nowhere looking for grassy areas to train on! The students were still in residence, so it got pretty rowdy at night. I recall Trevor Aylott got fed up one night and shouted to a load of students that he would throw a bar of soap at them if they did not clear off. Obviously they were typical students – pretty dirty and smelly! In the end we moved accommodation after being disturbed by the students, only to end up sharing a residential block with a load of drunken journalists. There was a row about bonus payments for getting to the Final with Samesh. Up to the semi-final we got £20–£30 per match, then for the semi we were offered £1,000. When we got our pay packets there was about £97 each. When we protested Kumar said he had meant £1,000 between us! Anyway a meeting was called and Dean Peer, the quietest man in the squad but with the thickest Black Country accent, spoke up with evidence that the bonus wording was exactly the same as previous rounds, so it should be the same for the semi-final. Even then Kumar negotiated and said we could have £1,000 each if we won the Final! I think it was the beginning of the end for Lou Macari, because he refused to support Kumar and said 'Don't involve me'. Lou was a strict teetotaller and tried to restrict our intake, although he did allow us two pints each after beating Brentford in the League to clinch promotion. My impression of Wembley was that although the stadium was huge, the playing surface was not that large. We were pretty confident of success as the week before we did practise an open-top bus ride! The Sunday after the game was fantastic, from the Civic Hall reception until going to the Barley Mow pub in Solihull, which was normally pretty quiet but was suddenly full of singing Bluenoses. I believe that game kick-started the Blues' revival.'

John Frain remembers:

'Our dramatic 3–2 victory in the Final came as due reward for perseverance at the end of some pretty lean times. I think everyone knew about Lou (Macari)'s work ethic – it was unbelievable. We had a great run in the Cup but had a long three weeks from the end of the season until Wembley. Lou was a mad fitness man, and he said he was going to get us fit in that time. My God, it was the hardest training I've done in my life, and we never saw a ball each week until Thursday or Friday. He had us running all over Birmingham. But, at Wembley, we had an absolutely fabulous day, so he got his reward.'

Colin Tattum recalls:

'Manager Lou Macari invited the press to travel with the team to their pre-final hideaway. The day before the Final, in blistering heat, Macari put them through a gruelling session that included track work. And he ordered the media to join in, probably for light relief. The sight of Tom Ross trying to hold off a pursuing John Gayle in a 'hare and hounds' race around the 800m circuit was hilarious. And in one 11 versus 11 game I was fouled badly by Robert Hopkins and also berated by Gayle for not tackling Vince Overson hard enough. There were a couple of images that stuck. The sight of Ian Rodgerson at the back of the coach, almost in tears, knowing that he was unfit to play. And then there was Hopkins, one of the biggest Bluenoses you will ever find, being denied the chance to come on as substitute for the club he loved at Wembley, even for the last couple of minutes. He was so upset that he almost didn't turn up for the open-top bus celebration around Birmingham.'

PLAYER FACTFILE

JOHN GAYLE
Striker
49 + 6 appearances, 14 goals.

John Gayle was born on 30 July 1964 and, at the time of writing, is the manager of Devon County Football League side Newton Abbot. Gayley was born in Turves Green, Birmingham. A powerful target-man centre-forward, he worked in a printers and on a building site before beginning his professional career. He played for a number of non-League sides: Alvechurch, Highgate United, Tamworth, Stratford Town, Solihull Borough, Sutton Coldfield Town and Mile Oak Rovers, before joining his local side Bromsgrove Rovers. From there he moved to Burton Albion, from where he joined Wimbledon in March 1989 for a fee of £30,000. In November 1990, after only 20 League games and two goals for Wimbledon, John moved to Blues for £175,000, helping the team to promotion in 1992. He moved to Walsall on loan in August 1993, making four League appearances, scoring one goal. A day after the end of his loan spell, on 13 September 1993, Gayle was back in the top flight, with Coventry City paying £100,000 for his services. He had scored 10 goals in 44 League games for Birmingham, but failed to settle at Highfield Road, making only five League appearances without scoring before being transferred to Burnley on 17 August 1994 for £70,000. This again proved to be only a short stay, Gayle making 14 League appearances and scoring three goals before moving to Stoke City for £70,000 on 23 January 1995. He moved to Gillingham on loan on 14 March 1996, making nine League appearances and scoring three goals, which helped secure the club's promotion from Division Three. The following season Gayle was on the move again, joining Northampton Town on 10 February 1997 for a fee of £25,000. He had played 26 times in the League for Stoke, scoring four goals, with almost half of his appearances as a substitute. He remained at Northampton for over a year, scoring seven times in 48 League games, before joining Scunthorpe United on a free transfer on 16 June 1998. Four goals in 49 League games followed for the Irons, before he was on the move yet again, this time a free transfer taking him to Shrewsbury Town on 25 November 1999. Gayle played a role in keeping the Shrews in the League, injuries limiting him to 19 League games, in which he scored twice. On 14 December 2000, Gayle was released by Shrewsbury, joining a Torquay United side in need of a target man that up to that time, under manager Wes Saunders, they had never really had. He made his Torquay League debut on 16 December 2000 against Hull City at Boothferry Park, a rare 2–1 away win for the Gulls, but injured his hamstring during the game and was out for the next month. By the time he returned, Torquay were deeper in trouble at the foot of the League, but Gayle played his part in ensuring survival, appearing mainly as a substitute to add weight to Torquay's lightweight attack late in the game; however, when he came on as a late substitute in the relegation decider at Barnet on 5 May 2001, he missed several chances to put the game beyond Barnet's reach, or at least test their goalkeeper, only adding to the anxiety of the fans in the away end. It was no surprise that Gayle was released in May 2001, joining non-League Moor Green, where he ended his playing career.

In July 2006 Gayle was appointed manager of Devon League side Totnes and Dartington Sports Club. Prior to his appointment, he had been working for the Prince's Trust in Birmingham. In the summer of 2008 he left Totnes and Dartington to be appointed as first-team manager at Newton Abbot. John's time at Plough Lane was not easy, ending up with him being suspended after a training ground bust-up with their captain Keith Curle. He will always be a hero to the Blues' fans, with his two goals at Wembley which secured the Leyland DAF Cup in 1991 in front of over 50,000 Bluenoses.

Promotion

BLUES 1 SHREWSBURY TOWN 0

Date: 25 April 1992   **Venue:** St Andrew's
Attendance: 19,868

Blues: Dearden, Clarkson, Frain, Rennie, Hicks, Matthewson, Rodgerson, Cooper, Rowbotham (Mardon), Gleghorn, Sturridge.

Shrewsbury Town: Hughes, Clark (Henry), Lynch, MacKenzie, Spink, Blake, Taylor, Summerfield, Bremner, Hopkins (O'Toole), Lyne.

Although Blues won this game, it was Stoke City's defeat that secured their promotion, after a period of six years in Division Three, with two games to go. [Author's Note: Blues lost both of their last two home games to sacrifice the title of champions: 28 April away at Wigan Athletic 1–0 and 2 May away at Stockport County 2–0.]

Nigel Gleghorn, who had made his debut for Blues against Shrewsbury Town on 9 August 1989 in a 2–0 defeat at Gay Meadow in front of less than 5,000 fans, scored the vital goal after 34 minutes in front of nearly 20,000 supporters, and the Blues' days in the third tier were over!

The manner of the victory was made more significant as Blues had failed to beat the Shropshire-based outfit for 12 years. It was a one-sided game in which both sides had to deal with a gale blowing down the ground from the Railway End.

The deciding strike came when Simon Sturridge found Ian Rodgerson, who proceeded to deliver a long cross to the far post for Gleghorn to head home. Interestingly, the Shrewsbury side included ex-Blues player and 100 per cent Bluenose Robert 'Hoppy' Hopkins.

Ian Clarkson recalls:
'Regarding promotion the following year, the week before the final game we had beaten Shrewsbury and were therefore promoted; however, we lost in mid-week away at Wigan because I guess some of us were still getting over the previous weekend's celebrations. Anyway Terry Cooper was so annoyed he did not let the coach stop for our regular fish and chips supper. The away game at Stockport was a game we needed to win for the title and they needed to win for a Play-off

place. Their team contained nine 6ft players, and they were physical. Mark Cooper was sent off. Many said that we were not up for it, but we were; it didn't help conceding two early goals. So that's how the season finished – no title, no medal (which seemed odd when the losing Play-off finalists get medals). It was a massive anti-climax.'

NIGEL WILLIAM GLEGHORN
Midfielder
176 appearances, 42 goals
Joined Stoke City in October 1992.

Gleghorn worked as a firefighter, playing part-time for his local club Seaham Red Star in the Northern League Division Two, until successful trials at Ipswich Town led to the offer of a professional contract. Reluctant to give up a steady job to risk failing as a footballer, his wife convinced him to take the chance. Within weeks the 23-year-old Gleghorn was making his debut in the First Division away at Arsenal.

One season at Manchester City followed, in which City were promoted to the First Division, but after only a few games back in the top flight Gleghorn was sold to Blues, who had recently been relegated to the Third Division, for the relatively big fee of £175,000. He stayed for three seasons, helping the team to victory in the Leyland DAF Trophy Final in 1991 and promotion to the newly-designated Division One in 1991–92. In that season he was Birmingham's top scorer with 22 goals in all competitions and scored the winner against Shrewsbury Town in the last home game of the season when the club needed a win to be sure of automatic promotion. In October 1992 Gleghorn moved to Stoke City, where for the second season running he scored the goal that ensured his club's promotion to Division One. After four years at Stoke, where he made over 200 appearances, he moved on to Burnley in Division Two and finished off his League career in 1997–98 with loan spells at fellow Division Two clubs Brentford and Northampton Town. Once his full-time football career finished, Gleghorn went to work full-time in the Sports Studies department at South Trafford College. Meanwhile, he involved himself with coaching and management. Following an unsuccessful few months as player-coach at Altrincham – though after he left, the club went on to win the Northern Premier League – he joined Witton Albion in the Northern Premier League First Division as player-manager. In his first season the club finished level on points with the top two teams, missing out on promotion only on goal difference. He then had three years at Nantwich Town in the North West Counties League, leaving when they wanted him to take the job full-time, followed by runners'-up spot in the same League with Newcastle Town, still as player-manager, from where he was sacked in 2006. He runs courses for the Cheshire Football Association and works in talent identification for the FA. He was also a good cricketer, playing for Durham Under-18s and Under-21s with a highest score of 135.

Game Thirty-seven

Auto Windscreens Shield Final

BLUES 1 CARLISLE UNITED 0

Date: 23 April 1995   **Venue:** Wembley
Attendance: 73,633   **Referee:** Mr P. Foakes (Clacton-on-Sea)

Blues: Bennett, Poole, Barnett, Daish, Cooper, Hunt, Ward, Shearer (Tait 62), Claridge, Francis (Donowa 76), Otto.

Carlisle: Caig; Edmondson, Gallimore; Walling, Mountfield (Robinson 100), Conway; Thomas, Currie, Reeve, Hayward, Prokos (Thorpe 90).

Blues became the first Wembley winners of a golden goal decider.
Mark Ward was awarded Man of the Match.

The road to Wembley
Peterborough (a) won 5–3
Walsall (h) won 3–0
Gillingham (h) won 3–0
Hereford (h) won 3–1
Swansea (h) won 3–2 after extra-time, Southern Area semi-final, Tait scored sudden-death winner.
Leyton Orient (h) won 1–0, (a) won 3–2, won on aggregate 4–2

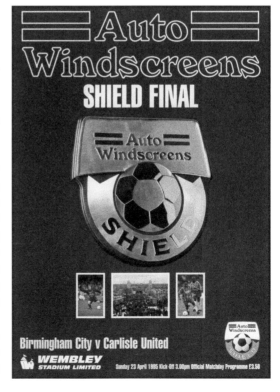

It was 1989 when the Blue Army last took over Wembley's Twin Towers to support their team to a trophy win. Close to 48,000 Bluenoses were dominating proceedings within the 73,633 crowd and, although never a game for the football purist or pundit, the day was a memorable one for the fans.

Jose Dominguez was away on international duty with Portugal, so Barry Fry made three changes to the

Barry Fry had used 28 players in getting Blues to North London:

Player	Starts	Substitutions	Player	Starts	Substitutions
Price	1	0	De Souza	1	0
Scott	2	0	Doherty	0	2
Frain	1	0	Shearer	4	0
Ward	7	0	Whyte	3	1
Barnett	8	0	Lowe	2	1
Daish	7	0	Cooper	4	1
Hunt	3	0	Tait	2	3
Claridge	7	0	Otto	5	0
Bull	2	0	Francis	3	0
McGavin	2	2	Saville	1	0
Wallace	0	1	Estevez	1	0
Bennett	7	0	Robinson	1	0
Donowa	5	1	Williams	0	1

side that had beaten Orient in the semi-final second leg at Brisbane Road. Gary Cooper came in at left back for Chris Whyte, Jonathon Hunt replaced Rui Estevez and Kevin Francis made the starting line-up in place of Steve Robinson. On the bench was Paul Tait, despite his 'sudden-death' winner over Swansea that had set up the Orient tie.

Blues were definitely firm favourites with the bookies, so it was no surprise that they dominated the early exchanges, Ricky Otto exploited the vastness of the Wembley pitch, but once Kevin Francis had suffered an early injury Otto's crosses, which Francis had been dominating against the Carlisle back four that included their Man of the Match Derek Mountfield, were no longer an effective form of attack.

At the other end Carlisle did little to trouble the Blues defence and Ian Bennett was left to enjoy the atmosphere as a virtual spectator for the majority of the first 45 minutes. At the break the score was 0–0.

The second half continued to be a lack-lustre affair which only sprung into life the manager made more substitutions with 13 minutes of normal time left. Paul Tait had already been tactically introduced into the game for Peter Shearer just after the hour mark, but the next change saw Louie Donowa finally replace the struggling Francis. Within minutes Louie had had two great opportunities to win the match but both were in the air, and he failed to trouble the 'keeper, which would probably have not been the case had a fully-fit Kevin Francise had been on the pitch. As the prospect of the 'sudden death' goal period became greater Blues almost won the game late on. Gary Poole had moved forward, and as his teammates expected a cross he let fly from outside the 18-yard box and his rifled shot went just wide of the upright. Extra-time began with the Blues increasing the tempo, with the turning point coming 10 minutes into the first period of extra-time, when Mountfield, who had been a rock in the centre of Carlisle's defence, left the field to get treatment following a cut to his forehead and was replaced by Jamie Robinson. Just three minutes later a floated cross by Otto fell into the territory Mountfield had dominated throughout the afternoon, but without his influence Tait rose to flick a header which cleared the outstretched arm of Caig and dropped into the corner of the net.

PLAYER FACTFILE

PAUL RONALD TAIT
Striker/Midfielder
169+43 appearances, 18 goals

'Taity' was born in Sutton Coldfield on 31 July 1971. After playing in local school and youth sides he joined Blues on a YTS in June 1987, signing professional terms in August 1988. He was a tough, tenacious player with a great attitude, excellent skills and the ability to not only play that defence-splitting pass, but also to ghost past the opposition. A serious knee injury in January 1991 left him with a synthetic knee ligament, which at the time appeared to be career threatening, but typical of Paul he proved the pundits wrong. After three loan periods with Millwall (February 1994), Bolton Wanderers (July 1994) and Northampton Town (December 1997), he signed for Oxford United on a free transfer in January 1999. He stayed there until May 2002, scoring three goals in 91 appearances.

MY INTERVIEW WITH PAUL WAS DUE TO APPEAR IN THE JUNE 2008 EDITION OF THE BLUES MAGAZINE. THE MAGAZINE NEVER MADE THE BOOKSTALLS AS THE OWNERS CLOSED THE BUSINESS DOWN.

'Can I help you with the door?' asks a concerned Paul Tait as a lady struggles to get through a door at Starbucks in Solihull. 'Thank you' replies the grateful female, as he tells me to get up and open the door! When you are in the company of 'Taity' it's a real pleasure, and there is always the unexpected. Relieved of my temporary doorman duties, I ask him about his early years.

'My dad is Scottish, and my mum's from Middlesbrough. They were living in Castle Vale when I came along, hence I was born at Good Hope Hospital in Sutton Coldfield. Two years later my sister Lauren was born and we were living in South Yardley. My dad, Ronald, is a Glasgow Rangers supporter, and I saw my first game at Villa Park when I was about five. The game was billed as a friendly fixture, but they didn't tell the Rangers' fans and they wrecked the place! I was watching from the safety of my uncle's box in the Trinity Road stand and thought it must always be like this. It was a riot and for me. It's been like that ever since!'

WHO SIGNED YOU FOR BLUES AND HOW?
'When I was at Byng Kendrick it was a rugby school, so it wasn't until my last year in the seniors that we managed to get one of the teachers to organise a football team. We did pretty well in our first and only season, winning a schools tournament. Matthew Fox, who played for Blues, was in the same team. After school I played for Hurley Colts, near Atherstone, and then 3 Cs, who were based in Chelmsley Wood. It was while playing for them that Norman Bodell spotted me, and Garry Pendrey signed me on YTS forms in June 1987 for a weekly age of £28.50. Blues were golden to me. When I was 12 I was playing with the Under-15s that included John Frain and Kevin Ashley. They would also take me on first-team trips — they made a real fuss of me.'

WHAT DO YOU REMEMBER OF YOUR DEBUT?
'It was also my most memorable game — I was just 16, and it was against Leeds United at St Andrew's. It was played on a Friday night (6 May) to reduce the threat of any trouble. I was really scared when I came on after 28 minutes, but I must have done alright as I got Man of the Match, which shows how bad it was! But it was a great experience, even though I froze in front of Mervyn Day, their 'keeper, and wasted a chance by hitting a post. It was the last match of the 1987—88 season and there was a crowd of 6,024. The team was: Hansbury; Frain, Roberts; Williams, Bird, Atkins; Handysides, Langley, Whitton, Russell, Wigley.'

WHAT WAS YOUR MOST MEMORABLE GOAL?
'That was my first, scored against Walsall in September 1989 in a 2—0 victory. I picked the ball up from a corner at the Railway End and cut in from the left before bending it into the top left-hand corner over Ron Green, which isn't that hard to do! I was originally a striker, and it was "Crackers" Dave MacKay and Bobby Ferguson that asked me to take on the midfield role as I was the best runner in the club. I've always hated it in midfield because I couldn't tackle, so I got lots of yellow cards!'

WHAT WAS IT LIKE AT BLUES IN THOSE DAYS?

'It was dire. We used to train wherever we could find some space — more often that not on the piece of parkland (well, it's got swings) opposite the Garrison Pub. After Garry left, we had a number of stand-in managers: Steve Fleet and Bill Caldwell before Terry Cooper was appointed.'

TELL ME ABOUT YOUR INJURY?

'It happened away against Leyton Orient on 12 January 1991. My knee was shattered, and I was in tears, I was only 19. Crackers was always reluctant to send on the trainer. You had to be virtually dead before he would sanction it. Anyway, eventually the trainer came on and asked me "Can you walk?" A lot of good that was! I was referred to Professor David Dandy at Addenbrooke's Hospital, Cambridge. He had sorted out Alan Shearer, but he took one look at my scan and predicted that I would never play at the top level again. I had to have a total knee reconstruction using bone from my hip, but I did get back to playing some nine months later. It was scary when I came on as a sub in a friendly against Bristol City at Wast Hills. Once I'd survived that first tackle I was fine and went on to score.'

'While I was lucky to get fit again, the timing of the injury ruined my move to Spurs for £500k. I was being watched by Liverpool, Wolves and Spurs as an up-and-coming midfielder along with Jamie Redknapp. Liverpool went for him and my move to Spurs was imminent. Because it was a done deal I did not sign the contract renewal offered to me. As soon as I was injured, seemingly never to play again, Samesh Kumar got me to sign the contract so he could claim the insurance money. Bad luck Samesh.'

WHY DID YOU CALL DAVE MACKAY 'CRACKERS'?

'Cause he was crackers. He was a mad fan of Simon Sturridge, and all he ever said was "Well done Simon".'

WHO WERE THE CHARACTERS DURING YOUR TIME?

'The whole team had that Wimbledon "Crazy Gang" mentality — we were like a prison team. Stand-out characters were Mark Ward, Liam Daish and Gary Cooper, he was a real cockney wide boy.'

HOW DID YOUR CAREER END AT BLUES?

'Initially Baz [Barry Fry] tried to get me off the payroll with a loan spell at Millwall and a trial for Bolton. I spent six weeks at Millwall and never played a game as I was either ill or injured. They put me in a bed and breakfast in Eltham near their training ground, and I got so bored I would drive back to Birmingham to see my mates and have a drink. On one occasion I missed training because of a late night/early morning, and Mick McCarthy (their manager) called the loan spell off.'

'Baz got me to go to Bolton, supposedly to play in a pre-season game against Liverpool at Burnden Park. When I got there I was due to play the following day in the reserves against Millwall. I told them to forget it, but it coincided with some bad press coverage on me, so I guess they were pleased with my decision.'

'Baz also nearly sold me to Watford for £250k; the fee was agreed, but before I went down I was told the deal was dead because someone from the West Midlands police had told one of their directors that I was trouble. So that put the kybosh on that deal.'

'Eventually, after nearly joining Dundee (I could never play against Rangers), I had a loan period with Ian Atkins at Northampton and played a couple of games; later, I joined Oxford

Blues Review

The agony of failure on the final day of last season was almost unbearable for the hoards of Birmingham fans up and down the country.

The taste of relegation was made all the more bitter by the fact that their midlands rivals West Bromwich Albion were the ones who survived to fight another day in the First Division.

But perhaps that disappointment has been made slightly easier to bear after one of the most exciting seasons at the club for years inside their newly developed St. Andrews stadium, now amongst the best in the lower divisions. And it has all been topped by their appearance in today's Wembley cup final that would never have been possible if they had remained in the First Division.

Those fans so disgruntled by last season's disappointment have been consoled this term by the charge from Barry Fry and his men which has left the Blues on the verge of a return to the First Division. And even if they miss out on automatic promotion, the Play-Offs will represent a lifeline and a possible return trip to Wembley in May.

Back in August, the task for Fry was to rally his men in a bid to recover from the disappointment of three months previous. The arrival of summer signings David Regis and Mark Ward, on a permanent deal after a loan spell, helped lift the gloom, but their opening day defeat at the hands of Leyton Orient knocked them back again.

The pressure was on Fry as Birmingham's chiefs were

Paul Williams, Barry Fry and Steve Claridge celebrate the semi-final victory over Leyton Orient

Mark Ward - Birmingham player/coach brought from Everton for £200,000

demanding an immediate return to the First Division. When the call came and the panic button was hit, the answer was emphatic. An unbeaten League run from early September until early January pushed the Blues firmly into the promotion chase and two impressive displays against the mighty Liverpool, eventually ending in a penalty shoot-out heartbreak at Anfield, showed what could be achieved.

But as one road to Wembley was cut off, their Auto Windscreens Shield progress gave cause for great excitement. The crowds being attracted to St. Andrews were creating more headlines in the media and breaking more records than the side's impressive run.

With more than 10,000 fans in attendance for the opening round group game against Walsall, a record was set for that stage of the tournament. They witnessed a thumping 3-0 win for the home side and next up were Gillingham with 17,086 seeing another 3-0 win.

Birmingham were handed another home draw and 22,351 witnessed an exciting tie against Hereford with the Blues firing another three goals, though 'keeper Ian Bennett was beaten on this occasion giving a final score of 3-1.

The semi-final created another record of a sort, with a Paul Tait goal in sudden death extra-time sending the Blues through to what proved to be a victorious Southern Area final against Leyton Orient.

Perhaps the only drawback from the Wembley run was a dip in League form that saw Birmingham fall from their lofty perch at the top of The League. But in recent weeks, they have returned to form and are knocking on the door of automatic promotion once again.

The form of striker Steve Claridge has been a key to that success. Ricky Otto's arrival from Southend boosted the side and Jose Dominguez, the tiny Spanish frontman, has been a big hit with the Birmingham fans. With the giant Kevin Francis now on board, the Birmingham ship is moving steadily towards a return to the First Division.

Perhaps a club as big and ambitious as Birmingham are in the wrong league, too far down the football spectrum. They will hope that today's Auto Windscreens Shield final will be their last in the competition at Wembley. A return next year will have meant failure to win promotion.

The managers of both finalists today will tell you promotion is far more important than any cup success. But for the hoards who will pack Wembley, cup glory would make a promotion season a perfect one. *Kevin Palmer*

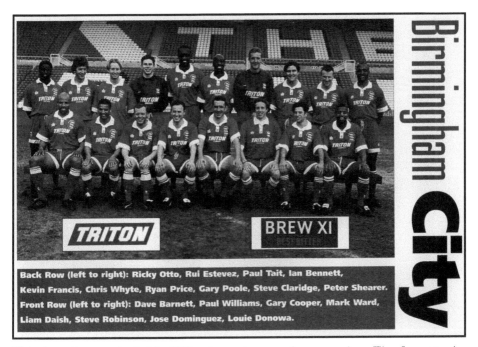

Back Row (left to right): Ricky Otto, Rui Estevez, Paul Tait, Ian Bennett, Kevin Francis, Chris Whyte, Ryan Price, Gary Poole, Steve Claridge, Peter Shearer. Front Row (left to right): Dave Barnett, Paul Williams, Gary Cooper, Mark Ward, Liam Daish, Steve Robinson, Jose Dominguez, Louie Donowa.

United on a free transfer in May 1999 and spent just over three years there. Then I went to play in Cyprus for five months. I stayed there for two years, but stopped playing when they never paid me. Eventually I did get paid in fivers — thank goodness my father-in-law, who is a Cypriot, acted as my interpreter. I knew things were going to be difficult when they showed me my club car. It was a very early Vauxhall Astra with flat tyres and no air conditioning!'

Author's note: If you ever get the chance to talk to Paul about his time at Oxford and an Irishman called Terry do so because the story is hilarious, as is his recollection of Malcolm Shotton's pre-match team talk.

WHAT HAPPENED AFTER THAT?

'While coaching in the evenings I did a number of jobs, notably working for a maintenance company, and for a year I was a postman in Redditch. After that the coaching got more and more and now I am full-time, running Midlands Soccer Coaching, which has centres in Redditch, Gloucester, Droitwich, Kidderminster and Banbury.'

HOW DO YOU SPEND YOUR TIME THESE DAYS?

'I have not got time for hobbies, although I'd like to play golf more, so I guess my real hobby is ensuring Rangers are always better than Celtic. Having said that, my best mate is Devs [Paul Devlin], who was my roommate when we played together, but he's a Celtic nut! I've also got four kids to keep me amused: Cameron (10) Adam (7) Luke (5) and Sasha (3).'

ANYTHING ELSE?

'When Craig Brown was the Scotland international manager he wanted me to play for Scotland as my dad was Scottish. I refused; why would I want to play for Scotland, I'm an Englishman. Tricky

Francis was shocked that I'd turned down an international career. After we had got promoted from Division Three in 1992, there was a celebration party at the Cobden Hotel on the Hagley Road after the Shrewsbury game. I remember Samesh was dancing with Joan Hill (Commercial Manager), and I grabbed him in a headlock and proceeded to drag him around the dancefloor. What a night! Joan Hill was a diamond to me as she would act as my taxi driver and get me home after a hectic post-match celebration.'

WHY DO YOU CALL TREVOR 'TRICKY'?

'At the start of every training session he would boot a ball as high as he could and then get it under control before it hit the ground. He had great skills.'

HOW DID YOU GET ON WITH BARRY FRY?

'I loved him, but if you were a true professional like John Frain it was murder. If training was called for 10 o'clock Frainy would be there dead on the dot, and then Baz would roll up half an hour later.'

Game Thirty-eight

Champions

Huddersfield Town 1 Blues 2

Date: 6 May 1995

Attendance: 18,775

Venue: The opening of the McAlpine Stadium

Referee: Mr J. Winter (Middlesbrough)

Blues: Bennett, Poole, Frain, Ward, Whyte, Daish, Hunt (Donowa), Claridge, Hendon, Williams (Tait), Cooper.

Huddersfield Town: Francis, Trevitt, Cowan, Bullock, Scully, Sinnott, Collins (Moulden 74), Duxbury, Booth, Jepson, Dunn (Billy).

It was a nervous Blues squad who were the first visitors to Huddersfield Town's new stadium. A single point was required to gain promotion as champions of the Second Division, so their nervous start was understandable!

Ian Bennett made a vital save from Jepson in the first two minutes, which served to settle the nerves of the 'boys in blue'. At half-time it was 0–0, and chances had gone begging to Jonathan Hunt and Steve Claridge, but if the score remained the same after 90 minutes then the Blues were up!

On 67 minutes the deadlock was broken in Blues' favour as Claridge sent the 4,000 travelling supporters delirious when he converted a cross following full-back Cooper's run. The nerves were settled at long last, and the visitors further spoilt the home side's celebrations when substitute Paul Tait scored the second on 82 minutes.

As usual, Blues had made it an uneasy last few minutes for their supporters, allowing the Terriers to score through Bullock's header with two minutes remaining. Blues had won their first League title since winning the Second

HUDDERSFIELD TOWN A.F.C.

SOUTH STAND

HUDDERSFIELD TOWN A.F.C.
V
BIRMINGHAM CITY
SATURDAY 6th MAY 1995
KICK-OFF 3:00 p.m.
ENDSLEIGH INSURANCE LEAGUE
DIVISION TWO

ADULT £7.50   CONCESSION £4.00
TURNSTILES:17-20
ROW   SEAT
K   127

TO BE RETAINED

147

Division title in 1954–55 season. They won the Championship with 89 points, a record seasonal points total to date, leaving them four points ahead of runners-up Brentford.

Steve Claridge remembers in his book *Tales from the Boot Camps*:

'Yet again, I was involved in a last match that had so much riding on it, this time against Huddersfield Town, who were a top-six team. It was a tense day and I did not help our cause early on when I missed a simple chance, my shot hitting a defender on the line. But I made amends by turning home a close-range shot to set us on our way and we eventually came through 2–1. It was my 20th League goal of the season – 25 in all competitions – making me the first Blues player since Trevor Francis, 20 years earlier, to reach that figure in a season, and won me the supporters' award for Player of the Year. I was particularly pleased because I played the end of the season with two broken ribs. About six minutes from the end of a game with Plymouth Argyle I was kicked under my chest and could not breathe. The bench were giving me stick but I stayed on and scored, although I knew something was not right. Every game after that I was in a lot of pain whenever I was elbowed or pushed, but I have always liked to play if I possibly could so I struggled on with a cricket thigh pad strapped around my rib cage. It had been a great season. We were averaging crowds of 20,000 in the Second Division, with very few away fans, the stand was finished and the ground was looking magnificent. I really felt that I was at what would very soon be a Premiership club, that finally I had a chance of getting in with the big boys. I really felt I could make an impression in the First Division.'

STEPHEN EDWARD CLARIDGE
Striker
116 + 4 appearances, 42 goals

Born in Portsmouth the year England won the World Cup, Steve played for his home-town club before beginning his journeyman life as a professional footballer. After spells with Fareham Town, AFC Bournemouth, Weymouth, Crystal Palace, Aldershot, Cambridge United, Luton Town and Cambridge United for a second spell, he signed for Blues in January 1994 for £350,000. Although he had an appearance that belied his abilities as a footballer, the fans loved his all-action, never-give-up attitude. He was always unkempt and always seemed to have his socks and his shin pads around his ankles right from the start of a game. On leaving Cambridge United he was quoted as saying: 'I knew I couldn't take anymore when, one day in training, a player shouted "feet" meaning that's where he wanted the ball – and he was punished by being made to do 40 press-ups'.

Not the most dedicated of trainers, with a love of gambling on the horses, he was good on the ball and possessed great stamina, although he did have his limits as the following story demonstrates. One morning he went to training having eaten a bowl of cornflakes in double-quick time. Feeling peckish, he devoured a fry up and some chocolate bars in a nearby café, but when he got to the training ground his stomach was rumbling (not surprisingly) and his remedy was additional chocolate bars! When training ended for the day his body had had enough and he flaked out, totally exhausted, in the back of the team's minibus. A few hours later he got out still feeling groggy and started to walk the streets of Cambridge. Some local residents, thinking him the worse for drink, called the police, who detained the wobbly Claridge for what was thought to be drunkenness. No action was taken as the truth eventually came out in more ways than one!

He scored a goal in every three games for Blues and eventually moved to Leicester City in March 1996 for £1.2 million, where he helped them win the League Cup in 1997 by scoring the extra-time winner against Middlesbrough. The previous year he had scored a 120th-minute Play-off-winning goal against Crystal Palace to take Leicester City into the Premiership.

Seven Away Goals

Stoke City 0 Blues 7

Date: 10 January 1998   **Venue:** Britannia Stadium
Attendance: 14,240   **Referee:** Mr T. Heilbron (Co. Durham)

Blues: Bennett, Bass, Charlton, Bruce (Johnson 51), Ablett, O'Connor, Marsden, Hughes, McCarthy, Furlong, Forster (Ndlovu 80).

Stoke City: Muggleton, Griffin, Myamah (Wallace half-time), Sigurdsson, Tweed, Keen, Forsyth, MacKenzie, Thorne, Stewart (Gabbiadini half-time), Kavanagh.

Blues matched their biggest away win in their history when Stoke were hammered 7–0 at the Britannia Stadium. The other was 104 years previous against Northwich Victoria on 6 January 1894.

The 'goalfest' began in earnest as soon as the fourth minute when Bryan Hughes headed in from close range. The goals continued virtually whenever the ball went into Stoke City's final third. Hughes again made it two after nine minutes as he curled in a great strike from 20 yards, and on 29 minutes Nicky Forster, turning sharply, hit a first-time shot which crept in the bottom corner of the bemused Muggleton's goal. At 3–0 the half-time break, with the game already in Blues' grasp, could not come soon enough for the

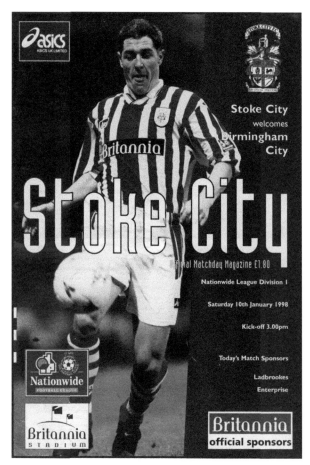

PAUL ANTHONY FURLONG
Striker
124+29 appearances, 56 goals
Joined Queen's Park Rangers in September 2002.

Born in London on 1 October 1968, Paul joined Coventry City from Enfield for £130,000 in July 1991. He moved to Watford a year later for £250,000 before joining Chelsea in May 1994 for £2.3 million. In July 1996 he became Blues' record transfer fee signing when he moved from Stamford Bridge for £1.5 million. His scoring record was four in 37 for Coventry City; 37 in 79 for Watford; 13 in 64 games for Chelsea. Furlong had two loan spells with Queen's Park Rangers in August 2000 and Sheffield United in February and March 2002 before returning to Loftus Road again in July 2002 and signing permanently in September 2002. Injury prone, he never realised his full potential, although he did play six times for England as a semi-professional, scoring one goal, and won the FA Trophy with Enfield in 1988. In 2007 he left Queen's Park Rangers with a goal haul of 54 in 162 appearances to join Luton Town, where he scored eight goals in 32 games. When Luton were relegated at the end of 2007–08 he signed a one-year deal with Southend United. He only made three appearances before being loaned out to Barnet.

home side. Blues were soon back on the attack, resuming intense pressure on the Stoke defence, and within five minutes Paul Furlong, unmarked in the penalty area, fired home the fourth and the first of his second-half hat-trick. John McCarthy, cutting in from the right wing, smashed a shot into the roof of the net to make it 5–0 on 57 minutes. It all became too much to bear for the Stoke faithful, and at this point several ran onto the pitch, which was a pre-cursor to future events.

Blues took complete control, and a pass from Jon Bass sent Forster clear again, and his neat lay-off found Furlong who in one movement side-stepped and shot home to make it 6–0. With two minutes remaining and riot police surrounding the gathering hordes of Stoke fans, Furlong got his third and Blues' record-equalling seventh, after a throw-in found him on the edge of the box, and he turned and lobbed the ball over a desperate Muggleton to complete the rout.

At the final whistle Stoke fans invaded the pitch, calling for chairman Peter Coates to stand down, but police with riot gear and horses kept the crowd reasonably orderly.

Game Forty

League Cup Semi-final Second Leg

BLUES 4   IPSWICH 1

Date: 31 January 2001   **Venue:** St Andrew's
Attendance: 28,624   **Referee:** Mr J. Winter

Blues: Bennett, Gill, Grainger, Purse, M. Johnson, Eaden (Hughes 109), Lazaridis (Burrows 118), O'Connor, Horsfield, , Adebola (A. Johnson 97).

Ipswich: R. Wright, Croft, McGreal, Venus, Hreidarsson, J. Wright, Holland, Magilton, Clapham, Stewart, Naylor.

O ne of the most dramatic matches ever seen at St Andrew's finished with Blues, of the Football League, defeating Premiership side Ipswich Town to win a place in the Final of the League Cup.

It was a long, hard night of football followed by lengthy celebrations before the Bluenoses got home. As well as extra-time being required, it also needed a Blues performance of grit and determination to ensure they defeated Ipswich 4–1 on the night (4–2) on aggregate to secure a place with Liverpool at the Millennium Stadium in Cardiff. Many fans who were there that night felt that if ever a game typified Blues style of play and the personality of Birmingham then this was it.

Two-goal Geoff Horsfield was the hero of the night for Trevor Francis's team. Goals either side of half-time by Martin Grainger and Horsfield reversed Ipswich's 1–0 lead from the first leg. Blues' lead, however, lasted

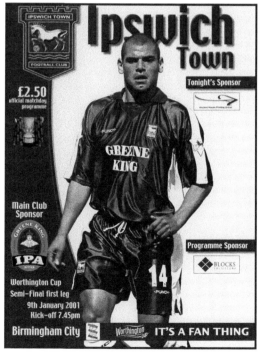

The programme for the semi-final first leg at Ipswich.

152

MARTIN JOHN O'CONNOR
Midfielder
216 + 7 appearances, 19 goals

Martin was born on 12 October 1967 and is the current assistant manager of League One side Walsall. He started his career at Bromsgrove Rovers in the early 1990s before moving to Crystal Palace, where he made only two appearances. He then spent the first of three spells at Walsall, joining on loan in March 1993 before signing permanently the following year. His most prominent role at the Saddlers was winning promotion to Division Two. In 1995 he scored 22 goals in 104 games in this spell.He then joined Peterborough United in 1996, scoring three in 18 games, followed by Blues, whom he captained in the 2001 Worthington League Cup Final against Liverpool. O'Connor rejoined Walsall in 2002, but his contract was not renewed at the end of the 2002–03 season. He then signed for Shrewsbury Town in July 2003, before ending his playing career with Kidderminster Harriers. O'Connor was also called up to the Cayman Islands national side. On 20 January 2009, he was named assistant manager to Chris Hutchings at the Bescot Stadium

less than a minute as James Scowcroft scored, but Horsfield and Andrew Johnson then struck in extra-time to ensure Blues created history.

If the 90 minutes preceding extra-time were difficult for the Bluenoses, then the extra 30-minute period is one that will live long in the memory for all the right reasons. Seven minutes into extra-time, TF sent on Johnson and the substitute's arrival turned the match around. It was Horsfield, though, who struck the definitive blow. Danny Sonner's astute pass caught the defence square, and Horsfield took the ball in his stride before stroking it perfectly across Richard Wright into the far corner of the goal. Johnson added the final blow, when with three minutes remaining Wright mis-kicked his clearance as the ball bobbled, allowing the Johnson to roll the ball into the empty net.

Martin O'Connor recalls:
'It was my happiest moment at Blues. I just knew we would get to the Final. It was destined to be our night. It was fantastic to be chaired off the field by the Bluenoses, who were trying to get hold of my shirt, shorts, everything!'

AN INTERVIEW WITH MARTIN WHICH APPEARED IN THE SUMMER 2007 EDITION OF THE BLUES MAGAZINE

In Pelsall, Staffordshire, lives Birmingham City legend Martin O'Connor with his wife and two daughters, Georgia and Ashton. When he's not involved with football his weekends are full of the girls' activities: horse riding, bike rides and shopping — which Martin manages to conduct from the comfort of a coffee shop at the Merry Hill Shopping Centre.

It's not often, however, that football's not on his agenda, for he is currently player manager of Halesowen Town and he cannot refuse a charity game when kid's charities are involved. 'I played in four charity games in the last week and my knee has started to play up'. This is his right knee, on which he had six operations during his professional career.

Martin, who was 40 that year, started his professional career late in life after being rejected by the Development Centres of Aston Villa and West Bromwich Albion at the age of 14. Although Martin has worked for the Wolves Academy and the Blues' College, he feels that 'the current scouting system lets a lot of kids down. It is virtually impossible to predict a boy's development and progress from the age of 7 through to 15.'

After his rejection at 14, Martin lost interest in football for two years before joining the Afro-Caribbean Centre team that was run by one of his mate's dads. Martin recalls 'My first game was at Swinfen Hall Prison – getting into the place was a problem – they had to unlock a door, get the team in, then lock the door behind us before they unlocked the next door and so on, and that's an open prison!'

'In my second season our goalkeeper passed his driving test, but he was dropped for the next game. What did he do? He parked his car in between the goal posts and demanded to be picked – our manager refused – the car stayed put, and the match was abandoned. You couldn't make it up.'

Martin had by now qualified as a freight train driver at Bescot, having completed his training in the shunting yard and as a guard. He'd been a train driver for six months when he began playing for Bloxwich Town, who were managed by Nicky Higgs. After half a season Higgs informed Martin that Bobby Hope (ex-Blues and West Bromwich Albion) had watched him and wanted him to go for a pre-season trial at Bromsgrove Rovers. He was offered a two-year contract and Martin recalls, 'Bobby Hope and later Chris Nicholl, at Walsall, were the two managers who helped make me a better player. Bobby taught me a lesson – I wanted to go to a party on a Friday night, so I told him on the Thursday that I would not be available for the following Saturday's match. Bobby said OK, but you will have to tell your teammates that you no longer wish to play with them. I told them, a huge row broke out – outcome? I didn't go to the party and played on the Saturday.'

'I was about 25 when Bromsgrove informed me that Cambridge, Bournemouth, Oxford, Wimbledon and Premiership side Crystal Palace were interested in signing me. After a trial at Cambridge for John Beck, I signed for Palace in June 1992 for £15,000 and moved to London. The PFA organised the move on my behalf and it included free hotel accommodation, which I didn't enjoy. It was all a bit too much for me living in London and moving to the Premiership. When I arrived for pre-season I was so unfit compared to the other lads that they sent me to Lilleshall to improve my fitness levels. I originally went for one week and stayed for four! There was huge competition for midfield places at Palace: Gareth Southgate, John Solako, Geoff Thomas, Alan Pardew and Simon Osborn, but I was in the Premiership, albeit as captain of the reserve team. Kenny Hibbitt was Walsall's manager at the time, and he travelled to watch me at Southampton, and he took me on loan in 1992–93. I helped the Saddlers get into the Play-offs and scored my first League goal against Darlington. Then it was back to Palace, who had been relegated, to join the first-team squad on a pre-season trip to Portugal. I had made it to the first-team squad, but just never broke through. I travelled to and from the Midlands with Stan Collymore, who eventually went to Southend, and I had the choice to go to either Chesterfield or Walsall. It was no contest – I moved to Walsall in February 1994 for £40,000, half of which was paid for by the supporters!'

Martin was an instant success at Walsall, becoming captain and making 80 appearances, scoring 19 goals. He was also picked for the Division Three Representative side for consecutive seasons (1994–95 and 1995–96). At the end of the season Martin was out of contract, and Derby had had a £350,000 offer refused. 'Walsall only offered me a one-year contract, obviously hoping to cash in on me early the next season. I was disappointed and refused the deal.'

HOW DID YOUR MOVE TO BLUES COME ABOUT?

Barry Fry answers that in his book *Big Fry*: 'I talked to a couple of players who were out of contract about coming to join Peterborough and the position with them was that their fees would be fixed by a tribunal. I did manage to get hold of O'Connor for £350,000, which was a club record.' Martin spent four months at Peterborough, scoring three goals in 18 games. During this time Graeme Souness, the Southampton manager, offered £1 million for Martin's services, but the deal was for £500k plus players and Barry refused. 'Barry was always saying he would get a million pounds for me, then we were drawn against Cheltenham in the FA Cup. On the Saturday we drew and therefore had a replay on the following Tuesday at Cheltenham. It was important to the club to win the game as they needed the cash. Unfortunately during the weekend my daughter had an asthma attack and was hospitalised. Barry was more than happy to let me miss the replay, but I just had to be there, so I played and we won, and on my way back to the hospital Barry rang to say Trevor Francis wanted to speak to me. It all happened so quick. I met Trevor on the Wednesday, had a medical and signed on the Thursday and met up with the lads on the Friday night prior to an away game at Norwich. I roomed with Dave Barnett, who told me how great the Blues were, and I responded by scoring the winner the next day.'

Barry Fry takes up the story: 'Then I sold Martin O'Connor to Birmingham for £528,000 up front and everybody said what a great deal it was. Oh yeah? It was a shit deal. I would have got a million for him if I had not been put under pressure. Trevor Francis had me by the short and curlies.'

WHAT WERE YOUR INITIAL THOUGHTS OF THE BLUES?

'Everything was so much bigger and more professional than I had been used to – the training for instance. At Peterborough it was predominantly all five-a-sides, while at Blues it was fitness, technique, drills etc. My mum used to say it was noisy at St Andrew's, unlike the other clubs I had been at. Dave Barnett told me that I would be a success with the Bluenoses because they loved players that gave their all.'

WHAT WAS YOUR PROUDEST MOMENT?

'Being given the captaincy by Trevor, who for me was 100 per cent; it was prior to an away game at Barnsley. I was captain in a side that included senior pros like Bruce, Ablett, Furlong and Newell – what an honour. I just lead by example, which I would do with or without the armband.'

HOW MANY TIMES DID YOU PLAY FOR THE CAYMAN ISLANDS?

'Twice. I qualified because my dad was born in Jamaica, and I had an English passport. The first game was a warm-up match against Jamaica prior to a World Cup qualifying game against Cuba. We had a 60-year-old Brazilian coach who trained us on the beach. Normally 200 or so people turn out to see the Cayman Islands play, and they normally get beaten 10–1. On this occasion

6,000 fans were there to see us lose 1—0. We lost the Cuba game by the same margin. TF was great about letting me have the time off! I didn't get a cap, you got a medal for each game. My mum's got them!'

HOW DID YOUR CAREER END AT BLUES?
'Once Steve Bruce was appointed manager I was his first departure, I think it was Bryan Hughes who replaced me. I played 24 games in that promotion season. Colin Lee was manager at Walsall, and I was signed on a free in January 2002 and immediately made captain and remained at Walsall until the end of 2002—03.'

WHAT DID YOU DO THEN?
'I was disillusioned with the game and turned down a number of opportunities before joining Jimmy Quinn at Shrewsbury, which enabled me to get my coaching qualifications (I have my A Licence). During my time at Gay Meadow we got them back into the Football League before I joined Stuart Watkiss as player-coach at Kidderminster Harriers. After Stuart was sacked I spent three months as caretaker manager. After spells with Wolves and Blues youth schemes, six months ago I joined Halesowen Town as player-coach when they were third from bottom, and we got very close to the Play-offs. I am with two ex-Blues favourites at Halesowen: Graham Hyde and Paul Devlin.'

HOW DO YOU SPEND YOUR LEISURE TIME?
'Avoiding going shopping with the girls. No, seriously, I play golf with a handicap of 28, and I have a number of apartments locally that I rent out. I am 40 this year, and my wife is threatening to take me to Las Vegas, so life's never dull.'

Game Forty-one

League Cup Final

BLUES 1 LIVERPOOL 1 (AET)

LOST 5–4 ON PENALTIES

Date: 25 February 2001　　　　　　　　　**Venue:** Millennium Stadium, Cardiff
Attendance: 74,434　　　　　　　　　　**Referee:** Mr D. Elleray (Harrow)

Blues: Bennett, Eaden, Purse, M. Johnson, Grainger, McCarthy, Sonner (Hughes), O'Connor, Lazaridis, Horsfield (Marcelo), Adebola (A. Johnson, half-time).

Liverpool: Westerveld, Babbel, Henchoz, Hyypia, Carragher, Gerrard (McAllister 78), Hamann, Biscan (Ziege 96), Smicer (Barmby 83), Heskey, Fowler.

The road to Cardiff
Round 1 First Leg v Southend (a) won 5–0 (Eaden, Marcelo, M. Johnson, Hughes, Adebola)
Round 1 Second Leg v Southend (h) drew 0–0
Round 2 First Leg v Wycombe (a) won 4–3 (Horsfield 2, A. Johnson 2)
Round 2 Second Leg v Wycombe (h) won 1–0 (Ndlovu)
Round 3 v Spurs (a) won 3–1 (Adebola 2, Burchill)
Round 4 v Newcastle (h) won 2–1 (Adebola, M. Johnson)
Quarter-final v Sheffield Wednesday (h) won 2–0 (Sonner, Adebola)
Semi-final First Leg v Ipswich (a) lost 1–0
Semi-final Second Leg v Ipswich (h) won 4–1 (Horsfield 2, A. Johnson, Grainger)

With Wembley unavailable due to its refurbishment, Wales became the temporary home of English Cup Finals. So it was that Cardiff's Millennium Stadium hosted the Worthington Cup Final of 2001. Premiership Liverpool were the bookies' bet, and initially they controlled the game. Not unexpectedly, on 29 minutes Heskey flicked on Westerveld's deep goal kick for Fowler to volley home from 25 yards.

At 1–0 the expected demise of the Nationwide team did not happen – it only inspired Blues to fight back, and by the end of the game it was agreed by everyone outside of Liverpool that the Blues came close to a major upset. Darren Purse was impressive, with a firm defensive display; after being beaten by Heskey for the opening goal, he did not make any further errors, giving Blues the chance to take the game to the Scousers.

In the second half a great chance was spurned by substitute Andrew Johnson, who should have converted his shot from a driven cross from Nicky Eaden. With the end of 90 minutes fast approaching, Blues threw everything into attack looking for an equaliser,

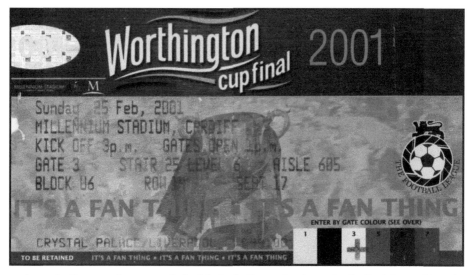

and eventually a good move ended with the ball running loose in the Reds' area. Captain Martin O'Connor reached it, and just as he was about to deal with the ball Hamann's outstretched leg brought him down, and referee Elleray immediately awarded a spot-kick. After a nervous wait while O'Connor received treatment for his injury, Purse, with 35,000 Blues fans praying behind the goal he was facing, fearlessly struck his penalty to Westeveld's left into the corner, giving the 'keeper no chance.

During extra-time the pressure from Blues was incredible, epitomised by a tremendous 35-yard chip from Bryan Hughes which almost caught out the Reds' keeper, his flailing hand pushing the ball just wide of his post. Then came the moment all Bluenoses will never forget. Hughes broke away and played the ball to Eaden who knocked it into the path of the advancing Andrew Johnson and, just like what had happened to O'Connor, as he was about to control the ball he was tripped by a defender. Amazingly, Elleray, who seemed to have a perfect view, waved play on. In the final minute of extra-time a deep Liverpool free-kick found Hamann whose fierce shot hit the Blues post and rebounded off into safety. So at 1–1 the match was to be decided on a penalty shoot out. Liverpool's fortune held when Johnson missed Birmingham's sixth penalty, and they took the Cup, the first of a superb treble-winning season.

Martin O'Connor remembers:
'I am never nervous before a game, but that day I had butterflies in my stomach and felt nauseous. I knew it was probably my last chance to win a major trophy, and as captain I would be the one to lift the trophy in front of 50,000 Blues fans. I remember at the beginning witnessing Trevor telling Gilly [Jerry Gill], Bugsy [David Burrows] and David Holdsworth that they were missing out. As captain I had to try and reduce their disappointment, but there was nothing I could say. At the end of the game I felt totally gutted knowing that David Elleray had copped out (or should that be Kopped?) in not giving us a second penalty. Robbie Fowler was great after the game going round shaking all the boys' hands and inviting us into their dressing room for a drink.'

PLAYER FACTFILE

DARREN JOHN PURSE
Defender
167 appearances, 9 goals.

Purse was born in Stepney, London and attended Cardinal Pole Roman Catholic School in Hackney. Having played in the same Sunday League side as Lee Bowyer when he was younger, he was offered a YTS deal by both Arsenal and Tottenham Hotspur, but turned them down in order to complete his A levels. On hearing that he had been offered deals by the two clubs, Leyton Orient showed their interest and told him that they would hand him a professional contract when he turned 17 if he signed for them. On signing his contract with the club he made his debut just three days later and established himself in the side before moving to Oxford United in 1996 for £100,000. Before moving to Oxford, Purse had a loan spell at Finnish Second Division club BK-IFK (now Vasa IFK) in the summer of 1996. Purse played just a handful of games for the club because of his move from Leyton to Oxford that summer. He spent just 18 months with Oxford before he joined Blues for £700,000 in 1997. Purse moved to West Bromwich Albion for £750,000 in the summer of 2004. He spent a single season with Albion, making 24 appearances in all competitions. In July 2005, Purse moved to Cardiff City, where he was appointed team captain. He played twice for the England Under-21 side.

PENALTY SHOOT-OUT

No.	Player	Team	Score	
1	McAllister	Liverpool	1–0	
2	Grainger	Blues	1–0	Missed
3	Barmby	Liverpool	2–0	
4	Purse	Blues	2–1	
5	Ziege	Liverpool	3–1	
6	Marcelo	Blues	3–2	
7	Hamann	Liverpool	3–2	Missed
8	Lazaridis	Blues	3–3	
9	Fowler	Liverpool	4–3	
10	Hughes	Blues	4–4	
11	Carragher	Liverpool	5–4	
12	A. Johnson	Blues	5–4	Missed

Game Forty-two

First Division Play-off Final

BLUES 1 NORWICH CITY 1 (AET)

BLUES WON 4–2 ON PENALTIES

Date: 12 May 2002   **Venue:** Millennium Stadium, Cardiff
Attendance: 71,597   **Referee:** Mr G. Barber (Tring)

Blues: Vaessen, Kenna, Vickers (Carter 71), M. Johnson, Grainger, Mooney (Lazaridis 69), Tebily, Hughes, Devlin, Horsfield (A. Johnson 113), John. Substitutes, unused: Bennett, D. Johnson.

Norwich: Green, Kenton, Drury, Mackay, Fleming, Rivers (Notman 90), Holt, Mulryne, Nielsen (Roberts 83), McVeigh (Sutch 102), Easton.

It had taken 16 years, four failed attempts in the Play-off semi finals, 120 minutes and eight penalty-kicks, but Blues had finally made it back to the top flight of football. When Darren Carter smashed in the winning spot-kick the noise in the Millennium Stadium reached a record-high level on the Richter scale. Blues fans were left glorifying the club's biggest win for years, an unforgettable day that still brings a smile years later to the faces of those fans lucky enough to be there. Blues started the game as the bookies' choice, having beaten Norwich twice in the regular season 4–0 at St Andrew's and 0–1 at Carrow Road. Blues were also the team with the best current form, unbeaten in their last 12 games. Norwich scraped into the Play-off places on the last day of the season, on goal difference over Burnley, but showed in the two-legged semi-final against Wolves that they were not going to be beaten easily.

Blues got off to a great start, and on 15 minutes Stern John was given a glorious chance after a ball from Bryan Hughes sent him clean though on goal; however, with just the 'keeper to beat he tried to bend the ball round Green with the outside of his boot, but he got it totally wrong and the ball drifted well wide of the target. Blues continued to go forward and were denied another chance of a goal via the penalty spot when Geoff Horsfield was apparently tripped by MacKay, but referee Barber ignored the incident.

Norwich, who had not troubled the Blues goal, suddenly became a threat and ended the first 45 minutes looking the side most likely too, even though they still could not force a save of any real description from Nico Vaesen in the Blues goal. It was the opposite at the other end, and right on the stroke of half-time Green produced a magnificent reflex save to prevent a volley from Horsfield entering the net after he had been put clear just a few yards out by Tommy Mooney's header.

With the pressure being felt by everyone, chances started to dry up in the second half.

DIVISION ONE PLAY-OFF FINAL

BIRMINGHAM CITY

- 1 Ian BENNETT
- 2 Nicky EADEN
- 3 Martin GRAINGER
- 4 Danny SONNER
- 5 Darren PURSE
- 7 Jon McCARTHY
- 8 Stern JOHN
- 9 Geoff HORSFIELD
- 10 Bryan HUGHES
- 11 Stan LAZARIDIS
- 13 Graham HYDE
- 14 Curtis WOODHOUSE
- 15 Jerry GILL
- 16 Tommy MOONEY
- 17 Michael JOHNSON
- 18 Nico VAESEN
- 19 Andrew JOHNSON
- 20 Tom WILLIAMS
- 21 Tresor LUNTALA
- 22 Damien JOHNSON
- 23 Chris WARD
- 24 Dele ADEBOLA
- 25 Paul Furlong
- 26 Olivier TEBILY
- 28 Jonathan HUTCHINSON
- 29 Clint DAVIS
- 32 Neil BARNES
- 33 Darren CARTER
- 34 Craig FAGAN
- 35 Steve VICKERS
- 36 Jeff KENNA
- 37 Paul DEVLIN

NORWICH CITY

- 1 Robert GREEN
- 2 Brian McGOVERN
- 3 Adam DRURY
- 4 Malky MACKAY
- 5 Craig FLEMING
- 6 David NIELSEN
- 7 Philip MULRYNE
- 8 Gary HOLT
- 9 Iwan ROBERTS
- 10 Zema ABBEY
- 11 Chris LLEWELLYN
- 12 Darel RUSSELL
- 13 Arran LEE-BARRETT
- 14 Alex NOTMAN
- 15 Darren KENTON
- 16 Steen NEDERGAARD
- 17 Daryl SUTCH
- 18 Paul McVEIGH
- 19 Marc LIBBRA
- 20 Gaetano GIALLANZA
- 22 Ian HENDERSON
- 23 Neil EMBLEN
- 24 Clint EASTON
- 25 Lewis BLOIS
- 26 Danny BLOOMFIELD
- 27 Mark RIVERS
- 28 Paul CRICHTON
- 29 Andy OXBY
- 30 Paul HAYES

OFFICIALS

REFEREE	REFEREE'S ASSISTANTS	FOURTH OFFICIAL
G Barber (Hertfordshire)	D Richards (Carmarthenshire)	P Dowd (Staffordshire)
	M Tingey (Buckinghamshire)	

 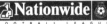 NATIONWIDE FOOTBALL LEAGUE

Team line ups.

The best chances, however, both fell to Blues and Olivier Tebily. Two minutes into the half, his header was cleared off the line by Drury, and four minutes from the end his snap shot from eight yards just cleared the crossbar. At the other end a timely interception from Jeff Kenna stopped the ball running to Norwich substitute Roberts, which presented him with a real goal opportunity. Roberts soon got his chance to hit the target, and Norwich took the lead 43 seconds into extra-time. Grainger badly misjudged a pass to Notman on the right, and from his beautifully flighted cross Roberts rose unmarked in the area to steer his header into the bottom corner of the net. Blues battled back, and Norwich frantically defended for 12 minutes before they finally gave in to a well-deserved equaliser from Horsfield's header after a great knock down from John. Blues continued to stream forward looking for a winner, and with three minutes of extra-time remaining Michael Johnson almost snatched a dramatic winning goal, but his headed effort struck the bottom of the post.

So the result of the game rested on the outcome of a penalty shoot-out, and Blues were given the early boost of winning the toss. They would take their penalties in front of their own 33,000 fans, but they also wanted to avoid the goal where they lost the shoot out against Liverpool in the Worthington Cup Final.

Paul Devlin recalls:
'This was my most memorable game. Taking my penalty was the worst experience of my life. In fairness, those of us who were nominated penalty takers had practised, but it does not prepare you for the emotional aspects. In my mind all I could think of was, "Don't let me be the one to miss". I had a further problem because I was suffering from cramp and therefore could not take the long run up I usually take. I just blasted it; when it went in there was no joy, it was just pure relief. The next three to four days were something of a blur, as we shared a few "shandies" to celebrate!'

PAUL JOHN DEVLIN
Forward
101 + 22 appearances, 37 goals.

Brummie 'Devs' was born in 1972 but did not join Blues until February 1996 after time at Stafford Rangers and Notts County. He was another all-action player with a big heart who endeared himself to the St Andrew's faithful. He was transferred to Sheffield United for £200,000 in March 1998 and spent loan spells at Notts County and Blues before rejoining permanently in July 2002 for £200,000. He was selected for Scotland's full international squad in October 2002, making his international debut in a friendly against Canada, going on to make 10 appearances. He joined Watford for £150,000 in September 2003 before moving to Walsall on a free transfer in January 2006. He is still playing on in non-League circles as he fast approaches 40 years of age.

PENALTY SHOOT-OUT

No.	Player	Team	Score	
1	Roberts	Norwich	1–0	
2	John	Blues	1–1	
3	Mulryne	Norwich	1–1	Missed
4	Devlin	Blues	2–1	
5	Sutch	Norwich	2–1	Missed
6	Lazaridis	Blues	3–1	
7	Easton	Norwich	3–2	
8	Carter	Blues	4–2	

AN INTERVIEW WITH 'DEVS' WHICH APPEARED IN THE JANUARY 2008 EDITION OF THE BLUES MAGAZINE

I was one bite into a bacon sandwich in the Gordon Blue café in the Jewellery Quarter when Paul arrived for our interview, desperate for the toilet and 'a white coffee with sugar' in that order. His coffee is served in an England mug that is something of a disappointment for a man who won full international honours for the Auld Enemy.

'Devs' was born in Dudley Road Hospital, Birmingham, and he grew up in Erdington, where his parents still live. His football at school was 'sparse', impacted by the industrial actions of teachers, only playing in his first and last year at senior school. He played his football for local teams and never thought he would have a career in football. 'I trained as a chef when I left school, working at what was the Post House at Great Barr. I got my first pass for City and Guilds and really enjoyed it. I was playing for various Sunday teams and progressed to Boldmere St Michaels, Paget Rangers, Tamworth and the like before I joined Armitage 90, which was run by a pal of mine, Joe Nugent. It was there that my football career kicked off at the age of 19 without having previously attracted the attention of the scouts of the big local professional clubs. I went to Stafford Rangers in the

Conference, Chris Wright signed me for about two grand, a kit and a friendly. I was there for less than a year when Notts County paid £40,000, and I met my best friend in football, Michael Johnson.'

Paul played 168 + 12 games for County during his four-year stay, scoring 31 goals before gaining the move he was 'desperate for'. Paul's father was Scottish and a big Glasgow Celtic supporter, so it was therefore inevitable that 'Devs' would follow in his footsteps, but he had an uncle who took him as a lad to St Andrew's: 'my first game was to see the Blues, so I have followed them ever since. It was great when Barry Fry signed Andy Legg and me for a combined fee of £500,000, and I was going to the Blues, because as well as achieving a boyhood ambition I was back as a teammate of Michael Johnson, who had joined Blues earlier.'

WHO WERE THE CHARACTERS AT BLUES?

'Obviously Johnno, but Benno [Ian Bennett] was a great lad, as were Jonathan Hunt and Gary Breen. The trouble was there were 40 of us in the squad, so it was hard to remember them all. I owe Barry a great debt of thanks for signing me for Blues, because for Bluenoses like me, Taity [Paul Tait] and Hoppy [Robert Hopkins], it is a fantastic thing to play for your team. You have such great empathy with the fans! Barry is, I think, one of the great characters in football.'

WHAT DO YOU REMEMBER OF YOUR DEBUT?

'Not a lot, but it was a televised game at home to Sunderland. But I really remember my second game, it was a night match at St Andrew's, it was a fantastic atmosphere and we won 2—0. I got both goals, one of which was a penalty. When Barry signed me he had asked me if I could score penalties as Blues had missed the last 12 or so they had been awarded. I said "Yes, I just blast them" so it was great to break that hoodoo so quickly.'

WHAT BROUGHT ABOUT YOUR MOVE TO SHEFFIELD UNITED?

'Under Barry I scored something like eight goals in 15 games and was playing really well, but when Trevor Francis was appointed manager it became clear fairly early on that he didn't rate me. Every opportunity he had to either drop me or substitute me, he took. I think he would have liked to have got rid of me, but he had a problem because in that first season I was top scorer and the fans' Player of the Season. In this spell I played 72 games plus 17 as substitute and scored 34 goals, which is virtually one goal in every two games. It was obvious my contract would not be renewed, so in March 1998 Steve Thompson signed me for Sheffield United. He wasn't there long before a new player-manager was appointed, Steve Bruce! It was his first managerial appointment.'

HOW DID YOU GET ON WITH STEVE?

'He's a top bloke. I was really sorry to see the way it ended for him at the Blues. He gave me one piece of advice that I still follow: it was a night match at Sheffield against Sunderland. Steve and I had both played, and we'd lost 0—4. Michael Bridge had scored a hat-trick, and Steve was devastated. Here was a bloke who had won everything with Manchester United and yet this defeat hurt him, and obviously time was running out for him as a player. He told me that night to "play for as long as you can". I have remembered that ever since, which is why I am still playing non-League and charity games at the age of 35! Steve has been a big influence on my career in so many ways. He loaned me to his pal, Sam Allardyce, when he was manager at Notts County because at Sheffield the two strikers were Dean Saunders and Graham Stuart, and I was not going to play, so

I got five games during November and December 1998. Neil Warnock took over from Steve, when he went to Crystal Palace, and offered me a four-year contract, but I refused it as I had heard that Steve might want me at Selhurst Park. As we know, Steve did not last too long at Palace, and his move to Blues was blocked, but I knew that as soon as he was released from "garden leave" I would be in his thoughts.'

SO YOUR SECOND SPELL AT BLUES BEGAN?
'Yes, I went on loan from Sheffield in February 2002, and played 12 + 2 games, before signing permanently in May for £200,000.'

WHAT WAS YOUR MOST MEMORABLE GOAL?
'I got the first Premiership goal at St Andrew's, which was against a high-flying Leeds United. We won 2−1, and I scored the first with Damien Johnson getting the second. I had been sent off in a pre-season friendly, so I missed the first three games, but as soon as I was available the boss put me in, and I rewarded him with a goal. That's a piece of history no one can take away from me, unlike my fastest goal record of 16 seconds against Luton − Bryan Hughes holds the record now with 12 seconds!'

WHAT WAS YOUR FUNNIEST MOMENT?
'There have been so many. My mate Johnno has the worst dress sense ever, which always raises a laugh, particularly when he wore a blue pinstripe jacket with brown trousers.'

'I roomed with Robbie Savage, and it was always the case that "Sav" went to the room first. When I went in he would jump on me from either the wardrobe or the shower and we would fight. It was just like Kato and Clousseau in the *Pink Panther* movies. I would always win and enjoyed choking him into submission.'

TELL ME ABOUT YOUR TIME WITH SCOTLAND?
'Prior to that I could have played for Mick McCarthy's first Republic of Ireland squad. Barry told me he was interested in me, but when I spoke to him he explained that FIFA had changed the eligibility rules and you could only go back to your grandparents, not great-grandparents. This change of rule meant my Irish connections were invalid, so I had to wait another 10 years before I got international recognition.'

'"Sav" predicted I would be "a one-cap wonder", but I proved him wrong (once again), and after making my debut on the bench against Iceland my first action was in a friendly against Canada.'

'Although the Division One Play-Off was my most memorable game, it is run a very close second by a European Championship qualifier against Germany at Hampden Park. The emotion you feel when the "Tartan Army" fills the ground and starts singing...you have a lump in your throat and a tear in your eye, it's exceptional. The "Tartan Army" is a special breed; there is never any nastiness.'

WHAT WAS THE PREMIERSHIP LIKE?
'In terms of pace and the physical side of the game, the Championship is quicker and harder, but in the Premier League you are playing against much better players who are clinical in their approach to the game. You get fewer chances to score as a striker, and any mistakes are invariably punished.'

HOW DID YOUR CAREER END AT BLUES?
'I had two years of my contract to go, but I was in and out of the team, not playing regularly, so when Ray Lewington of Watford offered me a three-year deal I accepted it. I had just over two years at Vicarage Road, playing 83 + 5 and scoring six goals.'

WHAT HAPPENED AFTER THAT?
'I let my heart rule my head when I moved to Walsall in 2006. I wanted to get back to the Midlands and Paul Merson wanted me. He left soon after to be replaced by my pal, Kevan Broadhurst. I lasted two months before retiring from full-time football on the eve of my 34th birthday after a game against Bournemouth. I wanted to keep on playing (remembering Brucie), so when Gareth Farelly (a pal of mine) was managing Bohemians in Ireland I went over weekly and played eight games. Then I went back to where I started at Tamworth, Sutton before joining my mates Martin O'Connor and Graham Hyde, who at the time were managing at Halesowen.'

ANY OTHER HIGHLIGHTS?
'I've been injury free throughout my career, only suffering from an arthritic toe, so I've been lucky to have no breaks, plus I've made two Wembley appearances, both for Notts County in the Finals of the Anglo-Italian Cup, one of which we won, in 1995.'

HOW DO YOU SPEND YOUR TIME THESE DAYS?
'I have a design and build company that works in the bar/restaurant market. I live with my partner in Walmsley in a house we bought about 10 years ago, where we have had three children: two girls, eight years and 20 months, and a boy aged five. I still play for the Birmingham City All-Stars with Tom Ross.'

The First Derby in Sixteen Years

BLUES 3 VILLA 0

Date: 16 September 2002   **Venue:** St Andrew's
Attendance: 20,505   **Referee:** Mr D. Elleray

Blues: Vaessen, Kenna, Purse, Cunningham, Grainger, Devlin (Powell 79), Savage (Hughes 87), Lisse, Johnson, John, Morrison (Horsfield 69).

Villa: Enckelman, Mellberg, Alpay, Staunton, De la Cruz, Kinsella, Johnson, Barry, Samuel, Allback (Vassell 45), Angel (Dublin 45).

It was a night for Peter Enckelman to forget, but Blues' fans will never forget his gaffe and a brilliant result. This was the first League derby since December 1987, and very was eagerly awaited and lived up to all Blues' hopes and expectations.

Before the game had even started, while Steve Bruce kept his own counsel Villa did all the talking, with Olof Mellberg motivating the opposition players by suggesting that he 'didn't know' any Birmingham players. Blues took the lead courtesy of a first-half strike by Clinton Morrison, and Enckelman allowed a throw-in by Olof Mellberg to slip under his studs and roll into the goal which doubled the lead for Steve Bruce's men at a critical time and set Blues up for Geoff Horsfield to score a third.

It was a typical derby – open and passionate – and one that saw Blues take the spoils. Villa had their patches of good play but, in the final analysis, they were found wanting when events required composure. Villa had only conceded three goals in their previous five games, so a 3–0 defeat was totally unexpected. In a very keenly contested game Darren Purse set the tempo with an outrageous tackle on Juan-Pablo Angel which almost took off his kneecap. David Elleray, who owed Blues one for that non-penalty in the Worthington Cup Final, let play go, and Villa knew they were in for a difficult time.

Blues were more direct and confident. It was inevitable, then, that they should take the lead. In the 31st minute, Jeff Kenna hooked the ball towards the penalty spot and, with Villa's offside trap breached, Robbie Savage was able to touch the ball to Morrison whose right-footed shot beat Enckelman. Darius Vassell thought he had equalised in the 57th minute, but while his volley beat Nico Vaesen the Villa striker was ruled offside. Villa boss Graham Taylor did not agree, however, and the lengthy argument with the official resulted in an official rebuke from Elleray, the Middlesex-based referee who had yet to endear himself to the Villa faithful.

And then, in the 74th minute, came one of the most bizarre goals seen at St Andrew's. Mellberg threw the ball back to Enckelman, who inexplicably allowed the ball to bobble under his boot and trickle into the goal. While Enckelman suffered the humiliation, it was

PLAYER FACTFILE

CLINTON HUBERT MORRISON
Striker
87 appearances, 14 goals

Clint was born on 14 May 1979 in London. He initially made his name as a player for Crystal Palace, making his debut on 10 May 1998 as an 82nd-minute substitute, capping his performance with an injury-time winner over opponents Sheffield Wednesday. The next season, his first full year-long tenure at the club, was packed with 13 goals, turning Morrison into a light among the darkness for a team who were struggling both on and off the pitch. While Palace were in administration, Morrison agreed to play for the club for free. Fourteen goals during 1999–2000 continued this reputation, as he played more than 30 games and scored 14 goals. His 2000–01 season gave him 14 goals, but he really made a mark the following year with 26 goals, and a move to Premiership side Blues capped his season perfectly. This year also saw his debut for the Republic of Ireland against Croatia, a 2–2 draw on 15 August 2001, in which Morrison entered the game at 53 minutes and scored the second Ireland goal. He also travelled to the 2002 World Cup, but did not participate. He joined Blues in a total deal of £4.25 million, with Andrew Johnson moving in the opposite direction; however, Morrison struggled somewhat in the top League, scoring only six goals in his first season and four goals in his second. Due to pressure for first-team places, Morrison left Birmingham on 24 August 2005. Palace agreed a £2 million fee for the 26-year-old, which resulted in a return to scoring form, with 13 goals in 33 starts and eight substitute appearances. He signed a two-year deal with Coventry City on 7 August 2008.

ironic that the 'mouthy' Mellberg was also involved. There was a minute of confusion when a number of players from each team surrounded Elleray, but the conclusion was inevitable. Blues were 2–0 ahead.

From Villa's point of view, the third goal was also self-inflicted. Alpay Ozalan lost the ball 18 yards from his goal and allowed Horsfield, a substitute, to beat the Villa keeper with a low shot from 10 yards. With Blues 3–0 up and the ground vibrating to the anti-Villa song, *S**T ON THE VILLA!*, the feeling from the players was very much to let Mellberg know something like 'You know who we are now, don't you, you so-and so!'

Game Forty-four

Double Over Villa in the Premiership

VILLA 0 BLUES 2

Date: 3 March 2003   **Venue:** Villa Park
Attendance: 42,602

Blues: Vaessen, Kenna, Cunningham, Upson, Clapham, Johnson, Savage (Carter 83), Clemence, Lazaridis (Devlin 76), Dugarry, Morrison (Horsfield 72).
Substitutes, unused: Bennett, John.

Villa: Enkelman, Samuel, Johnsen, Mellberg, Wright (Crouch 90), Gudjonsson, Hendrie, Barry, Vassell, Dublin, Moore (Hadji 45).
Substitutes, unused: Hitzlsperger, Edwards, Postma.
Bookings: Cunningham and Devlin (Blues), Gudjonsson (Villa). **Sendings off:** Dublin and Gudjonsson.

With a 3–0 home win already under the Blues' belt, the Bluenoses were ready for one of the rare doubles over their local neighbours, as it was 25 years since it had last been achieved.

Blues had to wait until the 74th minute for the first goal. From a throw-in on the right, deep into the Villa half, Dugarry and Clemence managed to work the ball through to Kenna. Kenna turned Alan right in front of the Holte End and sent a perfect cross flashing past Enkelman's goal. Horsfield missed on the near post, but Lazaridis was there at the far post, ahead of the sleeping Samuel, to head the ball home from a yard out.

Against 10-man Villa, Blues were not to be denied and secured the three points three minutes later when Savage's forward header was met by the retreating J. Loyd Samuel but, under pressure from Horsfield, his attempted back header was too weak, allowing the sub striker to nick the ball past the hesitant Enkelman before tapping into an empty net.

DARREN CARTER
Midfielder
32+21 appearances, 5 goals

Brummie Darren played for the England Under-20 international team before making his debut for Blues as a 19-year-old during season 2001–02. After a short loan period with Sunderland he was transferred to West Bromwich Albion for £1.5 million in the summer of 2005. In August 2007 he joined Preston North End for £750,000.

Game Forty-five

Dugarry's Day

BLUES 3 SOUTHAMPTON 2

Date: 21 April 2003   **Venue:** St Andrew's
Attendance: 29,115

Blues: Bennett, Kenna (Devlin 64), Cunningham, Upson, Clapham, Johnson (John 79), Savage, Clemence (Lazaridis 54), Hughes, Horsfield, Dugarry.
Substitutes, unused: Purse, Marriott.

Southampton: Jones, Telfer (Tessem 85), Lundekvam, M. Svensson, Bridge, Fernandes (Higginbotham 76), Oakley, A. Svensson, Prutton, Beattie, Delap (Ormerod 45).
Substitutes, unused: Williams, Blayney.
Bookings: Bridge, Telfer.

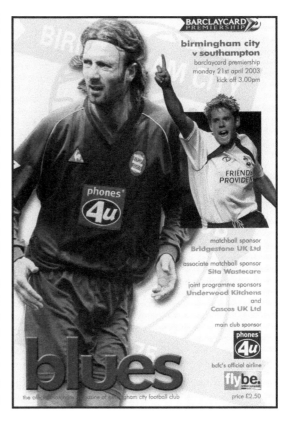

The threat of relegation hung over the Blues when they went into this home fixture against the FA Cup finalists, Southampton, and they were worrying times. Had the Blues fans known the result prior to the game, however, then they need not have worried because Christophe Dugarry was in the side. The former French international striker, a World Cup winner with France five years before, was so good on the day that even the Southampton supporters would come to applaud him.

Many older Bluenoses considered this to be the best individual performance by a Blues player at St Andrew's, since Eddie Brown in the 1950s and Trevor Francis in the 1970s, but even they would have struggled to achieve the quality of performance that

CHRISTOPHE JEROME DUGARRY
Striker
30 appearances, 6 goals

Frenchman Dugarry played 55 times for his country, scoring eight goals. He was born in Bordeaux on 24 March 1972, signing as a professional for his home-town club in 1989. While at Bordeaux they won the French Second Division Championship in 1992 and got to the UEFA Cup Final in 1996. He had a season at AC Milan before joining Barcelona in June 1997 and returning to France with Olympique Marseille in January 1998. While at Barcelona he won the Spanish League Championship in 1998. He rejoined Bordeaux in October 1999 after winning the World Cup with France the previous year (1998). In 2000 he won the European Championship with France and the Confederations Cup in 2001, while he gained a League Cup-winners' medal with Bordeaux in 2002. The 2003 season brought his unexpected move to the Blues, who were struggling in the Premiership. This led to a brief 'golden period' for both parties that was demonstrative of Dugarry's true value as a player. His scoring rate per game was not much better than his average at any level, although an impressive run of five goals in five games cemented the club's Premiership status. Most astonishing, however, was his effect on the players around him. When Dugarry played well, the team played above itself with flair and style. In particular, the archetypal English centre-forward Geoff Horsfield added new movement and ball skills to his repertoire, at odds with his hard-man image. Watching a football club totally transformed, it was easy to see why he had held his place in the French national side for so long. It also seemed that Dugarry had never been so loved in his career. The more the crowd chanted his name (Du-du-du-garry), the better he played. He joined Qatar in 2004 and retired on 1 February 2005.

Dugarry achieved on this afternoon in 2003. Dugarry scored twice, but his inspiration was such that his teammates, 10 professional footballers in their own right, were demoted to the role of bit-part players. He was the critical factor, if had not been in the team then Blues may well have endured relegation.

The Saints took the lead against the run of play as Swedish midfielder Svensson raced on to Beattie's pass and clipped the ball passed the advancing Ian Bennett. Dugarry equalised in the 75th minute after Damien Johnson had been fouled. From 25 yards out the Frenchman's free-kick struck the wall but was ordered to be re-taken by referee Bennett. With his second attempt, Dugarry curled the ball around the wall and past the dive of Jones into the bottom corner of the net.

Brett Ormerod restored Southampton's lead two minutes later when he latched on to Svensson's flick before firing a bullet-like shot into the top-left-hand corner of the net. Bryan Hughes restored the score to 2–2. Horsfield broke clear and picked out Hughes, who tucked the ball past Jones. Just when the Blues thought it could not get any better, substitute Stern John produced a superb cross from the corner flag, and the Frenchman was on hand to head a vital winner past Jones, sending St Andrew's into delirium. Stern John as a late substitute helped Blues and gave freedom to Dugarry. In the end Blues avoided relegation with relative ease. What the fans did not know then was that Dugarry would never again be as effective for City.

Colin Tattum remembers:
'Dugarry even had referee Steve Bennett eating out of his hand. Bennett tried to bring Dugarry to heel after a foul, but the forward simply shrugged and ambled away, back turned. Several sharp blasts on his whistle to no avail, Bennett actually made up the 20 or so yards to Dugarry. Priceless. Afterwards, Saints boss Gordon Strachan accepted that Dugarry was magical and quipped: "I've just gone past the referee's dressing room, and he was there giving Dugarry a rub down!"'

100 Years at St Andrew's

BLUES 2 QUEEN'S PARK RANGERS 1

Date: 26 December 2006   **Venue:** St Andrew's
Attendance: 32,000

Blues: Taylor, Kelly, Sadler, Jaidi, Upson (Larsson 89), Johnson, Nafti, Clemence, McSheffrey, Campbell (Jerome 59, Muamba 89), Bendtner.

Queen's Park Rangers: Royce, Rehman, Stewart, Mancienne, Milanese (Rowlands 76), Smith, Bircham, Cook (Bailey 59), Bignot, Furlong, Blackstock (Jones 81).

The gypsy's curse might have been lifted, but it was ex-Villain John Gregory who so nearly put a new hex on Blues' house. A sell-out holiday crowd came to watch the table-toppers and celebrate the St Andrew's centenary. It was a fun-filled atmosphere with stilt-walkers, fire-eaters, jugglers, face painting and a stirring pre-match rendition of *Keep Right On* by a female soloist. Why, you even thought Queen's Park Rangers had entered into the spirit of things, as war-horse Paul Furlong, who was knocking on 40, got a run. And, according to legend, the curse placed on Blues by travellers who had to be removed from the site in order to build the ground in 1906 would be no more.

The trouble was, Queen's Park Rangers came with a plan and left having given Blues a different kind of heebie-jeebies. They played with three centre-halves and another, Zesh Rehman, as a deep-lying right wing-back. The territory on the other side was patrolled by ex-Blue Marcus Bignot, giving Queen's Park Rangers a resolute look. And they even made Blues kick towards the Tilton Road from the kick-off.

Although Queen's Park Rangers lived on their nerves at times, and Blues were wasteful of good opportunities, it seemed as if they were going to frustrate and poop the party. It took substitute Jerome's first Championship goal on home soil to provide Blues with another victory, their 11th in 13 League outings, after some quick interplay created a hole that Queen's Park Rangers could not plug. It was not classic viewing, nor was it irresistible stuff from Blues, but, as so often that season, they did enough and got the job done.

Midway through the first half Blues took the lead through Matthew Upson's towering header. Probably never in St Andrew's history has one been put away with such precision and power. Upson galloped towards Gary McSheffrey's inviting free-kick from the left, soared above all and sundry and sent it into the top corner. Stunning. It was not, however, the key to unlocking the vault of goals Blues had so bountifully plundered in their recent games. Queen's Park Rangers were level 10 minutes later when Lee Cook

Team Sheet 2006/07

Birmingham City Football Club

COCA-COLA F.L. CHAMPIONSHIP
Tuesday 26th December 2006, QPR, k/o 3pm

BIRMINGHAM CITY **QPR**

	BIRMINGHAM CITY			QPR
1.	Maik TAYLOR (gk)		1.	Simon ROYCE (gk)
2.	Stephen KELLY		2.	Marcus BIGNOT 'C'
24.	Radhi JAIDI		3.	Mauro MILANESE
5.	Matthew UPSON		5.	Zesh REHMAN
3.	Mat SADLER		8.	Marc BIRCHAM
12.	Mehdi NAFTI		17.	Lee COOK
22.	Damien JOHNSON 'C'		25.	Damion STEWART
6.	Stephen CLEMENCE		29.	Paul FURLONG
28.	Gary McSHEFFREY		32.	Dexter BLACKSTOCK
27.	Nicklas BENDTNER		37.	Jimmy SMITH
14.	DJ CAMPBELL		38.	Michael MANCIENNE

Substitutes From

Substitutes From

	Substitutes From			Substitutes From
13.	Colin DOYLE (gk)		12.	Jake COLE (gk)
7.	Sebastian LARSSON		9.	Nick WARD
26.	Fabrice MUAMBA		14.	Martin ROWLANDS
17.	Neil DANNS		23.	Stefan BAILEY
10.	Cameron JEROME		31.	Ray JONES

Today's Match Officials

Referee	K. Friend (Leics)
Assistant Referee (Red/Yellow flag)	I. Evans (W'hampton)
Assistant Referee (Yellow flag)	R. Smith (W. Mids)
Fourth Official	W. Barratt (Worcs)

TODAY'S MATCH SPONSERS ARE BRMB

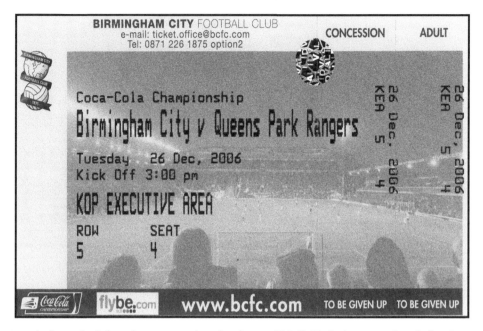

cut in from the left and sent a curving shot beyond Maik Taylor's grasp, via a deflection. Simon Royce made an acrobatic stop from a long-range effort by DJ Campbell, and Stephen Clemence was inches away from turning in Damien Johnson's ball back across the goal.

Allied to Nicklas Bendtner's failure to beat Royce when clean through in the 14th minute, it was an unsatisfactory opening period for Blues. Matters continued in the same vein early in the second half when Campbell got his feet in a twist with the goal at his mercy after McSheffrey wriggled through near the byline. Jerome entered the fray, replacing Campbell, and within two minutes had collected Blues' second goal, and ultimately the winner. Bendtner steered the ball behind Queen's Park Rangers's flat-footed defence to McSheffrey, who drew Royce to the right of the penalty area and squared for Jerome to tap-in.

The move came about due to Jerome's introduction as well. He chased down a through-ball that Royce, on the dodgy pitch, knowing the forward's rapid speed, could only hoist high and 30 yards, allowing Mehdi Nafti to nod it to Bendtner, who, in turn, waited for the runners ahead. Blues should have made it safe four minutes later when Radhi Jaidi stole in unmarked to a McSheffrey free-kick, only to glance a diving header wide.

Blues had to negotiate six nervy minutes of stoppage time without defensive rock Upson, who had been substituted, but they emerged to dig out another win and extend their lead at the Championship summit. It was a fitting way to celebrate a 100th anniversary.

MATTHEW JAMES UPSON
Defender
113 appearances, 5 goals

Matt Upson was born on 18 April 1979 in Hartismere, Suffolk. He joined Luton Town as a trainee in 1994, signing professional forms in April 1996. He only made one appearance for the Hatters in the following August against Rotherham United.

He joined Arsenal in May 1997 in a £2 million deal; however, faced with the longevity of Arsenal's existing centre-backs, Tony Adams, Steve Bould and Martin Keown, and struck by injury problems of his own, Upson rarely had a chance to break into the first team. After spending a year out of the game recovering from an anterior cruciate ligament injury sustained in 1999, Upson made only a handful of first-team appearances for Arsenal, in between loan spells at Nottingham Forest and Crystal Palace in 2000 and 2001 respectively. In his final full season at Arsenal, however, Upson did make 22 appearances; these included 14 in the League, earning him a Premier League winners' medal, but a broken leg in February 2002 ruled him out for the rest of the season and Arsenal's FA Cup-winning run as they won the double. After recovering from his broken leg, Upson joined Reading in September 2002 on a three-month loan. In total he played 56 times for Arsenal, never scoring. Birmingham City completed the signing of Upson from Arsenal in January 2003, for a fee of £1 million, rising to £3 million depending on appearances. He suffered a leg injury while preparing for the local derby against Villa in April 2006 and subsequently missed the rest of the season as Birmingham City were relegated. Upson remained with the club while he worked on regaining his fitness. On 18 January 2007 Birmingham rejected West Ham United's bid for Upson of £4 million, also rejecting an improved bid of £6 million a few days later. An offer of £6 million, with the potential to rise to £7.5 million depending on appearances, was accepted on the last day of the transfer window, and he agreed a four-and-a-half-year contract with West Ham; however, Upson suffered a calf injury less than 30 minutes into his West Ham United debut against Aston Villa.

Upson completed his first full game for West Ham in August 2007. One week later he made his first appearance as West Ham captain in the 1–0 away win against former club Birmingham City.

He won 12 caps for the England Under-21 team and scored two goals. His performances for Birmingham City led to his selection for the England senior squad, and he made his debut against South Africa in May 2003. He won seven full caps while a Birmingham player.

FA Cup Magic on TV

NEWCASTLE 1 BLUES 5

Date: 17 January 2007   **Venue:** St James' Park
Attendance: 26,099   **Ref:** P. Walton (Northamptonshire)

Blues: Maik Taylor, N'Gotty, Martin Taylor, Upson, Sadler, McSheffrey (Kilkenny 88), Larsson (Danns 86), Muamba (Nafti 82), Johnson, Campbell, Jerome.
Substitutes, unused: Doyle, Gray.

Newcastle: Given, Solano, Taylor, Ramage, Huntington, Milner, Dyer, Butt, Pattison (O'Brien 57), Sibierski (Carroll 80), Martins.
Substitutes, unused: Harper, Edgar, LuaLua.
Sendings off: Taylor (58).
Bookings: Taylor.

In April 2006 a stunned St Andrew's crowd had watched a goalless draw with Newcastle United confirm relegation back to the Championship. Because of Portsmouth's result on that day, the final game of the season a week later would prove meaningless – the 'yo-yo' club were down!

Many Bluenoses would like to think that the result achieved on this night was born out of revenge, but whether that was the motivation of the team or not, the fans certainly took this drubbing of the Magpies as sweet retribution.

Blues were performing well in the Championship, but as the fans arrived at St James' Park not even the staunchest Bluenose could have predicted the way the night would end. Look at the facts – Blues had a recent poor record in the FA Cup, were not great away from home, were up against a side doing well in the top tier of English football and the match was televised! No one has done the analysis, but from memory fans know the Blues have a tendenct to 'freeze' when the cameras roll.

So it was that when McSheffrey opened the scoring after five minutes by picking up Larsson's whipped cross to the back post and

DUDLEY JUNIOR CAMPBELL
Striker
43 appearances, 9 goals

'DJ' was born on 12 November 1981 in London. He had an unsuccessful trainee period with Aston Villa and was not offered a professional contract. In 2000 he moved into non-League football with Isthmian League Premier Division club Chesham United, scoring 16 goals in 29 League appearances. On 20 May 2001 he signed for Conference National League club Stevenage Borough. In two years at the club he made 23 League appearances, scoring three goals. In August 2002 Campbell was placed on the transfer list at his own request in order to gain regular first-team football, with the club chairman, Phil Wallace, saying: 'He's a very talented lad, and has every chance of playing higher so we won't let him go unless the terms are right for us.' In September 2002 he was loaned to Billericay Town, then on 4 February 2003 he moved to Yeading on a free transfer, where he had a hugely successful spell, scoring 83 goals in a total of 109 appearances in all competitions. He helped the club win promotion as champions of Division One North in the 2002–03 season. Later that season he won the Isthmian League Premier Division Championship with Yeading. At the end of the season, on 7 June, he signed for Brentford for £5,000 on a one-year contract with an option to extend it. On 28 January 2006 Campbell scored two goals to lead Brentford to a 2–1 victory over Sunderland in the fourth round of the FA Cup. He made a total of 28 appearances for Brentford, scoring 12 times, in his seven months at the club.

Three days later, Campbell was sold to Blues for £500,000, signing a three-and-half year contract. He made his Premier League debut as a substitute on 4 February 2006, playing the final 20 minutes in a 2–0 defeat to Arsenal. The club were relegated at the end of the season and Campbell scored his first goal for them in a 2–1 win over Colchester United on 5 August 2006. On 25 November he scored with his first touch of the ball after coming on as an 82nd-minute substitute to give Blues a 2–1 win over Burnley. Campbell started 20 games for Blues that season, scoring 12 goals in all competitions as they were promoted back to the Premier League.

On 20 July 2007, Campbell signed a four-year contract with Championship club Leicester City for an initial fee of £1.6 million. Ian Holloway, then manager of Plymouth Argyle, described the fee as 'absolute madness'. Unfortunately for DJ, Holloway was appointed manager of Leicester three months later. In the 2007–08 season, Campbell scored only four League goals. Leicester were relegated at the end of the season after Campbell had made a total of 32 appearances. After struggling to get a regular place in the first team, on 8 January 2009 Campbell signed for Blackpool on loan until the end of the season. He scored on his debut for them and then again on his home debut against Blues. After the match, Campbell said, 'I'd be lying if I said it didn't mean a lot more scoring against Birmingham. I love Birmingham. They are in my heart. I played for them for two years and had good times there. As you saw, their fans [who chanted Campbell's name at one point] haven't forgotten me which means a lot to me. But right now I am at Blackpool, and I am delighted that we got the three points, and I'm happy for the club because we deserved it.' Campbell has played for the England National Game XI (now known as England C) – the national team that represents England at non-League level.

slotting home, everyone felt it was just a case of Seb and Gary not reading the script, after all was this not the same Newcastle United team that had visited White Hart Lane the previous Sunday and beaten Tottenham Hotspur 3–2!

The good news for the Blues was that, while these were the same 11 players, this was a very disappointing performance from the home side, whose shots on goal in the first half could be counted on the fingers of one hand, so there was no surprise when on the stroke of half-time Cameron Jerome's break down the right and cross into the box resulted in Solano beating his own goalkeeper, Given, with ease. Half-time: Newcastle 0 Blues 2 – game on!

Everyone thought that the home side could not be as poor in the second half, and so it seemed when Milner pulled a goal back with a terrific strike from well outside the penalty area. Three minutes later, disaster struck for the surprisingly small crowd of just over 26,000. Instead of being on the cusp of a revival, the home side committed football suicide when Steven Taylor was given a straight red card for his tripping of the lively D.J. Campbell. The resultant free-kick on the edge of the 18-yard line fell to Bruno N'Gotty, who volleyed the ball into the top corner of Given's net.

The combination of being down to 10 men and losing 3–1 further dispirited the home side, and with the 'black-and-white' faithful leaving the ground in droves Blues scored their fourth and fifth goals on 83 and 89 minutes, the scorers being Larsson and Campbell respectively. The statistics showed that Blues had converted five out of 11 shots on the target, and that this was Newcastle's worst home defeat in the FA Cup since Sheffield United beat them 5–0 in 1914.

The goals:
5 minutes: 0–1 Larsson whipped in a ball to the back post, and Gary McSheffrey cut inside and calmly shot home.

45 minutes: 0–2 Jerome burst down the right, and his ball across the six-yard box was pushed past his own 'keeper by Solano under pressure from D.J. Campbell.

56 minutes: 1–2 James Milner gave the home side a glimmer of hope with a terrific 30-yard strike.

59 minutes: 1–3 A Blues free-kick on the edge of the area – after Stephen Taylor was red carded for tripping Campbell – fell to Bruno N'Gotty, whose right-footed half-volley found the top corner.

83 minutes: 1–4 A through ball from Jerome set up Larsson, who finished in style.

89 minutes: 1–5 Neil Kilkenny threaded a ball through to Campbell, who sealed a magnificent victory.

From the stats: Blues had 11 shots, all on target!

Return to the Premiership

BLUES 2 SHEFFIELD WEDNESDAY 0

Date: 28 April 2007   **Venue:** St Andrew's
Attendance: 29,317

Blues: Doyle, N'Gotty, Jaidi, Taylor, Kelly, Larsson, Muamba, Clemence, McSheffrey (Nafti), Cole (Vine), Bendtner (Jerome).

Sheffield Wednesday: Adamson, Simek (Clarke), Bullen, Wood, Spurr, Tudgay, Lunt, Whelan, Brunt (Johnson), MacLean, Burton.

A nd so it was that St Andrew's welcomed Play-off hopefuls Sheffield Wednesday for the penultimate game of the season. To say the game was full of nerves was an understatement, and at half-time it was goalless.

On 57 minutes things turned against Blues when midfielder Fabrice Muamba was sent off. Down to 10 men, the Bluenoses responded and drove their team forward, and it was no surprise when Jerome scored the opening goal. The match was won by arguably the goal of the season when Larsson ran from the halfway line to fire a shot past 'keeper Chris Adamson in front of the Tilton End. The fans went mad, as did the players, as they formed a human mound on top of Larsson, soon to be joined by the management and staff!

ALFE INGE SEBASTIAN LARSSON
Midfielder
108 appearances, 12 goals *

PLAYER FACTFILE

Seb Larsson was born in Eskilstuna, Sweden, on 6 June 1985. Initially he played for his home team, IFK Eskilstuna, before joining Arsenal at the age of 16. He made his debut against Manchester City on 27 October 2004. He joined Blues on a season-long loan from Arsenal in August 2006, with an option to make the move permanent. At Birmingham he made an immediate impact, scoring late winners in his first few games against Crystal Palace and Shrewsbury Town. At the end of January 2007 he signed permanently for Birmingham City on a four-year deal for £1 million. He made his debut for Sweden in February 2008, in a friendly against Turkey, after playing 21 times for the Under-21 side.
* Up until September 2009.

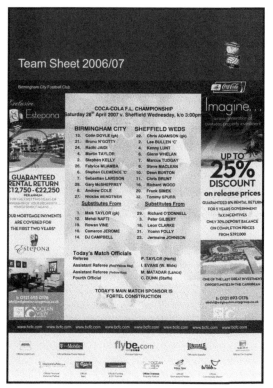

Stephen Clemence recalls:

'As soon as Fabrice got sent off, the fans really, really got going and gave us a lift. They were magnificent. We scored quite early after the sending off, and then that gave us something to hang onto, but I think when the second goal went in, it was like the roof was going to come off the stadium. It was electric. The fans were absolutely unbelievable.'

It was then onto Sunday when Palace played Derby; things were as tense in Birmingham as they were in London, and when Palace won 2–0 with a goal from ex-Blues forward Clinton Morrison that was enough to send Blues back to the Premiership.

Game Forty-nine

Big Eck's First

TOTTENHAM HOTSPUR 2 BLUES 3

Date: 2 December 2007   **Venue:** White Hart Lane
Attendance: 35,635   **Referee:** P. Dowd

Blues: Taylor, Kelly, Ridgewell, Djourou, Schmitz (Parnaby 63), Nafti, Muamba, de Ridder (Forssell 66), Larsson, McSheffrey, (Kapo 77), Jerome.

Tottenham Hotspur: Robinson, Chimbonda, Kaboul (Huddlestone 45), Dawson, Bale (Lee 75), Zokora, Lennon, Keane, Malbranque, Bent (Defoe 45).
Sendings off: Keane.
Bookings: Schmitz.

W ere the Bluenoses sceptical about the recent appointment of Alex McLeish to the job as manager of Birmingham City Football Club? I think the answer was 'Yes', but as always with the Blues' fans it was a case of let us give him a chance and have a reality check: 'Who else could we have attracted to St Andrew's?'

Steve Bruce had left to join Wigan Athletic (hardly a major step up in football terms), allegedly due to the inability of the Blues' board of directors to take appropriate actions after Carson Yeung, a Chinese businessman, had bought just under 20 per cent of the club and had recorded his intention to purchase the club.

So it was an interesting scenario that surrounded the arrival of 'Big Eck' to Birmingham in November 2007, having reputedly trebled his £400,000 salary! Some Brucie supporters may have thought to themselves that if the directors can make decisions like that, what stopped them satisfying the demands of the then incumbent manager?

Still, what had happened was over, and it was a new beginning for the club. But there were genuine concerns that this appointment was a little risky: Alex had no

experience of English football, let alone the Premier League. Having said that, his Scottish managerial time had been spent with Motherwell, Hibernian and Glasgow Rangers during a period of 13 years, and he had had a successful time with the Scottish International team, who just failed to qualify for Euro 2008.

I dare say even Alex would have preferred an easier baptism than a trip to White Hart Lane, but both teams were mid-table and Spurs also had a new manager, with Juande Ramos only being installed two months previous to this game.

The scoring began from the penalty spot when Younes Kaboul conceded the spot-kick for tripping McSheffrey, who picked himself off the turf to convert the penalty and give Blues the lead after 24 minutes. (Author's Note: Kaboul was purchased by Spurs in the Summer of 2007 for £8.2

Barclays Premier League
Sunday 2 December 2007
Kick-Off 4.00pm

Tottenham Hotspur				Birmingham City
1	Paul Robinson (GK)		(GK) Maik Taylor	1
2	Pascal Chimbonda		Stephen Kelly	2
4	Didier Zokora		Rafael Schmitz	5
5	Younes Kaboul		(Capt) Liam Ridgewell	6
9	Dimitar Berbatov		Sebastian Larsson	7
10	Robbie Keane (Capt)		Cameron Jerome	10
15	Steed Malbranque		Gary McSheffrey	11
16	Gareth Bale		Mehdi Nafti	12
20	Michael Dawson		Johan Djourou	16
23	Darren Bent		Daniel De Ridder	20
25	Aaron Lennon		Fabrice Muamba	26

Substitutes   **Substitutes**

12	Radek Cerny (GK)		(GK) Colin Doyle	13
3	Young Pyo Lee		Garry O'Connor	8
17	Kevin Prince Boateng		Mikael Forssell	9
18	Jermain Defoe		Stuart Parnaby	21
22	Tom Huddlestone		Olivier Kapo	23

Referee: Mr P Dowd
Assistant Referee: Mr C Richards
Assistant Referee: Mr P Norman
Fourth Official: Mr U Rennie

TO DARE IS TO DO

million. The Frenchman was substituted at half-time, and it seemed his career was over; he did in fact stay for the whole season, making 23 starts before joining Portsmouth.)

Robbie Keane was in his element against Ridgewell and Djourou and scored in the 50th and 53rd minutes, the first coming from a penalty when Djourou fouled Dimitar Berbatov. When Jerome equalised after 62 minutes it looked like a real contest was about to transpire, and Big Eck had certainly got the Blues more than holding their own; however, the game turned when Keane was sent off after 68 minutes for a two-footed lunge on Fabrice Muamba. To their credit, Spurs kept going and probably deserved a draw on the balance of play, but that was not to be as, with the referee looking at his watch, Larsson dispossessed Berbatov to strike the ball with great pace past the hapless Robinson from more than 30 yards.

This was Blues' first win at White Hart Lane for 24 years and broke a sequence of three defeats for Birmingham, lifting them above Spurs to 12th place in the League.

Statistics:

	Tottenham Hotspur	Birmingham City
Shots (on goal)	19(9)	7(5)
Fouls	9	12
Corners	11	2
Offsides	4	3
Possession	54%	46%
Yellow Cards	0	1
Red Cards	1	0

GARY McSHEFFREY
Midfielder
77 appearances, 20 goals *

Gary was born on 13 August 1982 in Coventry and began his football career at home-town club Coventry City. He made his first-team debut against local rivals Aston Villa at the age of 16 years and 198 days on 27 February 1999 to become the youngest player ever to play in the Premier League, a record he held for four years. During his time at Coventry he spent loan spells at Luton Town, Stockport County and Swedish side IK Brage. In the 2005–06 season McSheffrey ended up among the top scorers in the League, with 15 League goals. It was form like this that brought him to the attention of local rivals Blues during the summer of 2006. After weeks of bidding, Coventry accepted an offer valued at £4 million. The deal was completed on 16 August 2006, and McSheffrey became a Birmingham City player three days after his 24th birthday. He scored his first hat-trick for Blues against Preston North End on 9 December 2006. He converted a penalty in Birmingham's 3–2 win against Tottenham Hotspur to score his first goal in the Premier League. On 5 March 2009 he joined Nottingham Forest on loan and was allocated the number-22 jersey.
* Up until September 2009.

Game Fifty

Promotion to the Premier League

READING 1 BLUES 2

Date: 4 May 2009   **Venue:** Madejski Stadium
Attendance: 24,011   **Referee:** H. Webb (South Yorkshire)

Blues: Taylor (Maik), Carr, Traore, Jaidi, Taylor (Martin), McFadden (Larsson, 66), Johnson, Carsley, Fahey, Phillips (Bouazza, 72), Jerome (O'Connor, 80).

Reading: Hahnemann, Rosenoir, Harding (Doyle, 57), Bikey, Duberry, Tabb, Karacan (Matejovsky, 54), Long, Kitson, Hunt, Kebe.
Bookings: Jaidi, Phillips, Traore.

I am writing this section on the day that Manchester United won the Premier League for the third successive season. This is the second time they have achieved a successive treble of titles – a new record for the Red Devils. On Sunday 3 May 2009 Birmingham City set a unique record – they are the first club to be relegated, promoted, relegated and promoted to and from the Premier League in successive seasons. Birmingham City, therefore, retain the description of being a yo-yo club, which they have maintained throughout their history, as evidenced throughout this book.

After failing to secure the runners'-up spot, and thereby gaining automatic promotion against Preston North End at St Andrew's on 25 April, Blues needed a win the following week, the last game of the season, to ensure promotion to the Premier League.

After the team were booed off against Preston North End, the 2,000 travelling Bluenoses hailed one of the best performances of the season as Blues brushed aside a surprisingly uninspired Reading side to secure top-level football the following season.

If ever a Blues side had put in a performance that was defined by the club anthem, this was it. Brummie Lee Carsley was restored to midfield in place of the erratic Lee Bowyer and regained the captain's armband. He gave a captain's performance, covering every inch of the pitch, and was only robbed of the Man of the Match award by Keith Fahey, who edged the judges' vote by scoring the all-important first goal. Martin Taylor came in for the injured Franck Queudrue and, together with Radhi Jaidi, made up for their lack of natural ability with a rugged determination. They never missed a tackle, and both were in with a shout for the Man of the Match award. Other candidates included Steven Carr, James McFadden and Damien Johnson – it was that sort of game.

THE SEASON'S RESULTS WERE

Date	Result	Scorers
9 August	**Blues** 1 Sheffield United 0	(Phillips)
16 August	Southampton 1 **Blues** 2	(Phillips, O'Connor)
23 August	**Blues** 2 Barnsley 0	(Phillips, O'Connor)
30 August	Norwich 1 **Blues** 1	(Larsson)
13 September	**Blues** 1 Doncaster 0	(Jerome)
16 September	Bristol City 1 **Blues** 2	(Jerome, Larsson)
20 September	**Blues** 0 Blackpool 1	
27 September	Cardiff 1 **Blues** 2	(McFadden, Quincy)
30 September	Derby 1 **Blues** 1	(Quincy)
4 October	**Blues** 1 Queen's Park Rangers 0	(Phillips)
18 October	Burnley 1 **Blues** 1	(Jerome)
21 October	**Blues** 1 Crystal Palace 0	(O'Connor)
25 October	**Blues** 3 Sheffield Wednesday 1	(Phillips, O'Connor (2))
28 October	Queen's Park Rangers 1 **Blues** 0	
3 November	**Blues** 0 Coventry 1	
8 November	Nottingham Forest 1 **Blues** 1	(McFadden)
15 November	**Blues** 3 Charlton 2	(McFadden, Phillips, Queudrue)
21 November	Swansea 2 **Blues** 3	(Bent, Phillips (2))
25 November	**Blues** 2 Ipswich 1	(Ridgewell, Phillips)
29 November	Wolves 1 **Blues** 1	(Jerome)
6 December	**Blues** 3 Watford 2	(Phillips, Bent, Jerome)
9 December	Plymouth 0 **Blues** 1	(Carsley)
13 December	Preston 1 **Blues** 0	
20 December	**Blues** 1 Reading 3	(Phillips)
26 December	Ipswich 0 **Blues** 1	(McFadden)
28 December	**Blues** 0 Swansea 0	
17 January	**Blues** 1 Cardiff 1	(Bowyer)
24 January	Blackpool 2 **Blues** 0	
27 January	**Blues** 1 Derby 0	(Carsley)
31 January	Sheffield Wednesday 1 **Blues** 1	(Phillips)
7 February	**Blues** 1 Burnley 1	(Phillips)
14 February	**Blues** 2 Nottingham Forest 0	(Bent, Fahey)
21 February	Coventry 1 **Blues** 0	
24 February	Crystal Palace 0 **Blues** 0	
1 March	Sheffield United 2 **Blues** 1	(Morgan own-goal)
4 March	**Blues** 1 Bristol City 0	(Queudrue)
7 March	**Blues** 1 Southampton 0	(Fahey)
10 March	Barnsley 1 **Blues** 1	(Taylor Martin)
14 March	Doncaster 0 **Blues** 2	(Jerome, Bouazza)
21 March	**Blues** 1 Norwich 1	(Jerome)
6 April	**Blues** 2 Wolves 0	(Jerome, O'Connor)
11 April	Charlton 0 **Blues** 0	
13 April	**Blues** 1 Plymouth Argyle 1	(Queudrue)
18 April	Watford 0 **Blues** 1	(Jerome)
25 April	**Blues** 1 Preston 2	(Fahey)
3 May	Reading 1 **Blues** 2	(Fahey, Phillips)

The first goal came on 19 minutes from a corner after a teasing run from McFadden. After a clearance at the near post the ball fell to Phillips just outside the penalty area, and his flick found Fahey, who sent in a shot which Marcus Hahnemann got his hands on to but was unable to prevent the ball entering the net. With Blues leading at half-time, Reading came out for the final 45 minutes with their intentions clear, switching to a 3–4–3 formation. Although under pressure, it was Blues who extended their lead through Kevin Phillips in the 60th minute when Fahey returned the compliment by slipping him a delightful through ball. Phillips used all his experience and skill by rolling the ball beyond the 'keeper to score just inside the far post. It was 0–2 and Blues were back in the Premier League with only 30 minutes to go!

As Bluenoses know, Blues never do things the easy way and , within 60 seconds, Reading had pulled a goal back through their substitute Marek Matejovsky before Blues' fans had had time to celebrate Phillips's goal.

While all Bluenoses were thinking 'here we go again', Hameur Bouazza came on for Phillips and Blues reverted to a five-man midfield. It was a nervous period, and it seemed as if Garry O'Connor had sealed things with five minutes to go when, immediately after replacing Cameron Jerome, he got on the end of a Johnson pass and thumped a shot against a post. Reading took heart from this piece of good luck, and from then on they were camped in the Blues' penalty area. With the fans singing *Keep Right On*, the players responded by heading, tackling, harassing, chasing, blocking and giving their all as the clock ticked down until the celebrations could begin.

All Bluenoses would agree that in terms of performances it had been a poor season, but as David Gold said after the game 'In the summer I said "Alex, get us promoted pal." I didn't say how.' But Colin Tattum in the *Evening Mail* echoed the feelings of the fans with his comment 'Little could the chairman have known that McLeish would take him at his word and stretch levels of incredulity, agony and ecstasy to the limit.'

Alex McLeish achieved promotion at the first time of asking and, apart from wanting it achieved with better performances on the pitch, Bluenoses have to say 'he got the job done'. After failing to keep Blues in the Premier League in his first exposure to English football, he was required to perform that almost impossible trick – of reducing the wage bill but retaining sufficient quality to get promoted at the first time of asking. Mikael Forssell, Fabrice Muamba, Olivier Kapo, Daniel De Ridder and Rafeal Schmitz departed, but he was able to persuade the board to keep the jewels in the crown: McFadden and Larsson.

With McFadden and Larsson acting in midfield, the 'spine' of the team was completed by Maik Taylor, Radhi Jaidi, Liam Ridgewell in defence and Cameron Jerome and Garry O'Connor in attack. Major strengthening was required, and apart from Marcus Bent (a forward with the strike rate of a full-back), who could argue with the contributions of Lee Carsley and Kevin Phillips. So on paper the squad looked the best in the League – it was time to test it on grass!

The ability to score goals and kill off opponents is evidenced by the number of 1–0 victories – 10 during the season – and the total goals scored – 54 – which was beaten by three by relegated Norwich. Blues got off to a great start, achieving their best-ever start to a League campaign in their history on their way to the top by the end of October 2008.

Teams were raising their game against the Blues, and although defeats at home by Blackpool and Reading and a draw with Swansea proved to be just blips, they aroused questions as to whether McLeish was the man for the job. 'Big Eck' reacted and got rid of Quincy Owusu-Abeyie and Nigel Quashie and brought in loan signings Scott Sinclair, Hameur Bouazza and the questionable Lee Bowyer to bring more energy and skill into midfield. The unknown Irishman Keith Fahey was also signed from the Dublin side, St Patrick's Athletic of the Eircom League, and while Bluenoses thought 'Who are ya?', his impact was immediate as he brought pace and width to the midfield. Although performances improved, the score rate did not go up.

Controversially, Stephen Kelly was allowed to go on a £500,000 loan deal to Stoke City, leaving Blues without a recognised right-back. Surprisingly, Stephen Carr (ex-Newcastle United) was brought out of retirement to fill the gap, and his non-stop performances made him extremely popular with the fans. The defence proved to be the best in the League, keeping 17 clean sheets.

In April Blues showed the necessary grit and determination required for promotion and the spirit of the squad in being able to react positively to a number of incidents that could have easily derailed a lesser side. At St Andrew's on 6 April, Lee Carsley received a red card against League leaders and eventual champions Wolverhampton Wanderers, but the 10 men of Birmingham took all three points. Damien Johnson, after missing the early part of the season through injury, returned to perform doggedly in midfield.

Against Plymouth on 13 April Maik Taylor received a straight red card and Liam Ridgewell broke his leg; however, Colin Doyle performed such that the defence was not compromised by Taylor's absence, and Franck Queudrue deputised for Ridgewell in the next game against Watford on 18 April and scored the winning goal.

At Vicarage Road on 18 April David Murphy broke his kneecap and Traore came in and retained his place for the final two games. On 25 April against Preston Lee Bowyer received a straight red. Back came Carsley, Johnson fitted in while Queudrue was injured and Martin Taylor came in for the Reading game and performed heroics. In the final month of the promotion run-in, Blues had suffered three red cards, two broken legs and one major injury and still managed to achieve automatic promotion.

Season Statistics

LEAGUE APPEARANCES

Position	Name	Starts	Substitute	Goals
1	Maik Taylor	45	0	0
2	L. Carsley	41	0	2
3	L. Ridgewell	36	0	1
4	S. Larsson	35	3	2
5	R. Jaidi	30	0	0
6	D. Murphy	29	1	0
7	C. Jerome	27	17	9
8	K. Phillips	24	12	14
9	F. Queudrue	23	2	3
10	Martin Taylor	23	1	1
11	J. McFadden	22	8	4
12	S. Parnaby	19	2	0
13	M. Bent	16	17	3
14	L. Bowyer	16	0	1
15	K. Fahey	15	5	4
16	G. Agustien	13	5	0
17	S. Carr	13	0	0
18	Quincy	12	7	2
19	G. O'Connor	10	6	6
20	H. Bouazza	9	7	1
21	S. Sinclair	9	5	0
22	N. Hunt	9	2	0
23	D. Johnson	9	0	0
24	N. Quashie	8	2	0
25	M. Nafti	6	5	0
26	C. Costly	3	6	0
27	G. McSheffrey	3	3	0
28	D. Traore	2	1	0
29	S. Kelly	1	4	0
30	C. Doyle	1	1	0
31	U. De La Cruz	0	1	0
32	J. Wilson	0	1	0
	Own-goal			1

Team of the Decades

Football is a game of opinion, everyone recognises that, and it is undoubtedly one of the great appeals of the game. Sitting in the pub arguing with your mates about who was the best striker the club has ever had, the best goalkeeper, the best manager…the comparisons go on and on. Whatever people think, their arguments have to have some factual substance to gain credibility.

To find the most successful season in each of the completed decades covered in my book, I have chosen the measure of success in the League regardless of the status of that League, with the exception of 1955–65 because that is acknowledged as our best season ever. [Author's note: It is so difficult being objective!]. This means that the most successful season in each decade was:

Decade	Season	Position	Division
1890–1900	1892–93	First	Second
1901–10	1900–01	Second	Second
1911–20	1912–13	Third	Second
1921–30	1920–21	First	Second
1931–40	1931–32	Ninth	First
1941–50	1947–48	First	Second
1951–60	1955–56	Sixth	First
1961–70	1967–68	Fourth	Second
1971–80	1971–72	Second	Second
1981–90	1984–85	Second	Second
1991–2000	1994–95	First	Third

I then looked through the record books to find the 11 players with the most appearances in each of the above seasons in all competitions. This analysis is purely based on that and does not take into account position played, as I was looking for 11 players rather than a team of 11. The 11 for each season are presented in table format in reducing numbers of appearances. The player in the Number One position is designated STAR MAN. Where there is a tie for first position then the player scoring the most goals gains the STAR MAN accolade.

DECADE 1890–1900

MOST SUCCESSFUL SEASON: 1892–93

TOP 11 PLAYERS

Player	LEAGUE		TEST MATCH		FA CUP	
	Apps	Goals	Apps	Goals	Apps	Goals
G. WHELDON	22	25	2	1	1	0
W. OLLIS	22	1	2	0	1	0
T. HANDS	22	11	1	0	1	0
CAL JENKYNS	21	3	2	0	1	0
J. HALLAM	21	17	2	0	1	0
W.H. WALTON	19	14	2	1	1	0
F. MOBLEY	19	14	2	1	1	0
E.J. DEVEY	18	1	0	0	0	0
J.T. BAYLEY	18	0	2	0	1	0
C. CHARSLEY	14	0	2	0	1	0
G.F. SHORT	10	1	2	0	1	0

STAR MAN   GEORGE FREDERICK 'DIAMOND' WHELDON

G.F. Wheldon was born in Worcestershire on 1 November 1871 in Langley Green, Oldbury. He played in local football for Chance's Infants School, St Michael's Senior School, Rood End White Star and Langley Green Victoria and gained a trial with West Bromwich Albion in 1888, which was unsuccessful. Two years later, in February 1890, he joined Blues as a semi-professional. He made his debut against Darwen at home on 15 February 1890 and proceeded to score two goals in the 6–2 victory in front of a crowd of 500. For the record the other scorers that day were Jenkyns, Hallam, W. Devey and Wilcox.

He became a full-time professional in May 1890 and was an ever-present in that first season, scoring 14 goals, which included his first hat-trick for Blues in an 8–0 win over Hednesford in an FA Cup qualifying round. He developed a habit of scoring on his debuts, netting in his first Football Alliance, Division Two and FA Cup appearances. His stay at the Blues lasted just over nine years before he was transferred across the City to Aston Villa in June 1896 for the princely sum of £100 plus the receipts from a friendly game between the two rivals, which meant that the total transfer fee totalled £350. While at Blues he won the Division Two Championship in 1892–93, and eventual promotion to Division One the following season. He had a penchant for scoring hat-tricks, gaining six in less than two years:

'DIAMOND' HAT-TRICKS

FA Cup v Hednesford Town (h) 4 October 1890
Football Alliance v Bootle (h) 21 March 1891

League v Lincoln City (a) 7 January 1893
League v Northwich Victoria (h) 14 January 1893
League v Northwich Victoria (h) 2 December 1893 (four)

Fred, which was his chosen Christian name, gained two representative honours for the Football League against the Irish League and the Scottish League in season 1893–94 and for the Football League against Aston Villa in 1894–95. He will always be remembered for the fact that he scored Blues' first-ever Football League goal in 1892.

His career went into overdrive on moving to Villa Park. He won the Division One Championship for the three years 1897, 1899 and 1900 and won the FA Cup in 1897 in a period when he also gained four England appearances. In August 1900 he joined West Bromwich Albion for £100 to become the first player to represent Blues, Villa and West Bromwich Albion at senior level. Like many players he then transferred his dwindling football talent around the country for short periods: Queen's Park Rangers in December 1901, Portsmouth in August 1902, Worcester City in July 1904 and Coventry City in May 1905, before retiring in January 1907.

Fred played county cricket for Worcestershire from 1899 to 1926, scoring 4,938 runs in 138 matches for an average of 22.54. He hit three centuries, took 95 catches and was an occasional wicket-keeper and right-arm spin bowler. He also played cricket for Carmarthenshire. His brother Sam played for West Bromwich Albion and his son Norris played for Liverpool. He died on 14 January 1924 in St George's Worcester, leaving a Blues appearance record of:

| | LEAGUE | | FA CUP | | TOTAL | |
	Apps	Goals	Apps	Goals	Apps	Goals
1890–91	0	0	2	3	2	3
1891–92	0	0	7	8	7	8
1892–93	22	25	1	0	23	25
1893–94	28	22	1	1	29	23
1894–95	29	11	1	0	30	11
1895–96	30	7	1	0	31	7
Total	109	65	13	12	122	77

DECADE 1901–10

MOST SUCCESSFUL SEASON: 1900–01

TOP 11 PLAYERS

| Player | LEAGUE | | FA CUP | |
	Apps	Goals	Apps	Goals
A. ARCHER	34	2	5	0
W. WIGMORE	34	1	5	0

S.E. WHARTON	33	1	5	1
A. ROBINSON	33	0	5	0
A. LEAKE	31	3	5	0
J. ASTON	29	12	5	0
W.A. BENNETT	28	0	5	1
R. McROBERTS	26	13	3	0
G. ADEY	24	0	4	0
W.H. WALTON	24	2	4	0
W. PRATT	16	0	2	0

STAR MAN   ARTHUR ARCHER

Arthur was born in Ashby-de-la-Zouch in November 1877. He began his career playing for Burton St Edmunds in 1892 and 1893 when he moved to Tutbury Hampton for a further two years. He joined Swadlincote Town in January 1895 before joining Burton Wanderers. Blues signed him from Burton Wanderers for £50 in August 1897. He made his debut for Blues on 4 September 1897 away at Burton Swifts in a 3–1 victory in front of 1,500 fans (for the record, the scorers for Blues were Inglis [2] and Abbott).

He was an ever-present in seasons 1889–1900 and 1900–01 when he appeared in 96 consecutive League games and was a member of the team that finished runners-up in Division Two in 1901.

Arthur left Blues in March 1902 for £40 when he signed for New Brompton (now Gillingham). He stayed there for just over a year before joining Wingfield House in April 1903. In the six years before his retirement in the summer of 1909 he joined Queen's Park Rangers in August 1903, Tottenham Hotspur as a guest between 1903 and 1905, Norwich City in August 1905, Brighton & Hove Albion in June 1907 and finally Millwall in August 1908.

A talented coach, he pioneered English coaching techniques in Europe, beginning in Germany 1910–12, then Ghent (1912–14 and 1920–21), followed by Italy (1921) and then Belgium (1922–24), before returning to the United Kingdom to coach Watford in the 1924–25 season. He died in 1940.

APPEARANCES

	LEAGUE		FA CUP		TOTAL	
	Apps	**Goals**	**Apps**	**Goals**	**Apps**	**Goals**
1897–98	29	0	1	0	30	0
1898–99	33	0	6	0	39	0
1899–1900	34	1	4	0	38	1
1900–01	34	2	5	0	39	2
1901–02	24	1	0	0	24	1
Total	**154**	**4**	**16**	**0**	**170**	**4**

DECADE 1911–20

MOST SUCCESSFUL SEASON: 1912–13

TOP 11 PLAYERS

Player	LEAGUE		FA CUP	
	Apps	Goals	Apps	Goals
A. SMITH	37	2	1	0
W. BALL	36	0	1	0
J. BUMPHREY	34	2	1	0
W.H. JONES	33	16	1	0
F. WOMACK	30	0	0	0
E. ROBINSON	30	13	1	0
H. CROSSTHWAITE	28	0	0	0
A. TINKLER	27	1	1	0
A. GARDNER	23	8	1	0
J.H. HALL	22	2	1	0
A. McCLURE	19	0	0	0

STAR MAN   ARTHUR R. 'NIPPER' SMITH

One of the outcomes of the 'Star Man' system with an underperforming club like Birmingham City is that it occasionally elevates a player such as Arthur Smith. In the 1910s the best performing team was the 1912–13 squad that finished third in Division Two. Obviously for most other clubs coming third in Division Two would hardly be a 'record'. But for Blues it is, and Arthur, a nippy winger, was the top appearance maker with 37 appearances, making him the 'Star Man' for the 1910s.

Born in Stourbridge in 1887, 'Nipper' initially played for the local side Brierley Hill Alliance before moving to London in August 1911 to play for Queen's Park Rangers. He lasted less than a year before coming back to the Midlands in June 1912 to sign for the Blues. He only spent two seasons at the Blues before rejoining Brierley Hill Alliance in September 1914. He saw his playing days out at his first club and also took on the secretary's role until May 1934. Nipper was also employed as a teacher at St Peter's College in Saltley, Birmingham.

APPEARANCES

	LEAGUE		FA CUP		TOTAL	
	Apps	Goals	Apps	Goals	Apps	Goals
1912–13	37	2	1	0	38	2
1913–14	14	1	0	0	14	1
Total	51	3	1	0	52	3

DECADE 1921–30

MOST SUCCESSFUL SEASON: 1920–21

TOP 11 PLAYERS

Player	LEAGUE		FA CUP	
	Apps	Goals	Apps	Goals
J. CROSBIE	**42**	**14**	**1**	**0**
P. BARTON	42	5	1	1
A. MCCLURE	40	2	1	0
F. WOMACK	38	0	1	0
W.H. JONES	37	0	1	0
J. BURKINSHAW	35	6	1	0
J. LANE	34	15	0	0
J. WHITEHOUSE	33	11	1	0
D. TREMELLING	30	0	1	0
H. HAMPTON	29	16	1	0
J. ROULSON	22	0	1	0

STAR MAN   JOHNNY 'PEERLESS' ANDERSON CROSBIE

Johnny Crosbie was born on 3 June 1896 in Glenbuck, Ayrshire, in Scotland. His career began in local football with the Glenbuck Cherry Pickers, Muirkirk Athletic and Saltcoats Victoria before signing professional terms for Ayr United in August 1913. It was while with Ayr United that he gained his first representative honour for Scotland in a Victory International against England in 1919. He gained his first full international cap against Wales prior to joining Blues in May 1920 for a then record fee of £3,700. His Blues debut was on 28 August 1920 against South Shields, away in front of a crowd of 15,000, a game Blues lost 3–0.

During the 1921–22 season he gained his second full international cap starring in a 1–0 victory over England at Villa Park. This put Johnny in the record books for being the first Blues' player to gain full international honours for Scotland. He served Blues well for 12 seasons and during that time he won a Championship medal for Division Two in 1921 and a runners'-up medal in the 1931 FA Cup Final. He was recognised as one of the top Scottish players to play in the English League, being chosen three times to play for the Anglo-Scots against the Home Scots in seasons 1920–21, 1921–22 and 1922–23.

A button-maker by trade, he left Blues for Chesterfield in July 1932 before moving to Stourbridge as player-manager four months later in November 1932. He coached in Sweden for Gothenburg during the period February to August 1933, before returning to England, where in 1934–35 he ran a works team in Kidderminster.

Johnny died on 8 February 1982 having made 432 appearances for the Blues scoring 72 goals, a return of one goal in every six games, not bad for a creative inside-forward.

APPEARANCES

	LEAGUE		FA CUP		TOTAL	
	Apps	Goals	Apps	Goals	Apps	Goals
1920–21	42	14	1	0	43	14
1921–22	34	10	0	0	34	10
1922–23	32	1	1	0	33	1
1923–24	31	1	0	0	31	1
1924–25	40	8	2	0	42	8
1925–26	40	8	2	0	42	8
1926–27	39	6	2	1	41	7
1927–28	28	7	3	0	31	7
1928–29	38	4	2	0	40	4
1929–30	39	7	3	0	42	7
1930–31	31	2	7	0	38	2
1931–32	15	3	0	0	15	3
Total	409	71	23	1	432	72

DECADE 1931–40

MOST SUCCESSFUL SEASON: 1931–32

TOP 11 PLAYERS

Player	LEAGUE		FA CUP	
	Apps	Goals	Apps	Goals
L. STOKER	**39**	**0**	**2**	**0**
G. LIDDELL	37	0	2	0
G. MORRALL	37	1	2	0
J. BRADFORD	37	26	2	20
H. HIBBS	36	0	2	0
E. CURTIS	35	13	2	0
J. CRINGAN	30	0	2	0
G.R. BRIGGS	30	11	2	0
T. GROSVENOR	26	6	2	0
E. BARKAS	19	0	1	0
T. FILLINGHAM	17	0	0	0

STAR MAN   LEWIS STOKER

Lewis was born in Wheatley Hill, County Durham, on 31 March 1911, and his early career saw him appearing for Bearpark School, Brandon Juniors, Esh Winning Juniors, Bear Park FC and West Stanley.

Blues' manager Leslie Knighton invited him down from West Stanley for a month's trial in June 1930, which resulted in him signing professional terms in September 1930. He made his debut at home on 6 December 1930 against Huddersfield Town in front of 13,885 spectators. Blues won 2–0 with Bradford and Curtis the scorers. Lew made only seven appearances in the 1930–31 season and had the experience of being selected as a travelling reserve for the FA Cup Final in 1931 at the age of 20.

A year later he gained the first of his three full international caps for England against Wales in a 0–0 draw at Wrexham. He then played at Wembley against Scotland in April 1934 when he starred in a 3–0 victory. His final international appearance was against Hungary in Budapest in May 1934, a game that resulted in a 2–1 defeat.

A determined wing-half, Stoker also represented the Football League against the Irish League (1932–33) and was involved in three international trials, playing twice for The Rest against England in the early 1930s and for The Possibles against The Probables in the 1935–36 season. He left Blues for Nottingham Forest in May 1938 after making nearly 250 appearances in the Royal Blue shirt. Lew retired during World War Two in 1944 and became a charge hand at the Wimbush Bakery in Green Lane, Small Heath, just off the Coventry Road and a stone's throw from St Andrew's. Lew's younger brother Bob was also a professional footballer, playing for Bolton Wanderers and Huddersfield Town. Lewis Stoker died on 17 May 1979.

APPEARANCES

	LEAGUE		FA CUP		TOTAL	
	Apps	Goals	Apps	Goals	Apps	Goals
1930–31	7	0	0	0	7	0
1931–32	39	0	2	0	41	0
1932–33	38	0	5	0	43	0
1933–34	39	0	3	0	42	0
1934–35	37	1	4	0	41	1
1935–36	39	1	2	0	41	1
1936–37	19	0	0	0	19	0
1937–38	13	0	0	0	13	0
Total	231	2	16	0	247	2

DECADE 1941–50

MOST SUCCESSFUL SEASON: 1947–48

TOP 11 PLAYERS

Player	LEAGUE		FA CUP	
	Apps	Goals	Apps	Goals
F. HARRIS	40	0	0	0
H. BODLE	39	14	0	0

G. EDWARDS	37	2	1	0
G. MERRICK	36	0	0	0
T. DUCKHOUSE	36	0	1	0
K. GREEN	35	0	1	0
N. DOUGALL	34	5	1	0
D. JENNINGS	29	0	0	0
C. TRIGG	25	6	1	0
J. STEWART	17	7	0	0
J.W. GOODWIN	16	6	1	0

STAR MAN   FREDERICK HARRIS

Fred, who could play both wing-half and inside-forward, was born in Sparkbrook on 2 July 1912. As a local lad he first played for Formans Road School, before giving service to Sparkbrook FC, Birmingham Transport and Osborne Athletic. It was while he was with Osborn Athletic that he joined Blues in March 1933 at the ripe old age of 20. He made his debut against local rivals, Aston Villa, at St Andrew's on 25 August 1934, scoring in a 2–0 victory in front of a crowd of 54,200. The other scorer was Billy Guest. During his 10 seasons with the Blues he was a member of the team that became Division Two champions in 1947–48 season after winning the Football League South Trophy in 1946.

He was made captain by Harry Storer due to his leadership qualities both on and off the field. He gained a single representative honour playing for the Football League against the Scottish League at Ibrox in March 1949. He retired a year later in 1950 to set up a chiropody and physiotherapy business in Acock's Green. He died on 13 October 1998

APPEARANCES

	LEAGUE		FA CUP		TOTAL	
	Apps	Goals	Apps	Goals	Apps	Goals
1934–35	30	9	4	3	34	12
1935–36	42	17	2	1	44	18
1936–37	35	11	1	0	36	11
1937–38	19	7	1	0	20	7
1938–39	37	14	4	3	41	17
1945–46	0	0	10	0	10	0
1946–47	29	1	4	1	33	2
1947–48	40	0	1	0	41	0
1948–49	36	2	3	0	39	2
1949–50	12	0	0	0	12	0
Total	280	61	30	8	310	69

DECADE 1951–60

MOST SUCCESSFUL SEASON: 1955–56

TOP 11 PLAYERS

PLAYER	LEAGUE		FA CUP	
	APPS	GOALS	APPS	GOALS
G. ASTALL	39	12	6	3
G. MERRICK	38	0	6	0
J. HALL	38	0	6	0
E. BROWN	38	21	6	7
P. MURPPHY	38	12	6	5
A. GOVAN	36	4	3	0
N. KINSEY	34	14	6	3
L. BOYD	32	3	6	0
T. SMITH	30	0	6	0
R. WARHURST	30	2	4	0
K. GREEN	28	0	6	0

STAR MAN   GORDON ASTALL

Gordon was born in Horwich, near Bolton, on 22 September 1927. After playing school football, he went to Southampton as an amateur and to Bolton Wanderers on trial before signing professional forms for Plymouth Argyle in November 1947 while serving in the Royal Marines. While at Plymouth he helped them win the Division Three Championship title and gained an England B cap, becoming the first Plymouth player to achieve international recognition for 27 years. He scored 42 goals in 188 games for the Pilgrims in almost six seasons. His goalscoring exploits brought him to the attention of Blues' manager, Bob Brocklebank, who was looking for a replacement for Jackie Stewart, so Gordon was signed in October 1953. He made his Blues debut on 17 October 1953 against Bristol Rovers at Eastville. The match was a 1–1 draw in front of a crowd of 35,164, Ted Purdon scoring Blues' goal. Gordon started his scoring account with Blues in his third game, which was a 4–2 victory over Derby County. In his second season he helped Blues win the Division Two Championship in 1954–55, followed by a runners'-up medal in the 1956 FA Cup Final. His tremendous performances earned him England recognition with two caps in the 1955–56 season. The first cap was against Finland, in a game in which he scored, and the second was against the reigning World Cup holders, West Germany, when once again he got on the scoresheet. He was also selected for the Football League against the League of Ireland in season 1956–57. Before leaving Blues in July 1961 to join Torquay United, he gained a runners'-up medal in the Inter Cities Fairs Cup campaign of 1958–60.

He retired from first-class football in May 1963 and settled in the Torquay area, where for a period he coached a local Devon side, Upton Vale FC.

APPEARANCES

| | LEAGUE | | FA CUP | | LEAGUE CUP | | EUROPEAN | | TOTAL | |
	Apps	Goals	Apps	Goals	Apps	Goals	Apps	Goals	Goals	Apps
1953–54	24	6	2	0	0	0	0	0	26	6
1954–55	33	11	4	0	0	0	0	0	37	11
1955–56	39	12	6	3	0	0	0	0	45	15
1956–57	40	11	6	2	0	0	1	0	47	13
1957–58	37	5	1	0	0	0	3	0	41	5
1958–59	26	8	5	1	0	0	1	0	32	9
1959–60	19	4	1	0	0	0	2	0	22	4
1960–61	17	3	2	0	1	0	1	1	21	4
Total	235	60	27	6	1	0	8	1	271	67

DECADE 1961–70

MOST SUCCESSFUL SEASON: 1967–68

TOP 11 PLAYERS

| Player | LEAGUE | | FA CUP | | LEAGUE CUP | |
	Apps	Goals	Apps	Goals	Apps	Goals
B. BRIDGES	42	23	6	4	2	0
F. PICKERING	42	13	6	2	2	0
M. BEARD	41	2	6	1	2	0
J. HERRIOT	40	0	6	0	2	0
A. MURRAY	40	2	5	0	2	0
G. VOWDEN	40	17	6	4	2	1
R. WYLIE	39	2	6	0	2	0
J. VINCENT	36+1	14	3	0	2	0
T. HOCKEY	30	1	3	0	2	1
R. MARTIN	21+5	0	4+1	0	1	0
M. PAGE	20+1	1	4	0	2	0

STAR MAN   BARRY JOHN BRIDGES

Barry was born in Horsford near Norwich on 29 April 1941. After playing for Norwich & Norfolk Boys, he joined Chelsea as an apprentice in July 1956 aged 15, before signing professional terms in May 1958. He gained England international honours at both Schoolboy and Youth level before gaining four full caps, the first in April 1965 against Scotland at Wembley in a 2–2 draw.

A regular scorer, he amassed 205 senior appearances for Chelsea, scoring 93 goals, a return of one goal in every 2.2 matches. Blues paid a then record fee of £55,000 to secure his signature in May 1966. He made his debut on 20 August 1966 against Wolverhampton Wanderers at Molineux, a game which saw Blues win 2–1 in front of a crowd of 26,800. Both goals that day came from another ex-Chelsea player, Bert Murray, who was a factor in Barry's decision to join Blues. While he only spent three seasons at St Andrew's, he was a firm favourite with the crowd due to his all-out effort in every game and his trickery on the ball, a skill never better demonstrated than in his spectacular over-the-shoulder scissor kick that knocked Arsenal out of the FA Cup in 1968. He scored one hat-trick in the League against Rotherham United at St Andrew's on 28 October 1967. He left Blues for Queen's Park Rangers in August 1968, having scored 47 goals in 104 games, maintaining his return of one goal in every 2.2 matches.

Barry never stayed too long in one place, and after two years at Loftus Road he moved to Millwall in September 1970. After another two years he moved to Brighton & Hove Albion in September 1972, and in 1974 he went to Highlands Park in South Africa and then to St Patrick's Athletic in the Republic of Ireland as player-manager in 1976. In 1978 he moved into full-time management with Sligo Rovers before moving to Dereham Town, King's Lynn and Horsford, before deciding to concentrate on his hotel business.

During his career Barry made 567 League and Cup appearances, in which he scored 215 goals, a career return of one goal in every 2.6 matches.

APPEARANCES

	LEAGUE		FA CUP		LEAGUE CUP		TOTAL	
	Apps	Goals	Apps	Goals	Apps	Goals	Apps	Goals
1966–67	39	13	6	1	7	4	52	18
1967–68	42	24	6	4	2	1	50	29
1968–69	2	0	0	0	0	0	2	0
Total	83	37	12	5	9	5	104	47

DECADE 1971–80

MOST SUCCESSFUL SEASON: 1971–72

TOP 11 PLAYERS

Player	LEAGUE		FA CUP		LEAGUE CUP	
	Apps	Goals	Apps	Goals	Apps	Goals
R. LATCHFORD	42	23	5	4	1	0
A. CAMPBELL	42	4	5	0	1	0
R. HYND	42	1	5	1	1	0
T. FRANCIS	39	12	5	2	1	0
M. PAGE	38+1	0	5	1	1	0
G. TAYLOR	27+3	1	4+1	0	1	0
T. CARROLL	27	0	5	0	0	0

R. HATTON	26	15	5	2		0	0
G. SMITH	22+3	0	1+1	0		1	0
M. KELLY	19	0	0	0		0	0
S. HARLAND	19	0	5	0		0	0

STAR MAN   ROBERT DENNIS LATCHFORD

Born in Kings Heath on 18 January 1951, Robert played centre-forward for Brandwood Secondary School, South Birmingham Boys and Warwickshire County Schools before joining Blues as an apprentice in May 1967. He signed professional forms in August 1968, made his League debut in March 1969 and three months later played for England in the International Youth Tournament in East Germany. His progress at Blues was rapid, and he established himself in the first XI at St Andrew's in the 1970–71 season, scoring 13 goals in 42 senior appearances.

Part of a formidable trio comprising himself, Trevor Francis and Phil Summerill, and later Bob Hatton and TF, Latchford was strong and powerful, a sound header of the ball and could shoot with either foot. In the 1971–72 season he hit 30 goals, including 23 in the League, in 52 appearances as Blues won promotion to the First Division and reached the semi-final of the FA Cup. He followed up with another 20 goals in 49 outings in 1972–73 and then got 18 goals in 36 games the following season before his departure to Everton for a League-record fee of £350,000, a deal which saw Howard Kendall and Archie Styles switch from Goodison to St Andrew's. His record with Blues was excellent – 84 goals in 194 appearances.

Latchford was top League scorer in each of his first four seasons at Everton, and in 1977–78 he was presented with a cheque for £10,000 by a national newspaper for becoming the first player to reach 30 goals in a season in Division One for six years. He went on to net 138 goals in 289 appearances for Everton before moving to Swansea City for £125,000 in July 1981.

At Vetch Field he managed to score 32 goals in 1982–83 before being given a free transfer to Dutch side NAC Breda in January 1984, but within five months he was back in England with Coventry City. After a short spell at Highfield Road, he moved on to Lincoln City in July 1985. After a loan spell with Newport, he drifted into non-League football with Merthyr Tydfil in August 1986, gaining a Welsh Cup medal at the end of that season.

During his career, Latchford netted over 263 goals in 613 League and Cup appearances. He was capped 12 times at Senior level for England and scored five goals. He later became a Director at Alvechurch FC, before returning to St Andrew's on the community side during the late 1990s, taking over a coaching role in the 1999–2000 season. In the 2000–01 season Latchford resigned from his post at St Andrew's to start a new life in Germany. Truly a legend, he scored some great goals for Blues and for his other clubs too.

APPEARANCES

	LEAGUE		FA CUP		LEAGUE CUP		OTHERS		TOTAL	
	Apps	Goals	Apps	Goals	Apps	Goals	Apps	Goals	Goals	Apps
1968–69	4	2	0	0	0	0	0	0	4	2
1969–70	10	1	0	0	1	0	0	0	11	1

1970–71	35 +1	13	2	0	4	0	0	0	41 +1	13
1971–72	42	23	5	4	1	0	4*	3	52	30
1972–73	42	19	2	0	5	1	0	0	49	20
1973–74	25 +1	10	2	2	4 +2	5	2**	1	33 +3	18
Total	158 +2	68	11	6	15 +2	6	6	4	190 +4	84

* Third-place Play-off FA Cup (1972) ** Texaco Cup

DECADE 1981–90

MOST SUCCESSFUL SEASON: 1984–85

TOP 11 PLAYERS

Player	LEAGUE		FA CUP		LEAGUE CUP	
	Apps	Goals	Apps	Goals	Apps	Goals
W. WRIGHT	**42**	**2**	**4**	**1**	**4**	**0**
B. ROBERTS	41	0	4	0	4	0
W. CLARKE	40	17	4	0	3	2
R. HOPKINS	39	9	4	0	2	1
K. ARMSTRONG	36	0	3	0	4	0
D. SEAMAN	33	0	4	0	0	0
D. BREMNER	30	0	4	0	3	0
G. DALY	29+1	1	4	0	2	0
R. RANSON	28	0	4	0	0	0
M. KUHL	25+2	2	0	0	4	0
J. HAGAN	21+1	0	1	0	4	0

STAR MAN   WILLIAM 'BILLY' WRIGHT

Billy was born in Liverpool on 28 April 1958. At the age of 16 he became an apprentice at his beloved Everton, before turning professional in January 1977, following his uncle Tommy Wright who played right-back for Everton and England. During his time at Goodison Park, Billy also gained England recognition, earning two England B caps and six Under-21 caps. He joined Blues in June 1983 on a free transfer and made his debut on 27 August 1983 against West Ham United at Upton Park in front of 18,729 spectators. It was a game to forget as Blues lost 4–0.

Billy was a firm favourite with the fans due to his robust, never-give-up attitude, and in his three seasons at St Andrew's he scored 14 goals, of which 12 were penalties, taken in the style of 'if the goalkeeper got in the way they too would end up in the net'. The fiercest penalty taker at Blues since Stan Lynn in the 1960s, who was also a full-back, he was the captain of the side that became Division Two champions in 1984–85.

Billy was always in trouble with the management about his weight, often piling on the pounds during the summer break. He left Blues for Carlisle United in August 1986 on a free transfer after a two-month loan spell at Chester City in February and March. In August 1988 he joined Morecambe.

APPEARANCES

	LEAGUE		FA CUP		LEAGUE CUP		TOTAL	
	Apps	Goals	Apps	Goals	Apps	Goals	Apps	Goals
1983–84	40	5	5	3	8	0	53	8
1984–85	42	2	4	1	4	0	50	3
1985–86	29	1	0/1	0	3/1	2	32/2	3
Total	111	8	9/1	4	15/1	2	135/2	14

DECADE 1991–2000

MOST SUCCESSFUL SEASON: 1994–95

TOP 11 PLAYERS

Player	LEAGUE		FA CUP		LEAGUE CUP	
	Apps	Goals	Apps	Goals	Apps	Goals
I. BENNETT	46	0	5	0	4	0
M. WARD	41	3	4	0	4	0
S. CLARIDGE	41+1	20	5	0	3	2
L. DAISH	37	3	5	0	2	1
G. POOLE	34	1	0	0	4	0
L. DONOWA	21+10	9	5	0	0	0
P. SHEARER	24+3	3	2	2	3	0
J. HUNT	18+2	5	1	0	2	0
P. TAIT	18+6	4	2+1	0	0	0
K. FRANCIS	15	8	0	0	4	0
J. DOMINQUEZ	12+11	3	2+1	0	4	0

STAR MAN   IAN MICHAEL BENNETT

Goalkeeper Ian was born in Worksop on 10 October 1970. He joined Queen's Park Rangers as a YTS in 1988 and spent a year there before signing as a professional for Newcastle United in March 1989. He stayed at St James' Park for two years before moving to Peterborough United in March 1991 on a free transfer. Blues paid £325,000 for his signature in December 1993. 'Benno' made his debut on 28 December 1993 against West Bromwich Albion at St Andrew's in front of a crowd of 28,228. Blues won the game 2–0 with Saville and Peschisolido scoring. He spent 11 seasons at Blues, appearing in the double-winning side of 1994–95 that secured the Division Two Championship as well as the Auto Windscreens Shield. In 2001 he played in the Worthington Cup Final against Liverpool and assisted Blues to promotion to the Premiership a year later in 2002. In that double-winning season he had 10 successive clean sheets (27 in total from 62 matches). During the latter part of his career he went on loan to Sheffield United, Coventry City and Leeds United before making a permanent move to Sheffield United in the summer of 2006.

APPEARANCES

	LEAGUE		FA CUP		LEAGUE CUP		TOTAL	
	Apps	Goals	Apps	Goals	Apps	Goals	Apps	Goals
1993–94	22	0	0	0	0	0	22	0
1994–95	46	0	0	0	0	0	46	0
1995–96	24	0	1	0	8	0	33	0
1996–97	40	0	3	0	4	0	47	0
1997–98	45	0	3	0	5	0	53	0
1998–99	10	0	0	0	4	0	14	0
1999–2000	21	0	1	0	1	0	23	0
2000–01	47	0	1	0	10	0	58	0
2001–02	18	0	1	0	0	0	19	0
2002–03	10	0	0	0	2	0	12	0
2003–04	4/2	0	0	0	0	0	4/2	0
Total	**287/2**	**0**	**10**	**0**	**34**	**0**	**331/2**	**0**

So there they are, the Star Men from the history of the Blues: more arguments for the pubs and clubs around St Andrew's. In 4–3–3 format they could line up as follows:

IAN BENNETT

BILLY WRIGHT   **FRED HARRIS**   **LEW STOKER**   **ARTHUR ARCHER**

GORDON ASTALL   **JOHNNY CROSBIE**   **ARTHUR SMITH**

FRED WHELDON   **BARRY BRIDGES**   **BOB LATCHFORD**

Whatever your opinion of the individuals that have emerged as the Star Men, there are many Bluenoses that would welcome a team at St Andrew's in the early 21st century with the likes of Fred Harris and Billy Wright in the back four, a goalscoring midfielder like Gordon Astall or strikers with a goals-per-game return of Fred Wheldon and Barry Bridges.